Stories of Culture and Place

Library and Archives Canada Cataloguing in Publication

Kenny, Michael G., 1942–, author
Stories of culture and place : an introduction to
anthropology / Michael G. Kenny and Kirsten Smillie.

Includes bibliographical references and index.
Issued in print and electronic formats.
ISBN 978-1-4426-0794-1 (pbk.).—ISBN 978-1-4426-0795-8 (bound).—
ISBN 978-1-4426-0796-5 (pdf). —ISBN 978-1-4426-0797-2 (html)

1. Anthropology—Textbooks.   I. Smillie, Kirsten, 1979–, author   II. Title.

GN25.K46 2014   301   C2014-904974-9
                            C2014-904975-7

We welcome comments and suggestions regarding any aspect of our publications—please feel free to contact us at news@utphighereducation.com or visit our Internet site at www.utppublishing.com.

North America
5201 Dufferin Street
North York, Ontario, Canada, M3H 5T8

2250 Military Road
Tonawanda, New York, USA, 14150

ORDERS PHONE: 1–800–565–9523
ORDERS FAX: 1–800–221–9985
ORDERS E-MAIL: utpbooks@utpress.utoronto.ca

UK, Ireland, and continental Europe
NBN International
Estover Road, Plymouth, PL6 7PY, UK
ORDERS PHONE: 44 (0) 1752 202301
ORDERS FAX: 44 (0) 1752 202333
ORDERS E-MAIL: enquiries@nbninternational.com

Every effort has been made to contact copyright holders; in the event of an error or omission, please notify the publisher.

This book is printed on paper containing 100% post-consumer fibre.

The University of Toronto Press acknowledges the financial support for its publishing activities of the Government of Canada through the Canada Book Fund.

Printed in Canada

RECYCLED
Paper made from
recycled material
FSC® C103567

STORIES
of **CULTURE AND PLACE**

An Introduction to Anthropology

Michael G. Kenny and Kirsten Smillie

UNIVERSITY OF TORONTO PRESS

Contents

CONTENTS

Illustrations

Plates

Maps

Figures

Acknowledgements

We first of all acknowledge Anne Brackenbury, our editor at the University of Toronto Press, for her enthusiasm and encouragement over the course of this project. Fulsome thanks also to project manager Judith Earnshaw, copy editor Martin Boyne, and the anonymous reviewers of our draft manuscript.

Kirsten Smillie would like to thank Dusty, Georgia, and Charlie for all their love and support.

Michael Kenny thanks Angela Tai for being there, and his long-time colleagues in the Department of Sociology and Anthropology at Simon Fraser University for their intellectual stimulation over the years.

Preface

This book aims at providing you with an overview of social and cultural anthropology—its origins, its distinctive methods and concepts, and its place in the contemporary world. Anthropology is a rich and diverse subject, so it's difficult to give a precise definition of just what anthropology *is*. We think this end is far better served by seeing what it *does*, and that is our goal. You can then judge for yourself. However, to get things started, we should at least say the following.

What we now know as anthropology arose out of contact between western Europeans and the strange new worlds that were encountered during the great age of overseas exploration and imperial expansion. Previously unknown societies were "discovered," the true map of the globe outlined, trade routes established, and colonies founded. It was suddenly a much bigger world, and those events are the prelude to the story we want to tell. In its beginnings it is inevitably a Eurocentric story; but that would change.

Travelers, empire builders, missionaries, and scholars asked themselves how these new peoples and their unfamiliar customs fit into the broader scheme of things—their place in history, their status as human beings, and the value of their cultures. Anthropology as an academic discipline emerged from attempts to answer questions such as these. Encounters with human diversity provoked reflection and stimulated further inquiry; and these new worlds turned out to be incredibly diverse, ranging from small bands of hunter-gatherers to centralized empires.

As for theory, it shapes the questions one thinks worth asking, so theory, observation, and practice are intimately related. Even in the early days it came to be seen that much could be gained by *comparing* societies with one another in a systematic manner—that light could be shed on human nature and history by doing so. Anthropology was in the process of becoming a scientific endeavor, and this entailed the development of methods for analyzing, classifying, and comparing.

The most natural way to go about it was by comparing other societies with one's own. But difference, after all, is in the eye of the beholder! Conceptions about the nature of the non-European world were therefore an inverted mode of self-perception, seeing oneself through *the other*. One expression of this was a tendency to place particular societies on a scale ranging from the "primitive" to the "civilized." It had a historical dimension, the Europeans imagining that so-called primitive peoples resembled what their own ancestors had been like in the distant past.

That in turn raised the question of what historical processes were responsible for differentiating peoples along the great scale, making some more "progressive" and others less so. This was a fertile but misguided idea; be that as it may, so-called primitive peoples were once the distinctive object of anthropological inquiry, studied with the hope of casting light on earlier stages of social evolution, or even on the essence of humanity in its purist, simplest, most natural form. They were seen as a laboratory of human possibility, the beginning point for everything that followed. That is still a common stereotype about our subject, and it's not entirely wrong. But the world has moved on, and so has the discipline: it has gone global and as an academic discipline is now found everywhere, and with a much broader range of interests than its traditional subject—tribal societies. Contemporary anthropologists regularly turn their research lens on those who are "just like them," and they thus contribute to a better understanding of social issues that plague contemporary times, such as poverty, discrimination, and environmental degradation. Anthropologists are also regularly employed outside the world of academia, in fields including development, health, government, and law. In this text we will explore how the history of anthropology has shaped the discipline into what we see today, and how the lessons learned along the way have contributed to the development of a social science that is relevant, critical, and pertinent to understanding the world we live in. As you will see, some of our examples are taken virtually from yesterday's news. Of course, the world moves on, and what counts as newsworthy moves with it. We encourage you, therefore, to think about contemporary events from an anthropological perspective.

Our Approach

The typical introductory anthropology textbook is fat, heavy, and expensive, and attempts a comprehensive overview of the field with many examples illustrating particular issues. Our experience suggests that students (and instructors!) often find such an approach deeply boring, so we have opted for another. For many of you this may be your first and last formal contact with anthropology. No hard feelings; that's often the case with introductory courses, and then you move on to other things. What we hope to leave you with is a sense of what anthropology is all about and of its relevance to other aspects of life and academic endeavor. But some of you may be stimulated to go on and find out more; if so, all the better.

Given those facts of life, our view is that a few well-chosen examples are better than many superficial ones that can be memorized and quickly forgotten. Therefore, in each chapter we focus on a few specific cases that open up a discussion of the intellectual themes and wider anthropological issues involved. For example, in the following short introductory chapter we begin our story by examining three historically important "first contact" accounts. These accounts point to questions about the historical context in which anthropology arose, and to ongoing theoretical issues related to the situations we describe. In the chapter that follows we continue with this theme to describe the "first contact" experiences of three anthropologists from our own time, and to tell you more about anthropology itself. Each chapter of this book will follow a similar mode of presentation: beginning with a statement of what we intend to accomplish, followed by examples and discussion, concluding with a summary of the main points and suggestions for further reading.

Outline

Introduction: First Contact Columbus in the Caribbean; Cook in Hawai'i; Simon Fraser in British Columbia. Here we raise basic questions about what is seen and how it's seen—how theory shapes perception, how culture structures experience.

Chapter 1: Culture Shock The four fields of anthropology. An introduction to key anthropological concepts, including cultural relativity, culture shock, ethnocentrism and relativism, explained through three examples of the ethnographic experience.

Chapter 2: Life in the Field Fieldwork as practice; anthropological method; the problem of "objectivity"; ethnocentrism.

Chapter 3: Historical Beginnings The emergence of anthropology as a scientific discipline.

Chapter 4: Kinship The importance of the study of kinship to anthropology; encounters with difference; how we view and construct human relationships; reciprocity and exchange; kinship systems; kinship in our own time.

Chapter 5: Symbol, Myth, and Meaning Culture as a cognitive system; the social construction of the world and our place in it; the problem of language.

Chapter 6: The Politics of Culture Human rights; cultural identities and cultural property; alternative histories; land claims; applied anthropology; anthropologists as advocates and activists.

Chapter 7: Understanding Gender Problems of definition; biology, sexuality, and gender; gender roles.

Chapter 8: Race, Science, and Human Diversity Why "race" matters; the rise of genetic essentialism; taking control of evolution; the anthropological critique of race; race in the post-genomic age.

Chapter 9: Anthropology, Cultural Change, and Globalization We've always been global; the global and the local; colonialism; "modernization" and "development"; information technologies old and new; migration; caught between worlds; implications for anthropology as a discipline.

Introduction: First Contact

LEARNING OBJECTIVES

After reading this chapter, students should be able to

- outline the historical context that helped give rise to the anthropological perspective on cultural difference;
- explore the relationship between theory and observation of the social world (or of anything else)—what is seen and how it's seen;
- begin to appreciate the significance of concepts like "civilization" and "savagery" in the earlier history of our subject;
- understand why attempts to understand the nature of history and **social evolution** have been of such importance to the development of anthropology;
- get a sense of what the "comparative method" is—the kinds of insights that can be gained by comparing one society with another; and
- see through our specific examples why the question of "meaning" is so important to anthropology, and how difficult the problem of "interpretation" can be.

KEY TERMS

globalization	meaning	social memory
interpretation	social evolution	

The New World

This may well be your first encounter with anthropology, and so we begin with stories of three other first-contact experiences: those of Christopher Columbus with the peoples of the Americas in 1492, of Captain James Cook of the Royal Navy with the Hawaiians in 1778, and Canadian fur trader Simon Fraser with the native inhabitants of interior British Columbia during an 1808 journey down the great river that bears his name. Encounters such as these altered the course of history.

We will introduce anthropological concepts and questions as these stories are told. This will be the method of our book as a whole. It is our hope that, by the end, you will have acquired a fair overview of what modern socio-cultural anthropology is all about, and will be in a position to ask anthropological questions yourselves. We seek to illuminate the history and nature of a discipline and to document the emergence of a particular way of seeing. Call it the anthropological perspective. But we won't try to define just what that is. As we said in the Preface, that end is better served by seeing what anthropology *does*—through examples of anthropology in practice.

Columbus, Cook, and Fraser weren't anthropologists. The emergence of our subject was far in their future. At their best they were meticulous *observers*, and this tells us something about the difference between their perspective and that of modern anthropology. There's little sense of how indigenous peoples viewed *them*, and what their own world looked like from within. It's mainly a one-sided story that these explorers tell, from a "superior" outsider's perspective. Of course these were travelers who didn't come to stay. True enough, but we will show that this perspective was built into how Europeans of their time saw the world and its history. That would change as anthropology developed as a discipline and as the world changed around it. Broadly speaking, it can be said that the "anthropological perspective" has evolved from observation of "the others" to both collaboration with them and advocacy for them with regard to human and environmental rights.

A Mission from God

Of all these first encounters, that of Christopher Columbus with the native peoples of the Americas was the most consequential. From a European perspective it really was a "new world" that he had discovered. His three small ships set sail from Spain on Friday, August 3, 1492, and on Thursday, October 11, they at last reached land again, an island that "the Indians" called *Guanahani*, which we now know to be in the Bahamas, southeast of the Florida peninsula.

First Columbus took possession of these lands for his lords, the king and queen of Spain, and then he reflected on the nature of their inhabitants:

> … because I recognized that they were people who would be better freed from error and converted to our Holy Faith by love than by force—to some of them I gave red caps, and glass beads which they put on their chests, and many other things of small value, in which they took so much pleasure and became so much our friends that it was a marvel…. They took everything and gave of what they had very willingly. But it seemed to me that they were a people very poor in everything. All of them go around as naked as their mothers bore them…. Some of them paint their faces, and some of them the whole body, and some of them only the eyes, and some of them only the nose. They do not carry arms nor are they acquainted with them. They should be good and intelligent servants, for I see that they say very quickly everything that is said to them; and I believe that they would become Christians very easily, for it seemed to me that they had no religion. Our Lord pleasing, at the time of my departure I will take six of them from here to your Highnesses in order that they may learn to speak. (Columbus 1989: 72–73)

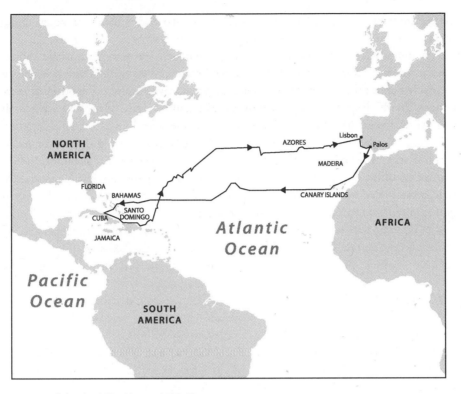

MAP 0.1 Columbus's First Voyage 1492–93

What the local people thought of these strange beings from another world is not recorded, and soon Columbus pushed off again in search of "Cipango"—Japan—the land that he believed had to lie nearby. Columbus had radically underestimated the circumference of the earth and truly believed that he had reached Asia; it took some years to clear that up. Meanwhile, in four voyages across the Atlantic, Columbus would visit Santo Domingo, Cuba, Jamaica, Trinidad, and the outer Caribbean Islands, then exploring the eastern coasts of Panama, Nicaragua, Honduras, and Guatemala. Near Trinidad he observed a vast current of fresh water flowing into the sea, which he correctly guessed could only have originated from a continental land mass. It was in fact the mouth of the Orinoco, with much of South America behind it.

Columbus died in 1506. In 1513, Vasco Nuñez de Balboa crossed Panama to reach the Pacific Ocean. In 1520, Hernan Cortes and his native allies toppled the Aztec empire, while Ferdinand Magellan rounded the southern tip of South America on his way to the Philippines. In 1533, the Incas fell to Francisco Pizarro. By 1540 the Coronado expedition had reached as far as central Kansas. Within a hundred years the peoples whom Columbus had encountered in the Bahamas and the Caribbean would be largely gone from the earth, the victims of disease, massacre, and slavery. Sometimes history moves very fast indeed, "dreams of empire that become other peoples' nightmares" (Gomez 2008: 411).

These are the bare bones of a complex story. But what we want to emphasize here is the fundamental idea that, then as now, theory shapes perception. Columbus's travels were motivated and his observations shaped by theories from a number of domains: geography, philosophy, theology, history, and "anthropology"—what was then known or believed about the kinds of people who inhabit our world.

Columbus thought that he was on a mission from God, part of a divine plan that was unfolding through the unification of Spain and the expulsion or forced conversion of Muslims and Jews. He had been present in May 1492 when Granada, the last Muslim state in Spain, had fallen to the Christian monarchs. Columbus's diaries and logs are full of references to the search for gold; but, in addition to enriching his family, what he wished to do with that wealth, if it should be found, was to enable his king and queen to launch a crusade to retake Jerusalem, as a necessary prelude to the Second Coming of Christ. So his venture into the western ocean was seen in terms of a vision about the direction of history. Anthropology, as we understand it today, has also been shaped by such visions, notably by the idea that history actually has a direction and that it's progressive in nature—onward and upward. We're less sure about that now.

As for the peoples of "the Indies," Columbus saw them as simple folk, childlike in nature and ready for conversion; others would see them as "natural slaves," witless and fit only to serve. In Todorov's words, "Columbus's behavior implies that he does not grant the Indians the right to have their own will, that he judges them, in short, as living objects. It is as such that, in his naturalist's enthusiasm, he always wants to take specimens of all kinds back to Spain: trees, birds, animals, and Indians; the notion of asking their opinion is foreign to him" (Todorov 1984: 48).

He searched the Hebrew scriptures for an answer to where the "Indians" might have come from, and he found one possibility in the ninth and tenth chapters of the book of Genesis, which tells of what happened to the sons of Noah—Shem, Ham, and Japheth—after they disembarked from the ark following the great flood (Columbus, 1991: 249). They dispersed from that point, "and from them came the people who were scattered over the whole earth" (Gen. 9:18). Columbus concluded that the "Indians" of the islands were of Japheth's line, because "from these the maritime peoples spread out into their territories by their clans within their nations, each with its own language" (Gen. 10:5).

He was also influenced by the geographical thought of the Greeks and Romans, such as the notion that the extreme parts of the globe—the arctic regions and the tropics—give rise to extreme forms of life: strange creatures and humanoid monsters. Drawings of such beings populate the margins of old maps (Friedman 2000: 34 and passim; Gomez 2008: 84–86). Monstrous in form, they were thought to be morally monstrous as well—incestuous cannibalistic savages (Gomez 2008:53; Pagden 1982: 81).

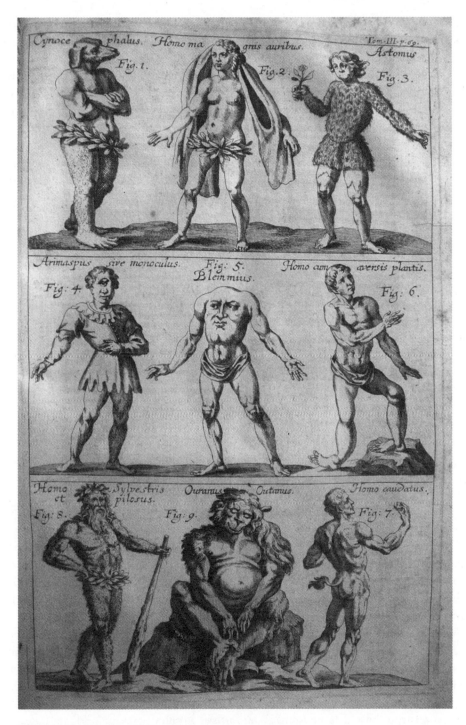

PLATE 0.1 The Monstrous Races

From Guanahani Columbus went on to Cuba where he heard, or thought he heard, some very strange things:

> These people are very gentle and very timid, naked, as has been said before, without weapons and without law. [The two sailors] … whom he had sent to see the interior told him [of] a settlement of 50 houses, where … there must have been a thousand inhabitants because many live in one house. These houses are like very large Moorish campaign tents. They said that the Indians received them with great solemnity, according to their custom. And everyone came to see them, men as well as women…. The Indians touched them and kissed their hands and feet, marveling, and believing that the Spaniards came from the heavens…. He understood … that, far from there, there were one-eyed men, and others, with snouts of dogs, who ate men, and that as soon as one was taken they cut his throat and drank his blood and cut off his genitals…. (Columbus 1989: 133, 137) (Plate 0.1)

There is a translation problem here; the Spanish had been in the area for less than a month, and how anything that they heard could have been correctly understood remains a mystery. Be that as it may, it is entirely possible that the local people had "others" of their own, strange beings who they imagined to live over the next mountain or across the sea somewhere. But it is more likely that Columbus projected his own pre-existing beliefs onto what he thought was being said to him.

As the voyages of Columbus and his successors unfolded, the true complexity and diversity of Indian society became apparent (but still no dog-headed men!). For example, the level of organization and technical sophistication of the Aztecs stunned the Spanish, as in this account from a member of the Cortes expedition: "When we gazed upon all this splendour at once, we scarcely knew what to think, and we doubted whether all that we beheld was real. A series of large towns stretched themselves along the banks of the lake, out of which still larger ones rose magnificently above the waters. Innumerable crowds of canoes were plying everywhere around us; at regular distances we continually passed over new bridges, and before us lay the great city of Mexico in all its splendor" (Diaz del Castillo 1928: 270).

Soon all that would be gone as well, the temples broken up, the stones used to build the churches of the conquerors, and the Indians reduced to serfdom. The early days of the Spanish Empire were savage times, documented in detail by an outraged priest named Bartolomé de Las Casas who, in the 1540s, wrote his famous book *In Defense of the Indians*. For Las Casas it was the Spanish who were the barbarians, and he put his argument in historical perspective, asking his readers to imagine what it had been like when the Romans invaded Spain under Caesar Augustus in the first century BCE:

> Do you think that the Romans, once they had subjugated the wild and barbaric peoples of Spain, could with secure right divide all of you among themselves,

handing over so many head of both males and females as allotments to individuals? And do you then conclude that the Romans could have stripped your rulers of their authority and consigned all of you, after you had been deprived of your liberty, to wretched labors, especially in searching for gold and silver lodes and mining and refining the metals? [Would you not judge] that you also have the right to defend your freedom, indeed your very life, by war? ... For God's sake and man's faith in him, is this the way to impose the yoke of Christ on Christian men. Is it not, rather, to act like thieves, cut-throats and cruel plunderers and to drive the gentlest of people headlong into despair. (de Las Casas 1992: 43)

If anything, the Indians were more "civilized" than the Spanish had been in Roman or even modern times. All that they had lacked was Christianity: "... long before they had heard the word Spaniard they had properly organized states, wisely ordered by excellent laws, religion, and custom. They cultivated friendship and, bound together in common fellowship, lived in populous cities in which they wisely administered the affairs of both peace and war and equitably, truly governed by laws that at very many points surpass ours" (de Las Casas 1992: 42–43).

Though his aim was moral and political, not "scientific," Las Casas was applying a "comparative method" in his attempt to understand the problem before him. He not only compared Spanish and Indian society at the time of contact; he also went back and compared previous stages of society with one another in the light of history, philosophy, and the teachings of his church. But, as we noted above, to compare anything you need some basis for doing it—some sense of what is relevant to the case at hand. It could be technology, the economy, government, religion, or the kinship system. Las Casas considered all of them in order to justify his claim that the Indians in fact lived in advanced societies similar in many ways to those of Europe.

As you will see, this kind of argument is still very much with us, and it is central to the evolutionary style of reasoning characteristic of anthropology in its earlier days (which we will explore in Chapter 2). Las Casas had a classification of societies in mind. It was largely derived from ancient Greek political science, particularly that of Aristotle, who asked about the nature of the state, about domestic life, about various forms of property and government, and about what it is that makes a person a slave, and distinguishes "civilized" from "barbarous" nations.

In 1992, the 500th anniversary of Columbus's "discovery" was marked by celebration in some quarters—but quite differently by protesting Aboriginal groups, who saw his accomplishment as the beginnings of genocide.

Captain Cook in the Islands of Paradise

In 1778, Captain James Cook of the Royal Navy unexpectedly came across the Hawaiian Islands during his third Pacific expedition.

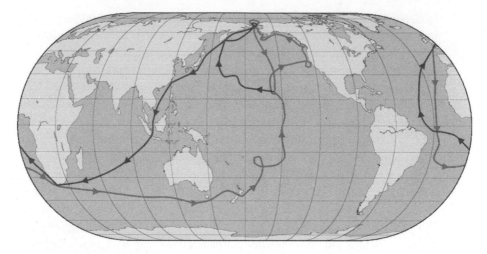

MAP 0.2 Cook's Third Voyage

The first two voyages (1768–71; 1772–75) had been sponsored by the Royal Society, which had been founded in the seventeenth century to promote the advancement of natural knowledge. These trips made Cook a famous man; their by-product was the expansion of the British Empire into Australia and New Zealand. The third voyage was aimed at establishing whether or not there was a usable northwest passage: an ice-free sea-route across northern Canada to the Atlantic Ocean and Europe. This time, commercial interests had a hand in the game, notably the Hudson's Bay Company, which sought to advance its fur trade in the region.

On Monday, January 19, Cook's ships *Resolution* and *Discovery* made landfall in Hawai'i on their way up from Tahiti. The immediate goal was the northwest coast of North America and the Bering Strait. The discovery of the Hawaiian chain was a total surprise; even though the Spanish had long been sailing the Pacific from Mexico to the Philippines, no Europeans had ever crossed this far north. No one knew of the Hawaiians, not even the closely related peoples of Tahiti and the other Polynesian Islands to the south; nor did the Hawaiians know of them, and it is possible that there had been no outside contact for hundreds of years (Beaglehole 1974: 574). Cook first spotted the island of Oahu, but the winds prevented them from reaching it; so they tacked toward the southern coast of Kaua'i:

> At this time we were in some doubt whether or no the land before [us] was inhabited, this doubt was soon cleared up, by seeing some Canoes coming off from the shore towards the Ship.... There were three and four men in each and we were agreeably surprised to find them of the same Nation as the people of Otahiete and the other islands we had lately visited. […] I never

PLATE 0.2 Hawaiian Temple

saw Indians so much astonished at the entering of a ship before, their eyes were continually flying from object to object, the wildness of their looks and actions fully express'd their surprise and astonishment at the several new objects before them and evinced that they never had been on board a ship before. (Cook 1967: 263–64)

Cook then went ashore himself near the present town of Waimca, where his statue now stands. He found the Hawaiians very hospitable and ready to trade just about anything for pieces of iron: "The very instant I leaped ashore, they all fell flat on their faces, and remained in that humble posture till I made signs to them to rise…. This, as I afterwards understood, is done to their great chiefs" (Cook 1967: 269). He had encountered a hierarchical society of a type already familiar to him on other Polynesian islands (1967: 284). Noting many similarities of language and culture, Cook asked himself, "How shall we account for this Nation spreading itself so far over this Vast ocean? We find them from New Zealand to the south, to these islands to the North and from Easter Island to the Hebrides; an extent of 60° of latitude … and 83° of longitude … how much further is not known" (1967: 279).

James Cook was a meticulous observer, with a keen eye for religious practice as for other things:

We observed at every Village one or more elevated objects. It proved to be a [*heiau*] which in many respects was like those of Otaheite…. It was 4 feet square at the base and about 20 feet high, the four sides was built of small sticks and branches.... On each side ... stood erect some rude carved boards.... At the foot of these were square places, a little sunk below the common level and inclosed with stone, these we understood were graves. About the middle of the [*heiau*] were three of these places in a line, where we were told three chiefs had been buried; before them was another that was oblong, this they called ... taboo and gave us clearly to understand that three human sacrifices had been buried there, that is one at the burial of each chief. (1967: 270)

In a structure nearby there were two effigies of goddesses, and the whole place was surrounded with an aura of *taboo*: "sacred, dangerous, set apart"—a term that entered the English language via the Polynesians, its first recorded use being by Captain Cook himself in 1777. The British had stumbled into a complex symbolic world of myth and ritual, as became evident when Cook was treated like a god on the Big Island of Hawai'i upon his return from the north Pacific in November 1778.

What happened in the meantime is a story in itself. *Resolution* and *Discovery* departed Kaua'i with an ample supply of fresh water and foodstuffs that they had traded for with the Hawaiians. They reached the coast of North America near the Straits of Juan de Fuca between what is now Washington State and Vancouver Island in British Columbia. Cook missed the strait and sailed up the west coast of the Island to Nootka Sound, where they had intense interactions with the locals—the people who now know themselves as the *Nuu-chah-nulth* ("along the mountains and sea")—who lived in houses made of boards, mainly subsisted on the products of the sea, and also had a keen interest in acquiring metal. We will return to them in Chapters 6 and 8.

They then passed through the Aleutian Islands and circumnavigated the Bering Sea up to the edge of the Arctic ice pack. After many encounters with local native peoples and with Russians on the Siberian side, Cook headed back to Hawai'i before winter set in. This time it was to the Big Island, where the British were astonished to find snow-capped mountains (Mauna Loa, 10,000 ft.; Mauna Kea, 13,000 ft.). The next events lead to questions about just what sort of being the Hawaiians took James Cook to be. His own diaries become spotty at this point, but they are supplemented by the journals of his officers, in this case by Lieutenant James King of the *Resolution*. Cook had established some degree of rapport with local men of evident importance, who now wanted him to participate in a ceremonial:

We landed on the Beech, & were receiv'd by 3 or 4 men who held wands tipt with dogs hair, & who kept repeating a sentence, wherein the word Erono was always mention'd, this is the name by which the Captn has for some time been distinguish'd by the Natives. At the [north] end of this beach is a Village, on the other an oblong pile of Stones & between a grove of Coco nut trees, with a stone wall separating it from the Beech; Not a Soul but those I have mention'd were to be seen on the beech, but close round the huts we saw numbers of the Inhabitants Prostrate, as they were at our first Visit at [Kaua'i]. We were conducted to the top of the pile of stones.... There was a stout Railing all round, on which there were stuck 20 Skulls, the most of which they gave us to understand were those of [Maui] men, whom they had killd on the death of some Chief.... There were 12 Images ranged in a semicircular form & fronting these opposite the Center figure was a [rotten] hog, placed on a stand.... On one side were two wooden Images; between these the Captain was seated.... While I was made to do the same to the other. [The priest] kept repeating in a very quick tone some speeches or prayers, to which the rest responded ... till at last he repeat'd only two or three words at a time & was answerd by the Croud repeating the Word Erono. (Cook 1967: 505–6)

The ritual went on for some time. The Lieutenant and his Captain were obliged to attempt to eat morsels of the rotten pig. King was mystified by "this long, & rather tiresome ceremony, of which we could only guess at its Object and Meaning, only that it was highly respectful on their parts, & seemed to promise us every assistance they could afford us" (1967: 506–7).

So here we face an anthropological issue that will concern us throughout this book: the problem of **meaning** and **interpretation**. How is a ritual of this sort to be understood? What is the nature of concepts such as "taboo"? Who or what was "Erono," and why was Captain Cook associated with this being in the eyes of the Hawaiians? What did it all mean? Anthropologists and historians have gone back over records such as King's in attempting to make sense of all this in the light of what is known about Polynesian religious belief and practice. What methods can we use to decipher such episodes? Evidently *culture* has something to do with it, but how is "culture" itself to be understood and interpreted when it comes to explaining events and practices such as these? As Cook's biographer wrote, "we may not unnaturally ask ... why Cook should have received such extraordinary notice at this particular island" (1967: 657). It wasn't like that on Kaua'i.

These questions take on added force given the unfortunate events that followed. After Captain Cook had been treated virtually like a god, the *Resolution* and *Discovery* took their leave but were forced to return within a week because of a broken mast. This time things didn't go well at all. Cook ended up in a dispute with the locals over the theft of a small boat; he and some of his party were killed in an attempt to get the boat back. His body was taken inland and dismembered, and his shipmates were only able to retrieve some of the parts. What was left of Captain Cook was put in a coffin and buried at sea in Kealakekua Bay, which had been placed under a do-not-enter taboo by a local lord so as to prevent further hostilities. As Lt. King reported, "we now assurd him we were entirely their friends, & as the Erono was buried all recollection of the affair was also buried" (1967: 567).

A monument to Captain Cook was erected on the shore of the Bay south of the town of Kailua on the famous Kona Coast; it is considered extra-territorial British property. As for Hawai'i itself, in 1810 the islands were unified into one kingdom by Kamehameha the Great. In 1893 the kingdom was overthrown in a bloodless coup organized by a group of American planters and merchants. In 1959 Hawai'i was admitted to the American Union as the 50th state. If you travel around the islands these days you may occasionally see the original Hawaiian flag flying by the roadside. A local man explained that it was to protest the illegal American seizure of the islands and to agitate for the restoration of the kingdom. On his t-shirt was written, "My people killed Captain Cook." Over the years Cook became for some "a symbol of the colonialism, dispossession and oppression that sometimes followed in the wake of his explorations." As one radical said, "the best part of Cook's visit was that we killed him … we can defend our honour by declaring that we rid the world of another evil white man" (Williams 2008: 170, 172).

You can think about these events as episodes in the history of **globalization** (which we will consider in Chapter 9). That's a trendy word these days, and a bit misleading. Such processes reach far back in time and are not just a feature of our own age of information technology, outsourcing, and global capitalism. Columbus was after gold, and the search for it was one of the driving forces behind the western European expansion, a fairly useless metal that nevertheless had—and still has—great symbolic value as an internationally recognized medium of exchange. His discoveries were profound, not least with regard to their biological effects. We often hear about the harmful ecological impact of invasive species. But try to imagine what things would be like without the New World food plants: corn, white potatoes, sweet potatoes, cassava (manioc), tomatoes, pineapples, papayas, avocados, and peppers, among others.

This flow also moved the other way. It makes an interesting footnote to point out that William Bligh was master of Cook's ship *Resolution* on that last fateful trip. In his subsequent career he captained the *Bounty* in a mission to bring breadfruit, which originated in the Pacific islands, to the Caribbean as a foodstuff for the African slaves who had been imported to work the sugar plantations. The native peoples of the region were largely gone by then, in the wake of the demographic collapse induced by the Spanish. Following the famous mutiny and an epic voyage in an open boat, Bligh tried again, and this time was successful; breadfruit is an important food crop in the Caribbean islands to this day. He then went on to become governor of the colony of New South Wales in Australia, which had been founded to offload Britain's convict population. A statue to him stands beside Sydney Harbour. William Bligh died an admiral and is buried in the yard of what is now the Museum of Gardening in south London, next to the palace of the Archbishop of Canterbury.

Simon Fraser's Quest

Simon Fraser was born in 1776 in what is now New York state. He moved to Montreal as a teenager and, through family connections, became involved with the western

MAP 0.3 The Pacific Northwest: Simon Fraser's Journey

fur trade. His story has connections to the previous one. Captain Cook's visit to the Northwest Coast was followed in 1792 by that of George Vancouver, who had served with Cook on two previous voyages. This one took Vancouver to the mouth of the Columbia River that defines the border between Washington and Oregon, and there he met an American merchant captain who had named the river after his ship. Vancouver was followed in turn by the Lewis and Clark expedition, which was organized by President Thomas Jefferson to explore the region recently acquired from France as part of the Louisiana Purchase. The Lewis and Clark party crossed overland from the headwaters of the Missouri River and spent the winter of 1803–04 at the Columbia's mouth near the present town of Astoria. Simon Fraser's mission was to determine whether the river his company had heard about from a previous expedition was or was not the Columbia. He and his party started down this unknown river by canoe in 1808, encountering numerous native groups along the way.

PLATE 0.3 James Teit and Wife

The story we want to tell now is a bit different from those above. Simon Fraser's journey took place in relatively recent times. At the end of the nineteenth century there were Aboriginal people alive who had heard stories of his visit from those who had actually witnessed it. Fraser's own account tells us something about the nature of the anthropological experience. How Aboriginal people regarded him gives us the other side of the coin; they were having an anthropological experience of their own. Fraser was a precise observer: What did he think about what he saw? What did the local people make of him and the other people on his expedition, including French-speaking employees of the North West Company, whom Fraser called "Canadians," and who were probably people that would now be recognized as Métis, men of mixed French and First Nations descent.

Fraser kept a detailed journal of his trip, while native people living in the vicinity of the present town of Lytton kept alive memories of his visit. They were told in 1900 to a self-educated anthropologist from Scotland, James Teit, who had married into a native family.

Teit's interest in interior First Nations culture and his knowledge of the local language came to the attention of Franz Boas, an anthropologist at Columbia University in New York, about whom we will have much more to say shortly. Teit was recruited as a research assistant and in the end produced a considerable body of work of his own. Here are two stories of first contact told by Simon Fraser himself, and by a woman named Semalitsa.

Simon Fraser, June 19, 1808

At 8 A.M. set out.... The natives ferried us over a large rapid river [the Stein River]. I obtained, for an awl, a passage to the next village, a distance of three miles through strong rapids. The others who went by land met some of the Indians on the way who were happy to see them. The Indians of this village may be about four hundred souls and some of them appear very old; they live among mountains and enjoy pure air, seem cleanly inclined, and make use of wholesome food. We observed several European articles among them, viz. a copper Tea Kettle, a brass camp kettle, a strip of common blanket, and clothing such as the Cree women wear. These things, we supposed, were brought from out settlement beyond the [Rocky] Mountains. Indeed the Indians made us understand as much.

After having remained some time in this village, the principal chief invited us over the river. We crossed, and he received us at the water side, where, assisted by several others, he took me by the arms and conducted me in a moment up the hill to the camp where his people were sitting in rows, to the number of twelve hundred; and I had to shake hands with all of them. Then the Great chief made a long harangue, in course of which he pointed to the sun, to the four quarters of the world, and then to us, and then he introduced his father, who was old and blind, and was carried by another man, who also made a harangue of some length. The old man was placed near us, and with some emotion often stretched out both his hands in order to feel ours.

The nation have many chiefs and great men, appear to be good orators, for their manner of delivery is extremely handsome. We had every reason to be thankful for our reception at this place; the Indians shewed us every possible attention and supplied our wants as much as they could. We had salmon, berries, oil and roots in abundance, and our men had six dogs. Our tent was pitched near the camp and we enjoyed peace and security during our stay. (Fraser 1960: 86–87)

Told by Semalitsa to James Teit, 1900

My grandmother told me that when she was a young girl she was playing one day in the summer-time (about the time the service-berries get ripe) near the river beach at the village of [Stein], when she saw two canoes, with red flags hoisted, come downstream. She ran and told her mother, and the people gathered to see the strange sight. Seeing so many people gathered, the canoes put ashore and several men came ashore. Each canoe carried a number of men, and many of them wore strange dresses, and everything about them was strange. Some of the men looked like Indians, and others looked like what we call white men. Among them was a Shuswap chief who acted as interpreter. Our people were not afraid of the strangers, nor were they hostile to them. The strangers produced a large pipe, and had a ceremonial smoke with some of our men. After distributing a few presents, they boarded their canoes and went on to Lytton, where they were presented with food of various kinds, and gave in exchange tobacco, beads, and knives. The Lytton chief ... went up the east bank of the Fraser, and conducted them to his place with considerable ceremony. All the Lytton people were assembled to meet them, and before they left they had many talks and smokes with the Indians. The Spence's Bridge chief ran on foot all the way [to Lytton] and arrived in time to see the strangers and to deliver a great speech. The Lytton chief at this time was also a great orator. The Spence's Bridge chief was presented with some kind of metal or brass badge, and a hat worn by the leader of the strangers whom the Indians called "The Sun." He was called this because of some kind of shining emblem he wore on his hat or cap, which resembled the symbol of the Sun. The Indians applied names to most of the strangers, all taken from some feature of their appearance or from certain marks or emblems on their clothing. (Wickwire 1994: 8–9)

Fraser was having a good day, though on a bad day he was likely to refer to his hosts as "savages." He noted unfamiliar cultural practices, such as the speech in which the orator pointed to the sun and the four quarters of the world. Fraser could not know that later generations in the Lytton area would call *him* "The Sun" or that some would remember him as having traveled in company with Coyote, Moon, and Morning Star. "Coyote" was a powerful figure among interior peoples, the trickster-transformer who gave the world its present form. Some said that Fraser's visit was foretold by prophets, and one version of the Fraser narrative tells it as though Fraser was *himself* Coyote. As Wickwire states, "This is the only time Coyote has appeared since the end of the mythological age" (1994: 10). A more recent and quite different account recalls that some member of Fraser's party molested a local woman. This is possible, of course, but it may also reflect the tensions that have arisen between whites and native people since Fraser's time.

When Fraser's party reached the river's mouth, he took latitude measurements and determined that this new river could not be the Columbia, but was well to the north of it. In years to come the peoples he had encountered along the way would be confined to small Indian reserves, a tiny fraction of the territory they had once used freely.

These contrasting stories point to the topic of "**social memory**"—the social factors affecting recollection and forgetting (see Fentress & Wickham 1992; Connerton

1989). The written accounts of Columbus, Cook, and Fraser are stories as well, told from the point of view of a particular time and place. In Semalitsa's story we see a process at work whereby long-ago events were assimilated into a First Nations style of storytelling. Things like this happen all the time. Memories of events, by being told and retold, change their shape over time. Events happen, but what do they mean? By themselves nothing much, unless they are combined into a story. Things that happened at different times may get absorbed into one story and begin to take on "mythological" qualities. Things and relationships that were highly important to your parents may mean little to you and are therefore forgotten. The chain of transmission is broken, while other things stand out and become part of the family's history. Ask yourself how many of your memories of early childhood are actually your "own" or are actually the result of what you've been told about what you were like as a child and the adventures you had.

Conclusion

Christopher Columbus, James Cook, and Simon Fraser were explorers; their first-contact experiences with foreign peoples were a by-product of expeditions that were undertaken for other purposes. Anthropologists, on the other hand, seek out such encounters. In the next chapter—"Culture Shock," we will explain why they do it, take a look at the kind of experiences they have, and examine the new perspectives that such experiences open up for them. Our task is to understand and to some extent explain the diversity of the human world. We hope that you will find the stories selected to discuss ideas of culture and place as interesting as we do, and that they serve as a starting point for discussions about your own culture and why people do the things that they do. As you'll see, anthropologists are storytellers too.

Study and Discussion Questions

1   What economic and political circumstances led the Europeans to go out in search of the new worlds that we've described? How is this related to the history of globalization?
2   How did the culture of his own time influence how Columbus saw the Native Americans?
3   How did what the Europeans found in those new worlds influence perception of the history of their own societies?
4   How would you go about understanding and interpreting things like Hawaiian "taboo" practices? What else would you need to know in order to understand them?
5   What is the relation between storytelling and memory?

PART I

THEORY, METHODS, AND CONCEPTS

CHAPTER 1

//

Culture Shock

LEARNING OBJECTIVES

After reading this chapter, students should be able to

- describe the four major sub-fields of anthropology and identify what makes cultural anthropology unique as a discipline;
- identify and explain the key research methods of cultural anthropologists, including participant observation, fieldwork, reflexive thinking;
- distinguish between *culture shock* and *ethnocentrism* and understand these terms in relation to the larger concepts of cultural relativism and moral relativism;
- define the term *ethnography* and describe the ethnographies of Malinowski, Fernea, and Small;
- understand the ethical implications of anthropology, the role of reflexive thinking, and how social position and category influence the work of the researcher;
- compare and contrast the comparative method and inductive approach, using examples from major researchers; and
- explain how the concepts of unity and diversity are related to the question of human nature and how this affects the work of anthropologists.

KEY TERMS

archaeology	ethnocentrism	participant observation
comparative method	ethnography	physical anthropology
cultural relativism	holistic approach	reflexive thinking
culture	inductive approach	socio-cultural
culture shock	linguistic anthropology	anthropology

Introduction

The experience of an anthropologist's first day in the field shares many of the same characteristics as that of an explorer—feelings of isolation, uncertainty, and wonderment at the people, customs, and location unfolding before them. The difference, however, is the objective of these excursions: the explorer was seeking a better understanding of geography in order to establish trade routes and other profitable endeavors; the anthropologist sets out in the field to gain a better understanding of the people who inhabit a particular space—their attitudes, behaviors, customs, and beliefs (or **culture**), and how they interact with others around them, whether in a neighboring town or a country on the other side of the world. The term "anthropology" is derived from the Greek words for "man" or "humanity" (*anthropos*) and "knowledge" (*logos*): "Knowledge of humanity." As we hope to show in the following discussions, the study of humanity that we call anthropology is as diverse and complex as its subject matter. What unifies the discipline, however, is a commitment to a cross-cultural perspective, to thinking about society in a comparative and global manner. What this commitment means in practice is that anthropologists investigate social life by participating in it—by being there in real situations and observing from a theoretically informed perspective.

The focus of this chapter is the ethnographic experience. Bronislaw Malinowski worked on the Trobriand Islands in the southwest Pacific during World War I; he had an enormous influence on the development of anthropological method. Elizabeth Warnock Fernea conducted research in the 1950s among the women of a small Iraqi village, while Cathy Small lived among American students in an undergraduate dorm in the early 2000s. Along the way we will introduce a few key anthropological concepts and also reflect on the nature and process of the research methods that anthropologists employ. First things first, however—just what *is* anthropology, and what do contemporary anthropologists actually *do*?

What Do Anthropologists *Do*?

What do anthropologists study? And what do they do with their findings? Most popular representations of anthropologists have them digging bones and fossils in exotic locations, or studying secluded tribes in the South Pacific. While both these portrayals are true, they do not begin to describe the diversity of subjects that anthropologists turn their lens on. The term anthropology encompasses four sub-disciplines that, on the surface, appear to have very little in common with one another. What unifies these sub-disciplines, however, is a desire to understand humankind. We will focus exclusively on **socio-cultural anthropology**, the study of human culture, social organization, and behavior. Because it is just as useful to know what one is *not* studying as it is to know what one is studying, we will briefly define the three other major areas associated with the discipline.

Physical anthropologists seek to understand human variation, adaptation, and change. Physical anthropology was once preoccupied with questions about the nature of "race," with classifying people according to their perceived physical types and explaining what such differences mean in historical terms. Physical anthropologists have moved on since those days, and, as you'll see, a critique of the concept of "race" was one of the formative influences on anthropology as it is practiced now. Today's physical anthropologists can be found studying nutritional issues in Africa, examining pre-human fossil remains, or using genomic evidence to reconstruct ancient human migrations. It is quite a diverse discipline in its own right. Two sub-fields of physical anthropology include *primatology*, the study of non-human primates and how their behavior and genetic composition compare with those of humans, and *forensic anthropology*, the focus on human skeletal remains found at crime scenes and at the site of accidents. **Archaeology** shares many research interests and methodological approaches with physical anthropology. Broadly speaking, archaeologists study the material remains of past cultures, but not exclusively. "Garbage Archaeologists" on Staten Island near New York City, for example, have been examining the Fresh Kills landfill to understand recent consumption practices and the rate of decomposition of materials. Finally, **linguistic anthropology** explores the relation between culture and language. Linguistic anthropologists explore everything from the structure, origin, and development of languages, to the relationship between language and social interaction. Linguistic anthropologists are also interested in exploring how communication is influenced by technology, such as email, social media, cell phones, and text messaging.

The focal points of the four sub-fields of anthropology are clearly very different from one another, and as one might expect, the methods employed to collect, analyze, and interpret these data also vary considerably. Cultural anthropology is primarily regarded as a social science, a classification based upon the type of research questions asked, the research methods used, and the approaches employed to analyze data. Throughout this text, we will explore these research components as they relate to pertinent topics such as gender, race, religion, and globalization.

Cultural anthropologists want to know how the elements in a cultural system are related to one another, and how they are expressed in individual lives. When we try to account for the behavior of other people, what we are really asking is: What does their behavior *mean*? What do they intend by it? What institutional structures constrain and direct it? What makes it sensible, rather than just random or crazy?' Culture is a system of meaning; it provides the standards of value through which action is judged and is usually an unconscious, taken-for-granted reality for the people who share it. It is one thing to experience a new city or country, meet new people or try a new activity, and quite another to consider how one will interpret or manage these experiences and findings so that others can make sense of them. For many anthropologists, considering how their own opinions and beliefs influence the way they see the people and activities around them is as important as considering how their participants might view these things. This is called **reflexive thinking**, and in a discipline in which the researcher is the instrument, it is extremely important.

Contemporary anthropologists seek to understand the similarities and differences between human cultures. Deconstructing the social world to fit into neat patterns and simple governing laws, as was the approach of early anthropologists, has largely been abandoned. Anthropologists conduct fieldwork in a specific location or with a specific group of people to gain an understanding of why they behave the way they do. Through **participant observation**, or joining and engaging in the culture and customs of the people who are the focus of one's study over an extended period of time, the anthropologist gains a **holistic** understanding of how the group works. How are social institutions related to one another in society? How does the economy impact the political system, and vice versa? Is religion a prominent feature in society, and why or why not? Is society highly stratified along class lines, or is it fairly egalitarian? The presence of an anthropologist in a community has a recognized impact on the way in which people act. Any account of an event, issue or group of people is a re-telling by a person who has their own values, beliefs, and experiences that influence what they see and how they see it. No matter how long one stays in the field and gets to know one's participants, one's own life experiences and worldview will affect what one deems important to document and discuss, and what one does not. Many cultural anthropologists will identify how their own life experiences and biases impact their observations.

The best way to gain an understanding of what anthropologists do, and how they do it, is to explore the product of their fieldwork and research. This is often presented as **ethnography**, a theoretically informed description and explanation of a way of life. We will consider three very different accounts of ethnographic fieldwork from three anthropologists. The first is from Bronislaw Malinowski and his pioneering ethnographic study *Argonauts of the Western Pacific*. The second ethnography by Elizabeth Warnock Fernea recounts her experience in a small isolated village in Iraq in the mid 1950s, before the 1958 overthrow of the British-established monarch. While *Guest of the Sheik* was written and published over 50 years ago, Fernea's description of her experience arriving late at night to the village and slowly getting to know the people and customs of her new home remains a relevant and compelling read. The third anthropologist whose work we will consider is Rebekah Nathan (a pseudonym), a professor of anthropology in the United States who went "undercover" as a freshman at the university where she taught. While these two experiences are clearly very different, we bring your attention to the notion of being on the outside looking in. You can

PLATE 1.1 Anthropologist Charlotte Whitby-Coles in India

likely relate to this feeling—have you ever traveled to a country where the language spoken was not your own? Have you ever moved to a new town or city where you knew very few people? Think about your first day of school or of a new job—did you find yourself wondering where to sit and who you would talk to over lunch?

Experiencing the Field

Bronislaw Malinowski

If you were to ask a random selection of anthropologists which ethnographic works they consider the most important to the development of the discipline, Malinowski's *Argonauts of the Western Pacific* would probably make the top five. One reason for this is its intriguing subject matter—his analysis of a system of ceremonial exchange known as the *kula*, which was conducted over great distances in sophisticated sailing canoes. The subtitle is: *An account of native enterprise and adventure in the archipelagoes of Melanesian New Guinea*. Malinowski also wants to tell us a romantic tale of adventure, in which the ethnographer comes across as an adventurer himself, one who goes off to exotic places and brings back important insights about the human condition.

The part of Poland in which Malinowski grew up was then part of the Austro-Hungarian Empire, ruled from Vienna. His father was a professor of Slavic languages and folklore at the University of Cracow, and the study of language also became an important aspect of Malinowski's career. At university Malinowski studied physics and philosophy, but along the way he became interested in anthropology and undertook graduate work at the London School of Economics (see Stocking 1995: 244–97; Young 2004). This led to an opportunity to go off to Australia and then to New Guinea, where he engaged in fieldwork in 1915–18 along the south coast of the main island, and in the Trobriand chain off to its northeast. The Trobrianders are yam-farmers, pig-raisers, fishermen, and traders, part of the wider "Melanesian" cultural and linguistic community in New Guinea and its adjoining island chains. World War I was under way—this "accursed war," as he called it. Technically Malinowski was therefore an enemy alien, but the Australian authorities let him continue with his work anyway. And he had met the daughter of a professor at the University of Melbourne, Elsie Masson, who—as his diary shows—he thought about obsessively while in the field. So ... what was it like "out there"?

> Imagine yourself suddenly set down surrounded by all your gear, alone on a tropical beach close to a native village. Since you take up your abode in the compound of some neighbouring white man, trader or missionary, you have nothing to do, but to start at once on your ethnographic work. Imagine further that you are a beginner, without previous experience, with nothing to guide you and no one to help you.... This exactly describes my first initiation into field work on the south coast of New Guinea. I well remember the long visits I paid to the villages during the first weeks; the feeling of hopelessness and despair after many obstinate but futile attempts had entirely failed to bring me into real touch with the natives, or supply me with any material. Imagine yourself then, making your first entry into the village.... Some natives flock around you, especially if they smell tobacco. Others, the more dignified and elderly, remain seated where they are. (Malinowski 1922: 4)

Of course the diary adds another dimension to this account. He was, as he says, troubled by "lecherous thoughts." Troubled quite a lot actually, since—in addition to the young woman in Melbourne—he thought about many others as well, both white and native. Malinowski was also a hypochondriac, constantly worried about his state of health, and occasionally down with what seem to have been bouts of malaria. This is a typical entry on a bad day, and they were many:

> Monday, November 26th, 1917: Yesterday I had what is usually called *an attack of feverishness, a touch of fever*. Physical and mental sluggishness. Yesterday, for instance, I felt no desire and was not strong enough to take a walk, not even around the island. Nor have I the energy to get to work, not even to write letters

to E.R.M. [in Melbourne] or look over my ethnographic notes. Moreover, I am extremely *irritable* and the yells of the boys and other noises get horribly on my nerves. Resistance to lecherous thoughts weaker. Tendency to read *rubbish*; I leaf through a magazine…. (Malinowski 1967: 131)

But he also had good days:

April 19, 1918: I was very tired and I could not think straight. I took a walk along the sandy, stony beach, then walked back. The bonfire cast flickering lights on the pastel-colored background of palms, night fell. Once again upsurge of joy at this open, free existence amidst a fabulous landscape, under exotic conditions, a real picnic based on actual work. I also had the real joy of creative work, of overcoming obstacles, new horizons opening up; misty forms take on contours, before me I see the road going onward and upward…. I came back late and slept well—oh yes, on my way back I went to the pool and delighted in the view of trees, water, and moonlight. It's a pity that I may leave this forever. I want to write about all this to E.R.M…. (1967: 257–58)

The diary also shows what he wanted to make out of his complex experiences, as on June 6, 1918: "I analyzed the nature of my ambition. An ambition stemming from my love of work, intoxication with my own work—*romance of one's own life*…. When I think of my work, or works, or the revolution I want to effect in social anthropology—this is a truly creative ambition" (1967: 289). In a mood like this, he found it hard to concentrate: "external ambitions keep crawling over me like lice," for example getting elected to the prestigious British Royal Society and being able to put F.R.S. (Fellow of the Royal Society) after his name (1967: 291).

There are also occasional references to the *kula* and how to establish some sort of order in the information he was collecting. He reflected on the relation between theory and observation and observed that "we cannot speak of objectively existing facts: theory creates facts"—in other words, without a framework to put them in, "facts" by themselves are meaningless (1967: 114). Malinowski noted that the Trobrianders have a practical approach to everyday affairs and are not in a position to see their society as a whole, as a set of related social institutions, values, and activities. That is the ethnographer's job, and he set out to do it for the *kula*, always keeping the "final goal" in mind: "to grasp the native's point of view, his relation to life, to realize *his* vision of *his* world" (1922: 25).

Argonauts of the Western Pacific was the result. Its title is taken from the ancient Greek epic of the hero Jason, who, to regain his rightful throne, must steal and bring back the golden fleece from the statue of a mythical ram. He assembles a crew, and they go off to find the fleece in a ship named the *Argo*. Many adventures follow. The Trobrianders also ventured off in search of valuable items—the decorative arm-shells and necklaces known as *vaygu'a*. *Argonauts* is a book about economics, about concepts of *value*—what it is that makes these things valuable in the eyes of the Trobrianders, and hence worth going to great lengths to obtain. The *vaygu'a* are not simple orna- ments; they are objects that carry a history, and that history is largely determined by memory of the exchanges between important men that they have been a part of. It's something like the Western market for fine art in which the value of a particular work is determined by the prestige of the item itself (a Picasso, say), and by what the last owner was willing to pay for it: "Every really good Kula article has its individual name, round which there is a sort of history and romance in the traditions of the natives" (1922: 89).

But there is a difference between the Western and the Trobriand scheme of things. In the West a precious item may be acquired in order to keep and admire, but in the Trobriands it is acquired in order to give away again to trading partners on other islands: "The main point of difference is that the Kula goods are only in possession for a time, whereas the European treasure must be permanently owned in order to have full value." A big man's status was determined by how well he played the game of *kula*—the game of giving and receiving, then giving and receiving again in a great round of exchange relationships: "Once in the Kula, always in the Kula" (1922: 83). Malinowski goes on:

> *The whole tribal life is permeated by a constant give and take*; that every ceremony, every legal and customary act is done to the accompaniment of material gift and counter gift; that wealth, given and taken, is one of the main instruments of social organization, of the power of the chief, of the bonds of kinship, and of relationship in law. (1922: 167)

Malinowski set out to document the structure of this social institution, how "it welds together a considerable number of tribes, and it embraces a vast complex of activities, inter- connected, and playing into one another, so as to form one organic whole" (1922: 63). This greater whole includes myth and magic. Malinowski had found that every impor- tant social undertaking had a magical element. He collected a great amount of material on the use of magic in ensuring the success of canoe building and the long-distance cer- emonial trading it made possible. He had a gift for languages, and paid close attention to magical spells as a kind of poetry, which he analyzed in detail in later works (Malinowski 1966). His method was to create an ethnographic picture of a society through detailed analysis of what he took to be a pivotal aspect of Trobriand culture.

And the Trobrianders themselves; what of them? Malinowski mentions many of his informants, but these people do not emerge as full human beings. Their value seems to have been mainly restricted to the information they could provide him. When he was successful in his work he thought well of them—"*native life and native society* had come to seem almost enough to me" (1967: 195). When he encountered difficulties, he grew more negative. On April 24, 1918, he recorded a "hatred for bronze-colored skin, combined with depression, a desire to 'sit down and cry,' and a furious longing '*to get out of this.*' For all that, I decide to resist and work today—'*business as usual*'" (1967: 261).

In the end, Malinowski got his golden fleece, and he was rewarded with considerable fame and a professorship at the London School of Economics, where he had a central role in educating the next generation of British anthropologists. In large measure he was actually successful in bringing off the "revolution in social anthropology" that he yearned for in his diary. He did indeed marry Elsie Masson, but he was never elected to the Royal Society.

Elizabeth Fernea

Elizabeth Warnock Fernea set out for a small isolated village in Iraq in 1956. She was going to join her husband, Robert Fernea, who was conducting two years of fieldwork in the village of El Nahra to complete his doctoral degree in social anthropology

MAP 1.1 Iraq

(R. Fernea 1970). Elizabeth Fernea was not an anthropologist, but despite a lack of formal training she had a keen eye for observation, a curiosity for learning, and an ability to "slip between countries and cultures with ease, never fully belonging but always at home" (Hassan 2001). Pairing these qualities with the fact that she was due to spend two years in an isolated village, Fernea became a skilled ethnographer and, most importantly, gained access to a group that her husband would never have had the opportunity to approach: the women of the village. Despite being game for this exciting adventure, Fernea had a difficult time when she first arrived in the village.

Fernea and her husband arrived in the village late at night, covered in mud and exhausted from their bumpy travels. Her heart fell as her husband opened the door to their new home: mud walls, a dirt floor covered in reed mats, a ceiling infested with birds, and trash and clothing littering the floor. Her husband had been there for three months and was clearly not much for keeping house. As she noted, "This wasn't what the romantic, roving life should be at all …" (E. Fernea 1969: 14). While Fernea eventually settled into her new lodgings, a more difficult task was adapting to the social organization of the village and gaining acceptance by the women.

At the time this book was written, men and women lived in segregation in El Nahra. When in public, women donned an *abayah*, a head-to-toe veil. They only removed this in the presence of their husbands and other women. It was expected that when doing errands around town one would bring little attention to oneself, and whenever possible the task should be done by servants, children or husbands. Shopping at the market was done by only those women of the lowest status. When visiting a household, women would sit with the women, and men with the men. These customs seemed strange to Fernea at first. She asserted before arriving in the village that she would not wear an abayah, telling her husband that "if they can't take me as I am—if we have to make artificial gestures to prove we are human beings too—what's the point?" (E. Fernea 1969: 6). After a few days of traveling unveiled and being the focus of much unwanted staring, Fernea quickly reconsidered her hastiness. Perhaps blending in would not be such an "artificial gesture" after all.

As her time in the village passed, Fernea gained a better understanding of women's roles in society. While at first she noticed only the restrictions and limitations that seemed to confine women to the private sphere, after time she began to see the different ways that women exercised control and authority. She learned the high importance placed on female friendship and companionship in the village. Women spent hours together and called on one another regularly—their social life may have taken place behind closed doors, but it was extremely rich and active. She learned of the negotiation of public space, of how the bridge connecting the neighborhoods to the village center had originally been built slightly removed from the center so that women could come and go undetected by men sitting in coffee shops or stores. The outer walls of homes had essentially no windows to provide complete privacy for women, but inside those walls open-air courtyards were found. She also learned of women's role in the family—in choosing a marriage partner for their sons, and how, in some cases, they negotiated the introduction of second and third wives to their own families. She also attended weddings and religious ceremonies and learned of the rituals and customs that governed these occasions.

While Fernea was gaining insight into the social organization of society, she was becoming increasingly frustrated with her slow progress in establishing personal relationships. When she first arrived in Iraq, her Arabic was basic at best. While she frequently visited the women in the village, she always had the suspicion that they were talking *about* her: "Were they talking about me or not? What errors in etiquette or custom had I committed? What in heaven's name were they *saying*? My uneasiness grew in this atmosphere of half hearing and part understanding" (1969: 70). After a particularly bad episode when a number of women visited her home, poked fun at her cooking, and implied she was a bad housekeeper, Fernea was surprised at how hurt and lonely these encounters were making her feel: "Six months before, I would not have believed that I could be so upset at being accused of laziness and incompetence by a group of illiterate tribal ladies…. It had now become important to me to be accepted by these people as a woman and a human being" (1969: 77).

Fernea was experiencing **culture shock,** or the feelings of confusion and insecurity that arise from living in a new culture or surroundings. Experiencing culture shock is not unique to anthropologists; you may have had your own culture shock experiences throughout your life. People are accustomed to believing that their own way of doing things—speaking, eating, dancing, dressing, worshipping, etc.—is the *best* way of doing things. After all, we have spent our whole life learning these activities, so it is not unreasonable to think that when presented with a different approach, people are surprised and taken off guard. There is a distinction, however, between the feelings of culture shock and those of **ethnocentrism**. Ethnocentrism is judging other cultures by the standards and values of one's own. There exist varying degrees of ethnocentrism: the mildest form we all exhibit by virtue of being raised in a particular social environment; the most severe form can be extremely harmful and can manifest as prejudice and racism. Ethnocentrism has appeared in some serious and world-altering ways: European colonizers not only explored and extracted wealth from countries all over the world, but also imposed their culture and way of life on the people that they encountered, as did (and, some say, continue to do) Christian missionaries. Can you think of any current events that are characterized by an ethnocentric mentality?

Cultural relativism is the idea that one should suspend moral judgment and assumption in order to appreciate and understand a culture on its own terms, rather than in comparison to one's own. While in the field, this is central to anthropologists' ability to move forward from their state of culture shock and gain an understanding of what is going on around them. The concept of cultural relativism, however, is complex. At its best, cultural relativism encourages engagement with and consideration of new ways of doing things—judgment is put on hold, as much as possible, until an understanding of what is going on is reached. At its worst, cultural relativity can lead to moral relativity, which makes it difficult for us to say that actions or behaviors that may be harmful to certain individuals are wrong. Anthropologists grapple with their sense of professionalism in the field as they do not want to judge a people according to their own values and ideals; however, at the same time, they must consider the issue of human rights and the idea that just because an act is deemed "cultural" does not make it free from criticism or even outrage. People view this position as an uncertain foundation for morality and political action, and anthropologists must walk a fine line between relativism on the one hand and ethnocentric judgments on the other. While there exists no instruction book on how to react to questionable behaviors and actions, there are now international agreements, such as the United Nations *Universal Declaration of Human Rights*, that define morality and human rights in absolute terms, regardless of culture. As you can imagine, this in itself is controversial.

For example, in the pages of her ethnography, Fernea recounts conversations where the discussion turned to beatings at the hands of one's husband. Never does Fernea voice her opinion about this matter, either to the women to whom she is speaking or in her narrative on the page. Given your understanding of cultural relativism, does an anthropologist have a moral obligation to speak up for human rights, or is it more important to gain an understanding of a behavior before any action is taken? Can you think of a time when you judged a situation without fully understanding it? What could you pay attention to in order to get a sense of what this event was all about? What pushes this situation beyond the parameters of "cultural" and into the realm of a human rights issue? As anthropologists, we can collect data and report the wonderful and the tragic in order to increase our understanding of human diversity.

Fernea's ethnography is an interesting and rich read—by the end of her two years in the village she had established many strong relationships and friendships. She went on to have a long career in academia and anthropology. In 1997, she published her last book, *In Search of Islamic Feminism: One Woman's Global Journey*, a personal account of women in a number of Islamic societies from Turkey to Egypt. Fernea died at the age of 81 in 2008.

We will now move on to our final ethnographic example, *My Freshman Year*, to consider the practice of conducting anthropology in one's own backyard. First, we will discuss the tension between directing the anthropological research lens abroad and focusing it locally. Next, we will consider the research methods used by Cathy Small, aka Rebekah Nathan, during her fieldwork at the university where she was employed as a professor, and some of the ethical implications that arose as a result of her covert approach to conducting fieldwork.

Collecting, Organizing, and Analyzing: Research Methods for Understanding the Social World

Anthropologists are social scientists—like other scientists, they pose a research question and determine what research methods to employ to capture data that will answer their carefully constructed question. Unlike a biologist or a chemist, however, anthropologists do not study in a lab, but on the street, in people's homes, in the classroom, or anywhere that people spend their time and go about their daily lives. This is not a closed and controlled setting like one would find in a laboratory. Due to the dynamic nature of the social world, anthropologists are skillful at adapting to their surroundings. This is all part of the joys and frustrations of fieldwork, and as we saw with Fernea's experience in Iraq, it may take some time before meaningful relationships are formed.

In order to fully acknowledge that the social world in which we live affects the way in which we view the world, we must consider how our own social position informs our actions, our beliefs, and our worldview. What do we mean by social position? Consider a few of the most obvious social categories that we use to understand those around us—gender, ethnicity, class, age, sexuality, ability, to name a few. Now consider what these categories mean to you and your own life—some of them may be very straightforward, some of them might not. How might one's social position influence what one deems interesting or important to study, and how one presents one's research? Because anthropologists are *their own research instrument*, it has become increasingly common for anthropologists over the last 20 years to reflect on their own position in relation to that of their research participants.

In Your Own Backyard: Turning the Lens

The experience of Cathy Small, aka Rebekah Nathan, conducting fieldwork among freshman university students in the United States offers a look at a relatively recent move in anthropology to conduct research in one's own "backyard." As a result of anthropology's colonial past, the discipline became the center of much criticism and critique during the 1970s and 1980s, no less than by anthropologists themselves. Why was this? The constant focus on those who were *not* of Western European background was called into question—what gave anthropologists the right to travel to a distant land, document, observe, and make conclusions about a group of people, and then publish this information for professional gain in a setting far removed from the locale in which it was based? What benefit was the interaction bringing to those being studied? And was there not great diversity everywhere, including one's own locale, without traveling across the world to observe and draw conclusions about others? This shift within the discipline reflects a realization that the prospect of studying the exotic "Other" is becoming increasingly problematic due, in part, to the continual self-reflection that the discipline has been undergoing over the last 50 years (Dyck 2000). For the most part, however, anthropology remains a discipline that is largely associated with regional specialization, culturally and spatially removed from the researcher's "home turf" (Amit 2000; Caputo 1995; Dyck 2000).

The term "native" anthropologist refers to those who study "their own"—that is, their own culture/ethnicity/community. As an "insider," there is an assumption that one will have greater and more intimate access to people's lives, and that this access will offer a more authentic portrayal than if the anthropologist hailed from a foreign land. This is not an obscure notion—as a local, you would know what types of food are eaten at which celebrations; the major holidays and traditions and who of the community is the most involved; the location of popular meeting places; what political party holds the most power, etc. Some may argue that it may in fact be *more* challenging to be an insider and be aware of the nuances and commonalities of the everyday that we take for granted. Being an "insider," however, is far more complex than simply speaking the same language, living in the same community, or being committed to the same cause. In reality, our identities are constantly shifting, and how (and with whom) we identify at one time in our life will likely be very different at others. Kirin Narayan, an anthropologist who conducts research in her home country of India, discusses why the "native" title is both problematic and outdated: "The loci along which we are aligned with or set apart from those whom we study are multiple and in flux. Factors such as education, gender, sexual orientation, class, race, or sheer duration of contacts may at different times outweigh the cultural identity we associate with insider or outsider status" (1993: 672). Think about your own identity—does it change depending on who you are around? Is it different around parents and your grandparents than it is around your university friends? Are you interested in the same things as you were 10 years ago? Our identities are not static but rather are influenced by experience—whom we meet, what we have seen, and what we have done.

As a cultural anthropologist, Cathy Small spent much of her professional life overseas conducting fieldwork in the traditional sense, that is, with people with whom she had very little in common. For three decades, Small conducted her research with Polynesian society in the kingdom of Tonga in the southwest Pacific. Small found that upon her return to the US, her experiences abroad had forced her to turn a critical eye on her own culture: "On your return from another world, things once unnoticed—our reliance on date books, for instance—seem glaring; what was a daily routine can resurface as an exotic American custom" (Nathan 2005: 1). A professor for over 15 years, Small began to feel as though she did not understand her students. Their behaviors and attitudes no longer made sense to her. She decided to investigate the lives of this now "foreign" group and to go "undercover" as a student on her own campus, which she refers to as "AnyU." Small registered as a freshman under the name Rebekah Nathan, moved into the freshman dorm, and took classes from professors whom she did not know. She did not tell her fellow students her profession or background, explaining only to those who asked that she was a writer. For one academic year, she lived as a student, attending classes, completing assignments, and waiting in line with the other dorm residents for showers in the morning.

Small employed a number of research methods during her year as a student. Participant observation was a major component of her work. She participated in dorm social activities, such as the orientation weekend before classes started, and movie and games nights organized to increase student morale. As a student, she was required to complete readings and assignments and to participate in class discussions. She became privy to the discussions of students sitting in the lecture hall simply because she was sitting *with* them rather than in front of them as a professor. She took notes about what was going on around her, including conversations in the cafeteria, in the classroom, and in shared spaces in the dorm. She posted questions on pieces of paper in the women's bathroom and recorded the responses. She documented the content displayed on students' dorm room doors: Who was featured in the photographs? What did the slogans say? Did people have a wipe board for messages or not? She also conducted formal interviews with individual students.

Before beginning a program of research, scientists formulate a hypothesis, or a research statement that the study aims to prove. Anthropologists also formulate a research question; however, their research is less likely to *prove* a hypothesis than to offer an interpretation and understanding of the issue. This can be done in many ways. The traditional approach is the **comparative method**, or considering how a particular theory fares when applied cross-culturally. The comparative method directs the anthropologist to collect information about the local factors that shape human action and perception. Small considered the college experience in the United States as "a rite of passage": "these are the rituals that shepherd individuals and groups from one stage in the life cycle to another" (Nathan 2005: 146). Small states that it is during these stages that people who may have different social status become equals while experiencing a new way of life: "undergraduate culture itself becomes this liminal communal space where students bond with one another, sometimes for life, and, amid rules of suspended normality and often hardship, explore their identities, wrestle with their parents' world, and wonder about their future" (2005: 147). Anthropologists have observed and written about these liminal spaces all over the world—rites of passage have been examined in small-scale hunter-gatherer societies as well as in large industrial societies. It is in these spaces that people challenge cultural norms, roles, and rules and where creativity and social change can be ignited. By comparing rites of passage cross-culturally, we see not only the power of social norms and values to have an impact on behavior, but also the profound diversity of human culture.

Another approach positions the actions and beliefs of those under study as central to determining what is important to be observed and documented, and what is not. This **inductive approach** favors what the people themselves have to say about their lives—understanding these subjective meanings is central to understanding the way in which people make sense of their world. A very well-known example of this type of research is Clifford Geertz's work in Bali studying illegal cockfights, recounted in the essay *Deep Play: Notes on the Balinese Cockfight*. Geertz investigated illegal cockfighting in a small Balinese town—why did people engage in such a high-stakes game? What significance did this immensely popular social gathering have to the locals?

Geertz begins his account with a story about a situation in which he and his wife had found themselves—being caught up in a police raid on a cockfight, which the Indonesian government had banned as a wasteful and primitive custom. The anthropologists fled from the police just like everyone else, and this was the ice-breaker. Before then, they had been treated by the locals as though they didn't exist: "As we wandered around, uncertain, wistful, eager to please, people seemed to look right through us with a gaze focused several yards behind us on some more actual stone or tree" (Geertz 1973: 412). Their actions during the raid made them real. It turned out that the local people had been acutely aware of these exotic strangers all along, but their code of etiquette blocked overt expression of curiosity. After the raid, "the next morning the village was a completely different world for us. Not only were we no longer invisible we were suddenly the center of all attention, the object of a great outpouring of warmth, interest, and most especially, amusement" (1973: 416).

Geertz now found it easier to get information about the cockfight and many other aspects of Balinese society. He was interested in the role of symbols in society. Through "thick description," or a close examination and analysis of individual cases, Geertz interpreted the symbols of a culture through an explanation of people's behavior, and the context in which this behavior occurred (Barrett 2000: 32). Geertz's close observations led to an interpretation of cockfighting in which the process and act of gambling encompass the social relationships of the village, including family and non-family relationships. Geertz also illustrated that the *cock* is a symbol of powerful men in Balinese society, and that the double entendre of the word exists in the Balinese language as it does in English. This approach makes less use of cross-cultural comparisons and generalizations, because local knowledge makes sense only when considered in the context from which it was created.

As Geertz notes, "What the ethnographer is in fact faced with ... is a multiplicity of complex conceptual structures ... which are at once strange, irregular, and inexplicit and which [the ethnographer] must contrive somehow first to grasp and then to render" (1973: 10). Analysis of the cockfight was a way for Geertz to get at broader cultural themes and to explore their relationship to one another. Through examination of very particular events, he sought to arrive at general conclusions about the nature of Balinese society. He found that "the cockfight ... is fundamentally a dramatization of status concerns. Its function ... is interpretive: it is a Balinese reading of Balinese experience, a story that they tell themselves about themselves" (1973: 437, 448).

That, in any case, is Geertz's interpretation. Other approaches are possible, depending on the anthropologist's background and theoretical goal. Consider what South African anthropologist Max Gluckman brought to the analysis of the opening of a newly constructed bridge in Zululand in the late 1930s. He begins, as Geertz did, with his immediate experience of a particular event: "In 1938 I was living in the homestead of Chief's Deputy Matolana Mdwandwe, thirteen miles from the European magistracy and village of Nongoma and two miles from the Mapopoma store. I awoke at sunrise ... and prepared to leave for Nongoma to attend the opening of a bridge in the neighbouring district of Mahlabatini" (Gluckman 1958: 2). The ceremony at the bridge was staged by the white-dominated local government. It was meant to connect the area to the administrative headquarters and the local maternity hospital—and to promote a moral bond between the African population and the government, even though the society as a whole was rigidly segregated into white and black, "two categories that must not mix, like castes in India" (1958: 12). The participants were white officials, the Zulu workmen who built the bridge, Christian missionaries, influential local tribesmen, and a representative of the Zulu royal family. And of course there was the anthropologist himself, who—being white, but living with Zulu and speaking their language—was acutely aware of his ambiguous status: "I, as an anthropologist, was in a position to become an intimate friend of Zulu as other Europeans could not, and this I did in virtue of a special type of social relationship, recognized as such by both races. Yet I could never quite overcome the social distance between us" (1958: 19).

In the ceremony itself, the white Native Commissioner drove his car across the bridge followed by a Zulu in full warrior dress. Having officially opened the bridge by breaking the tape, the Europeans went into their own tent for tea and cakes while the Zulu celebrated with local beer and feasted on roast meat. One of the Europeans was a labor recruiter for the gold mines, whose presence indicates the wider economic context of the encounter at the bridge.

Gluckman exploited his experience to comment on the "color bar," on the use of traditional ritual forms by both sides in this affair, and on how the two parties were both joined with and yet divided from each other because of their different roles in this social drama. Gluckman then went on to situate what he had seen in the historical context of South African race relations and the rise of the mining industry with its insatiable demand for cheap native labor. He saw this ceremony as an event that "crystallized" aspects "of the social structure and institutions of present day Zululand" (1958: 12). For Gluckman the concept of a "social situation" was an organizing principle, in that the analysis of such situations "reveals the underlying system of relationships" within the social structure of the community (1958: 9).

Geertz and Gluckman both examined events that they observed in the course of their fieldwork, but they did it in different ways and for different ends. Geertz was after the "deep" cultural elements expressed in the cockfight; Gluckman was interested in the interplay between race, class, and group organization in a divided society—a more "sociological" approach than Geertz's. In fact, Geertz knew a great deal about Balinese social organization—the kinship system for example—and wrote about it extensively elsewhere; but in his account of the cockfight he chose to highlight how such events fit in with other aspects of the culture. His aim was to achieve a "holistic" understanding of the Balinese world.

Likewise, Gluckman was well attuned to the nuances of both Zulu and white South African culture, but he represented what he saw in relation to the contextual demands of a particular social situation, in which—for a moment in time—the two came together at the bridge. Whereas Geertz saw Balinese culture as a thing in itself with its own internal integrity, Gluckman situated his analysis in relation to the expansion of European power and the spread of global capitalism into southern Africa. These are not mutually exclusive approaches. They do, however, represent different theoretical orientations originating in distinctive British and American anthropological traditions that we'll have more to say about later. What we wish to emphasize here is how both Geertz and Gluckman used particular events to inductively arrive at general conclusions about the societies they were studying.

Ethical Considerations in Anthropological Research

All research studies must go through a review process, usually conducted by an ethics review board at the university where the researcher is employed, to ensure that the research proposed is ethical and will not bring harm to the participants. The nature of anthropological fieldwork is such that researchers are frequently working and likely living closely with their research participants in often intimate and candid situations. A degree of trust must be established by all parties in order for this relationship to be fruitful. Consequently, there is a great responsibility on the part of anthropologists to present their research in a manner that does not bring harm or humiliation to participants. In much anthropological research, research is carried out with participants who are socially marginalized, meaning that for reasons such as income level, sexual preference, ethnicity, gender, age, ability, etc., people tend to be excluded by the wider society and may find it difficult to fully participate in the social world around them. As anthropologists are often educated and of the middle class, this calls into question the right and ability of an individual to accurately portray another's experiences. With this in mind, it is important to think about the relationship of the researcher to their participants.

Small's fieldwork adds another layer to this complex relationship because she did not disclose to those around her *why* she had returned to university and was living in a freshman dorm, unless they specifically asked (and according to her, only one person did). This is not standard practice for anthropologists, and Small's methodological approach received criticism and ignited debate within the academic community regarding her somewhat "covert" study. Small admits that she was surprised to find herself asking whether or not the observational data she had collected—observations and conversations she overheard in class or the halls when she was in her student "role"—could be ethically reported: "I realized that my level of comfort and certainty was shifting with the depth and quality of my relationships and with the lived concreteness of seeing the data in their human context, that is, as incidents, stories and conversations attached to real people and real encounters" (Nathan 2005: 164). Small recounts her experience running into a former classmate once she returned to her regular position as an anthropology professor: "We exchanged warm 'how you doin?' small talk. Then my friend asked where I was headed. 'To class' I answered. 'What is it?' she asked. 'Oh, an anthropology class … actually I'm teaching it.' 'No kidding!?' she exclaimed. 'How did you get to do that? I want to take it!' 'Well,' I answered sheepishly, 'it's cause I'm actually a professor too. I was a student last year to do some research, but now I'm back to being a professor.' 'I can't believe that,' she responded and then paused. 'I feel fooled'" (Nathan 2005: 167).

While reporting people's conversations and day-to-day activities is certainly an activity fraught with ethical questions, in the end Small's study posed little risk for those she was observing. This issue is complicated when the anthropologist is in a more volatile situation—for example, in 2007, anthropologists were employed in Afghanistan by the US military to collect information from Afghani people. The intent was to increase understanding between the soldiers and the citizens; however, this information could be used for many purposes other than what it was originally intended for. This created a great debate, both within academia and outside, about the ethical position of an anthropologist who conducts this type of research. The fundamental question was posed: "who should anthropological research serve—those paying the salary, or those under study" (Rhode 2007)? We will encounter these issues again in later chapters in the text.

If, generally speaking, anthropological research aims to break down barriers of understanding between groups of people, a logical next step is to consider just how profound those differences are. As a species, how much of who we are is biological, and how much is socially learned? In the next and final section of this chapter we will consider the themes of unity and diversity, and the meaning of these concepts from an anthropological approach.

Unity and Diversity

Unity and diversity are important themes that have been considered by anthropologists since the discipline's inception. The terms lead to important questions related to who we are as a species. On the one hand is the diversity of cultures across the span of world history and geographical space. On the other is the question of human nature—what underlying factors enable culture to exist in the first place? Perhaps one of the most fundamental questions in anthropological enquiry concerns what it means to be human. Are there shared characteristics and beliefs that are fundamental, regardless of specific cultural traditions and values? Are there fundamental similarities that unite us as humans or, as social beings, does our learned behavior negate or make obsolete the question? Are the differences between males and females rooted in biology or culture, or in some complex mix of the two? How is it possible that some humans can be responsible for the genocide in Central Africa and Bosnia, while others can become the saintly figures of various religious traditions? These questions are complex and do not have simple answers. Through anthropological research, however, aspects of these issues are investigated, usually on a local and individual level. As we have seen, anthropologists encounter and experience these issues first hand via their fieldwork.

Consider the concept of unity as it relates to Fernea's research in Iraq. As a woman, Fernea gained almost instant access to the other women of the community, a group her husband had not met and would in fact never meet. She was invited into their homes, asked to have tea and eat food and to participate in hobbies such as embroidery. This was simply because she shared their social position in society—as a woman. Their relationship, at least superficially, was characterized by a sense of unity gained by being members of the same group. As we know, however, it took some time for Fernea to develop true relationships with any of the women. Their social backgrounds—culture, education, upbringing, religion, etc.—were so different that the women in El Nahra found it difficult to relate to Fernea in the beginning. Simply being a woman was not enough to bridge the cultural gap that separated them. Classifying a group according to one characteristic, whether it is gender, race, age or ethnicity is problematic, for it ignores the great diversity within these groups. Classifying all the women of El Nahra into one group neglects the powerful roles of family heritage and social class. Anthropologists, particularly feminist anthropologists, have been very critical of generalizations made within and across groups (McGee & Warms 1996).

Small encountered the concepts of "diversity" and "community" during her fieldwork at AnyU. Those who identify as part of a community are announcing their membership in a particular group and, to varying degrees, a sense of unity among members exists. Establishing a "community" is advertised by college administrators as key to engaging freshman students in the college "experience." At AnyU, great lengths were taken to create a community-like atmosphere. One example was a seminar course that all freshman students were required to take. A novel was chosen, students were to meet in small groups to engage in debate and discussion (led by a professor), and then they were introduced to the author at the end of the course. This course was cancelled, however, after many attempts at offering it were met with a lack of enthusiasm and engagement. Through this experience, the university learned that *requiring* students to establish a community (in this case, the community of freshman students) is not a successful strategy. Small observed that real networks of engagement among students had more to do with shared experiences that occurred *before* college, as well as with demographic factors such as race, religion, and class (Nathan 2005: 47). Removing the element of choice to engage in a group goes against the fundamental individualism that is a cherished value in America. Small observed students struggling with this, particularly when they were encouraged to join in one of the many extracurricular activities or clubs offered at the university. While students voiced their interest in participating and may have even intended to join, they would "resist the claims that community makes on their schedule and resources in the name of individualism, spontaneity, freedom, and choice" (2005: 47). Small characterizes this as the "American way"—students are conflicted about wanting to be part of an entity that provides a sense of belonging, but are hesitant to give up their freedom.

While community is advertised as a key component of university life, so too is diversity. University administrators hope that students will engage with those from a different background, and that part of the learning experience in college that takes place outside of the classroom will lead to an increase in understanding between diverse groups of people. Small's discussions with international students, however, suggest that the notion of acceptance and understanding was not something that American university students had wholeheartedly embraced. International students talked of the friendly manner of American students—they would say hello and suggest getting together sometime, and then would never hear from them again. International students also discussed the lack of interest that many American students showed toward learning about those international students' home countries, as well as their lack of knowledge about other parts of the world. Small concludes that as with efforts to establish "community," embracing diversity is not something that comes easily to students who have been educated over their lifetime about the centrality of American culture and way of life.

Unity and diversity are complex concepts because not only are they abstract, but they also relate to fundamental questions about how we live and organize ourselves. In order to understand them in a specific context, we must look to how individuals experience them. This is the goal of the anthropologist. What Malinowski, Fernea, and Small illustrate through their research is that "culture"—whether in an isolated village in Iraq or a university campus in America—cannot be fully understood in bits and pieces. Rather, the components of culture, such as social organization, gender, and ethnicity, can be understood only when contextualized within the society in which they occur.

Conclusion

In this chapter we have introduced and defined a number of foundational anthropological concepts, as well as methodological and theoretical approaches. Through different examples of ethnographic fieldwork, we have explored some of the challenges and successes associated with anthropological research, such as the experience of culture shock and the challenges associated with developing new relationships with individuals whom one is observing and studying. While anthropologists often study those that they do not know and ways of life that they are not familiar with, a fundamental goal of much anthropological research is to break down barriers of understanding between groups of people. Ethical issues associated with how anthropologists conduct research and what is done with their findings have long been explored, debated, and critiqued. Rather than threatening the legitimacy of the discipline, however, these debates have required that those who practice anthropology remain vigilant, reflective, and adaptable.

Study Questions

1   Identify and describe the four sub-fields of anthropology.
2   Describe the discipline of cultural anthropology and identify three ways in which it differs from other areas of social and scientific research.

3   Define *reflexive thinking*, and explain the purpose of employing reflexive thinking while in the field.

4   Explain the terms *culture shock*, *ethnocentrism*, and *cultural relativism* using examples from the work of Fernea.

5   Compare and contrast the inductive approach as used by Geertz in Bali and Gluckman in South Africa.

6   How does Small's work at AnyU differ from that of Malinowski in the Trobriand Islands and Fernea in Iraq? Outline the ethical implications of this difference.

7   Define the term *native anthropologist*. Outline the origins of this term and the limitations it places on so-called native researchers.

8   Describe the concepts of *unity* and *diversity* and use examples to explain how they can coexist within the same context.

Discussion Questions

1   Describe the history of anthropology in terms of Eurocentrism, and discuss how the field has changed since the days when explorers first began to observe "primitive" cultures.

2   Consider the concept of cultural relativism and how it relates to moral relativism. Discuss how relativism influences the ethics of anthropology. Consider recent current events that might cause you, the researcher, to question the appropriateness of cultural relativism. Do you think that anything is universally wrong? When do you think an observer, such as a researcher or journalist, should intercede? If there are moral absolutes, when should anthropologists become activists?

3   Fernea gained access to a segment of the community closed to her husband, the trained anthropologist, by nature of belonging to a particular category: women, and more specifically, wives. What does this suggest about the limitations of anthropological research in general, and the body of knowledge we have about women in society?

CHAPTER 2

///

Life in the Field

LEARNING OBJECTIVES

After reading this chapter, students should be able to

- outline the British School of anthropology and identify its major figures;
- summarize and explain Richards's use of *structural functionalism* and her contributions to anthropological methodology;
- outline the American School of anthropology and identify its major figures;
- describe how the work of Franz Boas helped to move anthropology away from a biological understanding of racial difference and social evolution;
- summarize Mead's work in Samoa, her methods and findings, and their effect on the discipline of anthropology; and
- outline the opportunities for professional anthropologists and describe two major types of applied anthropology: medical and international development.

KEY TERMS

applied anthropology   medical anthropology   qualitative research

diffusion   purposeful sampling   structural functionalism

historical particularism

Introduction

In the last chapter we examined the social and intellectual climate in which anthropology developed as a discipline. If we were to characterize the nineteenth century by the theme of social evolutionism, where societies were thought to pass through stages of development, starting with the "primitive" and ending with the "civilized," the twentieth century would be characterized by the consideration of "culture" over biology in explaining human diversity. In this chapter we will look at the direction that anthropology took at the beginning of the twentieth century. We will briefly examine the development of two prominent schools of thought: the British school, as led by A.R. Radcliffe-Brown (1881–1955) and Bronislaw Malinowski (1884–1942), and the American school, pioneered by German-born Franz Boas (1858–1942).

Malinowski was instrumental in establishing fieldwork as a main component of anthropological enquiry. We will take a look at the work of one of Malinowski's students, Audrey Richards, to see the structural-functionalist approach applied in a fieldwork setting. Boas, along with many of his students, was influential in dismantling the racist ideology that was used by academics and politicians alike to restrict immigration and maintain racial segregation in America. We will consider Boas's most famous student, Margaret Mead (1901–78), and her best-selling ethnography *Coming of Age in Samoa* to explore how this way of thinking about the world was applied in ethnographic research. Finally, we consider where anthropology sits today as a discipline, both theoretically and methodologically. It is our hope that by gaining an understanding of where anthropology has come from and how the political climate of the time influenced what was deemed important to study, you will better appreciate where anthropology is positioned today. One small caveat before we proceed: we have selected what we believe to be compelling times and figures in the discipline's history. As we said in the previous chapter, this is by no means intended to be a history of anthropology. Rather, we offer a brief look at some influential figures and approaches to understanding culture and society.

Setting the Stage

The nineteenth century was the era of evolutionary anthropology, an approach to understanding the development of humankind grounded in comparisons between societies. Social development was considered on a unilinear scale, beginning in "savagery" and ending in "civilization." By the turn of the century, however, the appeal of evolutionism was waning. Science was progressing at a rapid rate, as was the recognition that the environment and social factors played a dominant role in shaping the "culture" of a people. Two prominent schools of thought developed at this time: the British and the American Schools.

The British School

Anthropology was a well-established discipline in the United Kingdom at the turn of the twentieth century. As the main tenets of evolutionary anthropology became more and more problematic, anthropologists were eventually forced out of their comfortable armchairs and into the field. British social anthropology became largely synonymous with **structural functionalism**. Through this lens, society is conceptualized as composed of major structures comparable to the organs of a biological organism—the heart, lungs, and blood. Each structure has a function, and "healthy societies" are those that are stable, well functioning, and orderly.

British anthropologists were committed to a scientific approach to understanding society. Their approach was synchronic, in that they did not consider the history of society, but rather restricted their analysis to the present. They also did not concern themselves with aspects of "material" culture, or the impact of the individual, ideology, and environmental factors on social life; instead, their analysis was restricted primarily to social structures, such as the family and the economy (Erickson & Murphy 2013). Structural functionalists believed that kinship systems, or the social organization of the family, had a greater impact on society than any other institution, particularly in pre-industrial societies.

There are two prominent figures associated with the British school: A.R. Radcliffe-Brown and Bronislaw Malinowski. Both were committed to a natural-science approach to the study of society. Radcliffe-Brown believed that there were three stages of scientific investigation: observation, taxonomy (i.e., classifying data), and generalizations. Generalizations across cultures were essential. Radcliffe-Brown wrote an innovative structural-functional ethnography called *The Andaman Islanders* (1922) based on his experiences with a tribal people in the Indian Ocean, and also conducted ethnographic research in Australia and Africa. He was interested in how ritual activity and social institutions such as kinship were factors in maintaining the social structure of a society (Erickson & Murphy 2013). His interests, like those of most British anthropologists at the time, lay in gaining an understanding of so-called primitive societies. Radcliffe-Brown was heavily influenced by Émile Durkheim (1858–1917), a prominent French sociologist who had a pronounced impact on social anthropology. As a greater understanding of the complexities of all societies emerged (including those thought to be "primitive"), Radcliffe-Brown's insistence on cross-cultural generalizations was limiting in gaining a full understanding of a particular society. His influence on the development of British anthropology, however, was considerable, both through his own work and through the work of the students he taught.

Bronislaw Malinowski is a somewhat heroic figure in British anthropology and, as discussed in Chapter 1, was influential in establishing fieldwork as a necessary component of anthropological research. Malinowski was committed to the establishment of anthropology as a scientific discipline with rigorous methods and a

PLATE 2.1 Bronislaw Malinowski

coherent theory. His focus—as outlined in his book *A Scientific Theory of Culture* (1944)—was on "basic needs" and how culture as an adaptive mechanism functions to supply them; some of these needs are biological in nature—nutrition, sexuality, control of aggression, nurturance of the young, care of the aged—while others are seen as intrinsic to culture itself, such as the coordination of activities so as to achieve at least a minimal degree of coherence in social life. Malinowski said that his version of functionalism was "meant primarily to equip the field-worker with a clear perspective and full instructions regarding what to observe and how to record" (Malinowski 1944: 145).

Malinowski's work illustrates the importance of getting out of the "armchair" and into the field, where one actually meets, observes, and participates in the lives of those one is studying. Whereas Radcliffe-Brown imagined society as a whole to operate and function like a biological organism, Malinowski put much of his emphasis on the *function* of social institutions in relation to the fulfillment of certain basic needs—for example, making a living and coordinating the social activities that make it possible. His influence is perhaps best understood by exploring the work of his students. Here we take a brief look at Audrey Isabel Richards (1899–1984), one of the earliest practitioners of "functionalist" anthropology and also one of the most noteworthy Africanists of her generation. In addition, "she was a sensitive interpreter of female interests and attitudes … she assumed rather than strove for equality with men" (Firth 1985: 344).

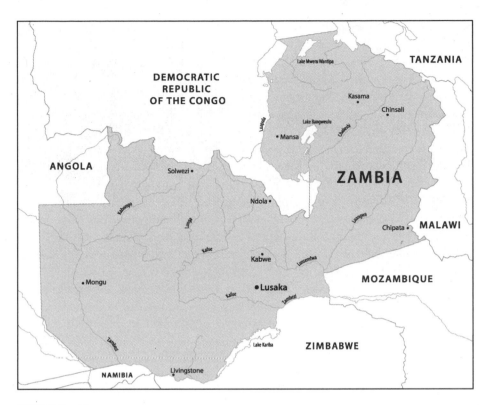

MAP 2.1 Zambia

Audrey Isabel Richards

In the 1920s, Richards was one of Malinowski's students at the London School of Economics. She applied his method to the letter in her study of food production, distribution, and consumption among the Bemba people of what was then the British Protectorate of Northern Rhodesia (now the independent nation of Zambia). She was in a doubly advantageous situation—treated by influential men as an honored outsider, and by women as one of their own. Indeed, her work with women led to *Chisungu* (1956), a groundbreaking study of a female initiation ritual.

The preamble to the Bemba research was her Ph.D. thesis, which was based on the existing ethnographic literature concerning food practices in southern Africa. It was subsequently published under the very "Malinowskian" title, *Hunger and Work in a Savage Tribe: A Functional Study of Nutrition among the Southern Bantu* (1948).

Malinowski himself wrote the Preface, in which he noted that Richards was something of an anthropological pioneer, venturing into a field that had never been systematically dealt with before. What he said about Richards's book could apply to the study of food practices anywhere (think about your own experience): "[A central motif] in Dr. Richards' book is her thesis that the traditional tribal or cultural attitudes towards food are among the most important cohesive forces in the community, which unite its members to each other and differentiate them from the surrounding tribes. The attitude to food, table manners, customs of common eating—the morals of food, as we might call it, the things permitted, forbidden, and enjoined—all form a complex and developed ideology of food" (Richards 1948: xv).

When Richards arrived in Northern Rhodesia in 1930, the Bemba lived mainly in small villages widely dispersed throughout a deciduous forest with an economy based on shifting cultivation. Her fundamental method was meticulously recording what went on in the daily life around her and making connections between the various facets of what she observed or was told. Like many central African peoples, the Bemba were matrilineal and matrilocal, village residence being determined by kinship established through women. The men of the village generally married in from elsewhere, and a new husband had to spend an extended period of time providing labor for his in-laws. He helped produce raw food for them, while they in turn provided him with cooked meals, a type of arrangement characteristic of social relationships between people of unequal status. The Bemba were dependent on one staple crop—finger millet—and suffered from periodic scarcity. The population density was very low, and yet the Bemba were politically fixated on their Paramount Chief, who was seen as having mystical powers with regard to the prosperity of both land and people: "The power of the chief rests ultimately on his people's belief in his supernatural powers over the prosperity of the land and the welfare of his individual subjects. By his inheritance of the guardian spirits of the line of dead chiefs, and his possession of the sacred relics of the tribe, he has power of approach to the tribal deities and he is responsible for the economic rites on which the food-production of these people is thought to depend" (Richards 1939: 25).

Food, of course, was one of Malinowski's "basic needs," but, as Richards found, the value of food went far beyond mere nutrition. It was the general focus and glue of social life; social relationships were created and defined through its production and consumption. By observing how people dealt with and talked about food—which they did incessantly—Richards was arriving at insights into the entire Bemba social order. Food was wealth, and there was little else to be had until the coming of the Europeans and the beginnings of the mining industry. Food meant followers, and much of the power of the Paramount Chief was traditionally based on its distribution, particularly in the form of beer:

> This giving or receipt of food is part of most economic transactions, and may come to represent a number of human relationships whether between different

kinsmen or between subject and chief. For this reason the whole question of handling or dividing food acquires tremendous emotional significance … and discussions of personalities or legal relationships tend to be ultimately expressed in this idiom.… For us it requires a real effort of imagination to visualize a state of society in which food matters so much and from so many points of view, but this effort is necessary if we are to understand the emotional background of Bemba ideas as to diet. (1939: 45–46)

Richards's use of the term "idiom" is an interesting one; it implies a form of discourse in which one thing is talked about in terms of another. For the Bemba the idiom of food was a largely unconscious way of talking about the *quality* of social relationships, and it contained fundamental notions of justice and reciprocity—"obligations to share and to give," the Bemba version of the Golden Rule (Richards 1939: 200). There were supernatural sanctions to back this up, since a relative who died with a grievance in his or her heart could visit misfortune on those who had provoked it. And if one offends the living, there is always the danger of witchcraft.

This sketch can only hint at the richness of Richards's ethnography. She systematically investigated the kinship system and village structure of the Bemba, their land tenure arrangements, the details of their agricultural practices, the place of ritual, their ideas about the natural world and the nature of chieftainship. How she went about this shows what the "functionalist" approach to social life was capable of, and there are many other studies like it from that period. Rather than just recording a collection of unconnected facts, Audrey Richards saw a social system at work, each element related to every other in sometimes very subtle ways. Of course, that is also how she chose to tell her story, and this was not one that could have been told by anthropologists of earlier generations. As we said earlier, "theory shapes perception." The anthropological movement known as functionalism was based on a theory of a very particular kind, with a history of its own (Stocking 1984).

Richards's work is transitional. In some ways it reads like a study of a more or less isolated and coherent tribe. But, as she knew very well, by the 1930s Bemba society was far from isolated and was in fact becoming increasingly *in*coherent. The very fact that she chose to study nutrition was due in part to Malinowski's influence, but also to concerns that had arisen from within the colonial bureaucracy and the mining industry about the health of the native population and its suitability as a workforce. Bemba villages were being sucked dry of younger men as they departed for the mines and rapidly growing towns of southern Africa, leaving women, children, and old men behind in the villages to live as best they could, supplemented by cash remittances from relatives working in the outside world. Zambia, which became independent from Britain in 1964, is now one of the most urbanized countries in sub-Saharan Africa.

There are many other influential names associated with developing and establishing the British School that we cannot, unfortunately, delve into here. We conclude our discussion simply by noting that the tidy framework put forth by structural functionalists proved to be too straightforward for studying complex and diverse societies. This approach played down conflict and seemingly ignored social change in favor of viewing society as patterned and stable. In stark contrast to this orderly approach, however, was that of the American School; rather than synchronic and tidy attempts to understand society, the American School approached the study of culture from a holistic perspective, where social, political, religious, and economic beliefs and behaviors across time were considered (Erikson & Murphy 2013). This holistic approach is also evident in their establishment of the "four fields" approach (archaeology, linguistics, physical anthropology, and cultural anthropology).

The American School

Franz Boas was born in 1858 in Germany. He was educated in the fields of physics, mathematics, and geography, and his first research expedition was a geographical investigation of the Inuit on Baffin Island in the 1880s. Boas was forever a scientist at heart, and his early training greatly influenced the meticulous manner in which he collected and analyzed data, whether it was investigating the color of sea water (the subject of his doctoral thesis) or describing the potlatch (a system of ceremonial exchange discussed in Chapter 6) among the Kwakiutl of the Alert Bay area in British Columbia. Where he slightly diverged from his scientific roots, however, was in the way in which he formulated his research questions. Rather than using data to prove a preconceived hypothesis or theory, Boas applied an inductive approach, whereby explanation and theory emerged from massive amounts of data that could be collected only through an extended period in the field (Barrett 2000: 55). This differed greatly from the approach taken by evolutionary anthropologists who attempted to "prove" their hypothesis through library research and debate with other academics, rather than collecting their own data via fieldwork. While Boas did not believe in an anthropology devoid of science, he argued strongly for a discipline that subjected scientific "truths" to criticism and further interpretation. Boas's approach is often labeled **historical particularism**, for he considered the unique history of each culture to be influential, and central to understanding the present.

Boas was instrumental in dismantling many of the problematic elements associated with social evolutionism. He disagreed with the notion that societies passed through stages of development, such as progressing from matrilineal to patrilineal forms of inheritance and organization. Instead, Boas asserted that each culture or society consisted of elements **diffused** from other cultures. Boas argued that changes in culture did not occur in a single, unilinear process, but instead in "a multiplicity of converging and diverging trends" (Freeman 1983: 30). Cultures could not be ranked in a hierarchy, as hypothesized by the social-evolutionary theorists. Unlike his evolutionary predecessors who embarked on massive studies that attempted to locate a culture in relation to the development of other societies, Boas argued that a study should be limited to one particular cultural area. He was wary of universal categories

PLATE 2.2 Franz Boas

and generalizations that attempted to convey scientific truths about groups of people, and instead he stressed the importance of diversity, the individual, and the need to historically contextualize research (Lewis 2001: 447). A strong proponent of cultural relativism, Boas asserted that each culture is unique and should be understood in terms of the beliefs and ideals of that culture and not judged according to another. Boas championed a rigorous approach to fieldwork, in which extensive notes and data were collected.

Boas believed that the value in anthropology lay in its ability to break down barriers that prevented a greater understanding between people, and in the consequent lessening of ignorance that would result (Lewis 2001: 450). Boas also strongly believed in social equality, particularly concerning race—as a Jewish German living in America, he had experienced racism in society and academia first hand (Lewis 2001). At the heart of much of his work was an attempt to dismantle and deconstruct aspects of early anthropology that served to strengthen scientific theories of biological and racial determinism, such as the idea that certain human "races" were more or less developed than others by virtue of their biological makeup (Mukhopadhyah & Moses 1997: 517).

It was with these goals in mind that Boas published his groundbreaking work *The Mind of Primitive Man* (1911), a book that set out to disprove biological explanations of the superiority of the white race and the consequent inferiority of all others, particularly Africans and Native Americans (see Chapter 8 for more on this topic). Boas used anthropometric[1] measurements and statistics to illustrate the large gaps that existed within scientific theories that purported to "prove" the biological differences between races. By 1918, Boas had published over 50 articles on racial and biological issues. He showed how nutrition and access to shelter and clothing affected physical growth and development (Mukhopadhyay & Moses 1997), and how socio-economic class and access to resources affected an individual's ability to thrive in certain environments. While this may seem fairly obvious to us in the twenty-first century, it was somewhat groundbreaking at the time. As with many new ideas that challenge the status quo, Boas's work was not well received by intellectuals and politicians of the day. However, the establishment of the Anthropology Department at Columbia University in 1890 under Boas ensured that his relativistic approach would be institutionalized and perpetuated by his eager American students.

By the early 1920s, the "nature versus nurture" debate was at its height, and the positioning of culture and environment against biology was driving a wedge between anthropology and the scientific disciplines. The resulting gap would have profound effects on shaping anthropology into the discipline that exists today. Boas and his students, most notably Margaret Mead, Ruth Benedict (1887–1948), and Edward Sapir (1884–1939), were pioneers of a discipline that sought to explain behavior in cultural and environmental terms (Freeman 1983: 48). They represented a major shift in thinking that occurred at the beginning of the twentieth century, when many academics and scientists began to realize that the diversity that characterized humankind did not represent snapshots of stages of development, but was rather illustrative of the ways in which groups of people adapted to their environments and the social world around them.

We will now take a closer look at the work of Margaret Mead, for it was her classic ethnographic tale *Coming of Age in Samoa* (1928) that not only introduced anthropology to the masses, but also ignited a debate about the validity of observations and ethnographic fieldwork that has continued long after the book's publication.

Margaret Mead

Coming of Age in Samoa was Margaret Mead's first foray into anthropological fieldwork. At just 23, Mead left the United States under the direction of her advisor Franz Boas to examine the lives of adolescent girls in Samoa. As discussed above, the intellectual climate at this time was rife with debates concerning racial determinism and the tension between culture and biology. Mead was intent on exploring this tension

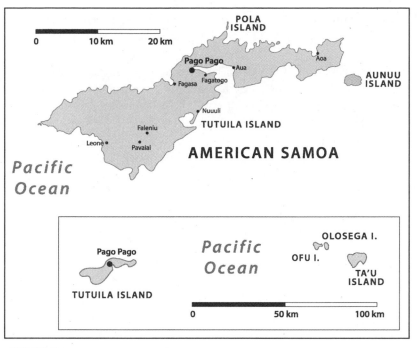

MAP 2.2 Samoa

through her fieldwork, and she set out to investigate if adolescence was "a time in the life history of every girl child which carries with it symptoms of conflict and stress as surely as it implies a change in the girl's body" (Mead 2001: 136).

Intent on traveling to an "untouched and undiscovered place," Mead was directed by Boas to American Samoa, primarily because of the frequency with which ships called on the island and the possibility of regular contact via written mail. After arriving with a letter from the surgeon-general of the US Navy, Mead decided on the island of Ta'u, one of the three small islands in the Manu'an archipelago and with a population of 600.

Before settling in Ta'u, Mead studied the Samoan language for approximately ten weeks in the port of Pago Pago. After ten days living with the family of a county chief, Mead moved herself into the medical dispensary, where she lived with the Holts, local representatives of the naval government in American Samoa and the sole white family on the island. The Manu'an people had been governed by the United States for about 21 years, and a government school had been established for at least ten of those years by the time Mead arrived (Freeman 1983).

Mead selected 50 girls for her study, 11 of whom were children showing "no mammary signs of puberty," 14 of whom would likely mature in the next 18 months, and the balance who were past puberty (Mead 2001: 180). Mead's **purposeful sampling** of her study subjects was based on her assertion that "a detailed investigation will be of more value than a more diffused and general study based upon a less accurate

PLATE 2.3 Margaret Mead, with Manus Mother and Child

knowledge of a greater number of individuals" (2001: 179). Due to the small number of participants involved and the nature of the data, Mead believed that a **qualitative research** approach was the most suited: "The composite of the background against which the girl acts can be described in accurate and general terms, but her reactions are a function of her own personality and cannot be described without reference to it" (2001: 180). Mead conducted interviews in the Samoan language and used intelligence testing, such as "color-naming, rote memory, opposites, substitution, ball and field, and interpretation" to gain what she believed was an understanding of the mental capacity of the girls (2001: 182). She examined the social organization of the community, including the various roles a girl would likely play and the relationships she would have. This included the differences between boys and girls at various stages of adolescence and young adulthood; the relationships girls established within the household, the community, and with those of the same age group; sex relations within and out of wedlock; and the case of the "deviant" and the consequences of existing on the perimeters of society.

After nine months in the field, Mead returned to the United States with findings in hand. In Samoa, there existed no great behavioral or emotional differences between pre-adolescents, adolescents, and young adults. Mead concluded that as the physical and biological development of girls was essentially the same in both Samoa and the United States, the turmoil and distress that American girls experienced were due to the cultural constraints placed upon them by American society. As assumptions concerning the disposition of *all* humans would have to be found true in *all* societies, Mead concluded that the despair and anxiety associated with adolescence was indeed an American cultural construction and not a universally experienced biological stage. Her findings were wholeheartedly supported by Boas and other colleagues.

Mead attributed the Samoan adolescents' seeming emotional calm to their social environment—because they did not establish intense personal relationships, and because they were exposed to all forms of experiences, such as birth, sex, and death at a relatively young age, they were far more accepting of a wider range of "normalcy" than their American counterparts. Mead described what seemed to her as a lack of choice for adolescent girls—because their lives were simple and straightforward, they were not bothered with decisions regarding education, extracurricular activities, career or other lifestyle issues that would contribute to their social status in society. Those who strayed from this easy-going nature were labeled as deviant. In contrast, American society offered children a plethora of religions, standards of morality and sexual practice, occupations, and family life from which to "choose." The social location of American children played a major role in the breadth of their "choices"—education, class location, and ability all combined to limit and expand their opportunities. The media also played a key role in perpetuating the idea of "endless possibilities," while at the same time disregarding the importance of social class and race. The downfall of American adolescents, Mead asserted, was the sheer plurality of choices in a society that championed "one standard" for all.

Now that we know what Mead's findings are, it is helpful to consider the social context in which she conducted her research. Mead was in Samoa at a time when there existed much opposition by Samoan chiefs to American administration (Gilliam 1993). In addition, the political circumstances of the people under study were often ignored by anthropologists, as was the position of the anthropologist in relation to their participants. Mead's identification with the foreign administration of Samoa never wavered during her time there, a relationship that certainly had an impact on how the Samoan people perceived her (Gilliam 1993). Furthermore, Mead believed the Samoan people to be "simple" and therefore ideal as an easy study subject: "… the anthropologist chooses quite simple peoples, primitive peoples, whose society has never attained the complexity of our own" (Mead 2001: 7). Mead relied on generalizations as a way of characterizing her subjects' "modal" personality type (Feinberg 1988). By portraying Samoan adolescence as representing one personality type, she could easily contrast this with the anxious and depressed American teen, another personality type. Mead's assumptions most certainly influenced the manner in which she approached and spoke to her participants, and in turn, the way that they spoke and interacted with her. This is not to say that her work is inadequate; rather, by making her assumptions clear we are provided with much-needed context for understanding her conclusions. Mead's approach and her portrayal of non-Western societies were similar to those of most anthropologists conducting research at this time, a fact that has undergone close scrutiny over the last few decades by anthropologists themselves.

Mead's work greatly contributed to the defeat of biological-determinist thinking in the United States. Her work also illustrated that childhood is not a universal experience and is just as susceptible to the environmental and social conditions as other stages of life, a concept widely ignored in the realm of social science until the 1990s. *Coming of Age in Samoa* was an enormously popular book. The American public could not get enough of reading about the carefree and sexually promiscuous lives of exotic

South Pacific Islanders, and it continued to be consumed by the public for decades to come. In the realm of academia, however, fellow anthropologist Derek Freeman (1916–2001) launched an attack on Mead's work after her death in 1978, asserting that Mead's conclusions on female adolescent sexuality were all wrong, and that her informants had essentially "duped" her. Freeman's criticism of Mead's work has been widely critiqued within academia and provides an interesting snapshot of how two people can observe and interpret the lives of others in vastly different ways.

Despite the criticism, Mead's contribution to illuminating one of the basic tenets of anthropological research—the power of research to increase understanding between diverse groups of people—cannot be ignored. As Mead herself said, "Realizing that our own ways are not humanly inevitable nor God-ordained, but are the fruit of a long and turbulent history, we may well examine in turn all of our institutions, thrown into strong relief against the history of other civilizations, and weighing them in the balance, be not afraid to find them wanting" (2001: 160). Mead went on to have a very high-profile career as a respected, if controversial, anthropologist—she was a professor at The New School, Columbia University (1954–78) and Fordham University (1968–70), was the executive secretary of the National Research Council's Committee on Food Habits during World War II, and served as curator of ethnology at the American Museum of Natural History from 1946 to 1969. Her research in later years continued to consider child-rearing practice and was greatly influenced by the field of psychology. Mead died of pancreatic cancer in 1978.

While the British school may be characterized by a focus on the "psychosocial solidarity" of societies, the American school institutionalized an approach that highlighted the diversity of culture. Structural functionalists were criticized for ignoring history, change, and diversity in order to develop concise explanatory theories, while the Americans were critiqued for a "descriptive approach" that lacked theoretical sophistication and depth (Erikson & Murphy 2013). Throughout the latter half of the twentieth century, scholars strove to develop a paradigm that drew on the strengths and abandoned the weaknesses of their earlier colleagues. We will not spend time here summarizing or debating the strengths and weaknesses of the myriad of approaches that characterized anthropology for the last half of the twentieth century. Rather, we will note that anthropology as a discipline has always been subject to the political, social, and intellectual climate of the time. While this can be said of almost all academic disciplines, anthropologists are perhaps the most forthright in recognizing the influence of these forces on their study and practice.

Today, anthropology sits at an interesting point that is unlike any time in the past. The discipline continues to be characterized by a diversity of theoretical and methodological approaches. Perhaps what has changed is the amount of energy spent debating the validity of a single "master narrative," or a "one size fits all" approach to how best to understand culture and society (Knauft 2006). In place of this debate is a recognition and embracing of a range of approaches that are critical, creative, rigorous, and, importantly, relevant to understanding the world we live in. To conclude this chapter, we will consider where anthropology is positioned today, in the early years of the twenty-first century, before we move on to exploring how contemporary anthropologists approach the study of powerful social categories (kinship, cultural identity, gender, and race) and institutions (science, religion, and globalization) in society.

Contemporary Anthropology

Thus far in our introduction to anthropology we have considered three major approaches associated with the discipline: social evolutionism, the British School, and the American School. Like other scholars hailing from both the social-scientific and scientific disciplines, anthropologists have traditionally subscribed to a particular approach to organizing and structuring their method of understanding how and why societies operate the way they do. Anthropologists continue to be engaged in vigorous theoretical and methodological debates about which approach is the best suited to accurately capture the complexities and diversity of the social world. The plurality of these approaches has led to the declaration of a discipline "in crisis" too many times to count, for how can anthropologists call themselves a unified discipline if there is no consensus around how to practice?

Academic debate is what keeps research relevant—these conversations challenge and critique theoretical and methodological approaches in order to identify and strengthen new ways of thinking. There has, however, been a wider acknowledgment and acceptance of anthropological study that is multidisciplinary in both perspective and practice. During the eras of Boas and Malinoswki, it was easy to identify one's particular school of thought—you were either A or B or were championing a new approach known as C. Today, however, anthropologists are better known for *what* they study rather than a specific theoretical approach. Anthropologist Bruce Knauft has described the current anthropological landscape as "the braiding together of different approaches or perspectives like strands of a rope configured specially for a new topic, issue or critical intervention" (2006: 408). So why is this? And why *now*?

Cultural anthropology occupies an interesting position—it is a discipline that is constantly critiquing, through rigorous research, the social world and the actors and institutions within it (gender, political movements, economy, etc.). While at one time anthropologists endeavored to *explain* the world, today many anthropologists aim to critically engage with the world through a diversity of professions (Herzfeld 2001). Many anthropologists are employed outside the realm of academia, in areas including, but not limited to, government agencies, non-profit organizations, and multinational corporations. Others straddle many of these professional roles and act as professors, activists, and consultants. As a discipline that embraces a wide range of methodological approaches, anthropologists can endeavor to answer complex research questions that are not limited by boundaries, be they geographic, methodological, theoretical or other. When we consider that, at least according to the North American approach, anthropology has always approached the study of humans from a four-field perspective—culture, biology, linguistics, and archaeology—envisioning a discipline that is secure in its multidisciplinary approach seems relatively natural. In the next section we consider how anthropologists are applying their research and theoretical skills in a diverse range of fields outside of academia, creating a sub-field referred to as applied anthropology.

Applied Anthropology

Applied anthropology is the application of anthropological theory, methodology, and knowledge to solving "practical" problems, usually at the request of a specific organization or client. As a result of their specialized and often intimate knowledge of how people live and get along (or not) in a given area, anthropologists are in demand in a diversity of fields, including health, education, and international development. The term "applied anthropology" may be somewhat misleading, for it implies that the discipline is split in two—on the one hand, a passive, theoretical, and disengaged anthropology and on the other, a "toolkit" anthropology where skills are simply applied to problem solving. This is certainly not the case, for the production of knowledge that leads to a better understanding of complex issues is certainly not passive or disengaged. Applied anthropology, however, is often framed as a problem-driven approach. Anthropologists are asked to *apply* their research, observation, and interpretation skills to a specific issue, such as policy planning, marketing, legal disputes or medicine. Below we will explore two popular areas of application, the first in the field of global health, and the second in the area of economic aid.

Medical Anthropology and Global Health

Medical anthropology is a sub-field of anthropology that has become increasingly prominent over the last three decades. It employs anthropological theory and method in exploring understandings of health and health care from a cross-cultural perspective. According to the Society for Medical Anthropology, "Medical anthropologists examine how the health of individuals, larger social formations, and the environment are affected by interrelationships between humans and other species; cultural norms and social institutions; micro and macro politics; and forces of globalization as each of these affects local worlds" (Society for Medical Anthropology 2014). The emergence of this sub-field speaks to the desire to investigate topics that are relevant, problem-driven, and increasingly multidisciplinary. Health is a predominant social category in all societies: how we define well-being and illness, how we go about maintaining and treating different conditions, who society considers an expert in the field, and what type of information we base our understandings on—these are all cultural constructs that vary drastically from one society to the next.

Nor is health simply a physiological state. In order to gain an understanding of how the wide range of political, social, economic, and cultural forces have an impact on a community's health, research that positions the experiences and beliefs of people themselves at the forefront of analysis is key. Those dedicated to the field of global health face seemingly insurmountable obstacles in attempting to improve health conditions in low-income countries. How on earth does one approach the serious challenges and daunting social circumstances that have led to these health crises? While philanthropic organizations such as the Bill and Melinda Gates Foundation and the US President's Emergency Plan for AIDS Relief (PEPFAR) have pumped millions of dollars into research, programs, interventions, and health facilities, the health crises facing the world's poorest nations continue to loom large.

Medical interventions and policies based on scientific evidence have emerged as central strategies used by many of these international funding organizations to assist in improving global health (Behague et al. 2009). There remains a gap, however, between the context in which this evidence is produced and the local reality for which it is intended. There is no doubt that scientific research is essential for illustrating the effectiveness of an intervention in a controlled setting; these situations, however, often bear little or no resemblance to the local context in which the intervention is to occur. The "inadequate translation of public health knowledge into effective action" as a result of clashing social and cultural beliefs is thus a major barrier to improving global health (Hahn & Inhorn 2009). This is where medical anthropology plays a crucial role.

The process of implementing an intervention or a program involves the interaction of a number of cultural and social systems, including the local people, the social institutions on a local and national level, the researchers, clinicians, and staff who are there to implement the intervention, as well as funding agencies, NGOs, and local and foreign governments (Janes & Corbett 2009). Anthropologists are well versed in attending to how these social systems interact and, ideally, coexist in a manner that facilitates the best understanding of issues. Ethnographic methods such as fieldwork, participant observation, qualitative interviews, and focus groups are effective strategies for gaining an understanding of how a program or intervention should be tailored and implemented to effectively reach community members and meet their needs. The importance of designing culturally acceptable prevention and treatment strategies is perhaps best illustrated when we consider the case of malaria, a disease that is avoidable and curable through simple interventions, yet continues to kill millions of people in low- and middle-income countries.

Malaria

The biomedical explanation of malaria is a disease "caused by a parasite that commonly infects a certain type of mosquito which feeds on humans" (CDC 2012). According to the World Health Organization (WHO), "half of the world's population—3.3 billion people living in 109 countries—are at risk for malaria. In 2000, malaria caused between 350–500 million illnesses and more than one million deaths" (WHO 2008: 2). As one scholar writes, this number is the equivalent of "filling seven Boeing 747s with children, and then crashing them, every day" (Attaran et al. 2000: 730). Health costs associated with the disease include both personal and public expenditures: "In some heavy-burden countries, the disease accounts for up to 40% of public health expenditures, 30% to 50% of inpatient hospital admissions and up to 60% of outpatient health clinic visits" (WHO). The toll on the economy in low- to mid-income countries as a result of infection is substantial: death and illness due to malaria cut economic growth rates by as much as 1.3 per cent in countries with high disease rates. Malaria disproportionately affects the marginalized and poor who cannot afford treatment or who have limited access to health care.[2]

Once a person develops malaria, early diagnosis and treatment are central to reducing the risk of illness and death (WHO). While drug therapies exist, the widespread parasite resistance to these drugs is making malaria control increasingly difficult (WHO; Maslove et al. 2009). Prevention of malaria is therefore key to effective malaria control. Prevention strategies focus on reducing the transmission of disease through the use of mosquito nets treated with insecticide (an approach effectively tested), and indoor residual spraying of insecticides (Woelk et al. 2009). The success of efforts to reduce malaria is difficult to assess, as there has been poor planning of major initiatives (Attaran et al. 2000), a lack of baseline data (Attaran et al. 2000), and unreliable data on incidence and mortality rates (Kamat 2009). Despite this uncertainty, research funds continue to be poured into treatment and prevention strategies—for example, since 2000 the Bill and Melinda Gates Foundation has donated nearly $250 million (McCoy et al. 2009: 1645). Attention to how individual communities understand the disease and consequently perceive treatment and prevention strategies is often neglected, however. One anthropologist writes:

> In order to assist the community in selecting and designing appropriate and potentially successful control programs, it is necessary to understand the context of the disease in the community. This context includes the community characteristics, the community perception of the nature and etiology of the illness and its symptoms, and health seeking behaviour for prevention and treatment, including the use of traditional and cosmopolitan medications.... Programs which take local concerns into account are more likely to be successful (and sustainable) than those that adopt a simple strategy for providing information. (Helitzer-Allen, Kendall, & Wirima, cited in Kamat 2009: 37)

Cultural understandings of illness dictate how individuals protect themselves from illness, when they will seek care, and to whom they will turn. Access to care, understandings of disease and prevention methods, and practices around seeking treatment are dictated by socio-cultural factors. Anthropologist Vinay Kamat conducted ethnographic research in Mbande, a peri-urban village in Tanzania, to understand care-givers' decision-making processes in seeking malaria treatment for their young children (2009). Through interviews with 45 village women, Kamat learned of local explana-tions for what causes *degedege*, "the indigenous name for a much feared life threatening illness that in many cases people do not associate with malaria fever" (2009: 43). The characteristics of *degedege* resemble the characteristics of cerebral malaria, a type of malaria that kills the majority of children. Kamat provides a description of *degedege* as told to him by women and the local elders in the village, which we include below:

> The Kiswahili word *degedege* literally translates into English as "bird bird." In coastal Tanzania, among the Zaràmo people in particular, the illness is believed to be caused by a coastal spirit (*mdudu shetani*) that takes the form of a bird that casts its shadow on vulnerable children on moonlit nights. Children who come under the bird's shadow subsequently become seriously ill, develop convulsions, and in many cases succumb to the illness and die....
>
> In the dominant local cultural model of fever, if *homa ya kawaida* is left untreated, it may lead to *homa kali*, which in turn, if untreated, may lead to *homa ya malaria*. Finally, if malarial fever is not successfully treated, it may lead to *degedege*—although some informants said that *degedege* is a distinct illness with an etiology that is not related to malaria. They believed that the illness is not an advanced stage of malarial infection but an illness that is caused by "spirits." While most mothers I interviewed shared the cultural understandings of the etiology of *degedege*, there was considerable variation and flexibility in how they interpreted the taxonomy of fevers and the trajectory of the illness or the "ultimate" cause of the illness....
>
> In Mbande, people consider "bad luck" or "God's will" to render particular children to be more vulnerable than others to *degedege*. Thus, when asked why some children are more prone to contracting *degedege* than others, the majority of the people in the village responded that it was just "God's wish" or "God's work" (*kazi ya mungu*) and that it was due to witchcraft (*uchawi*), sorcery (*kurogwa*), or someone's evil actions. This etiological belief significantly influ-ences their acceptance of the fatal outcomes of the illness. Interviews with key informants and with local *waganga* who are known for their expertise in diag-nosing and treating cases of *degedege* suggested that there is a general agreement that the illness is caused by a "spirit bird." (Kamat 2009: 45)

As this section illustrates, the local understanding of *degedege* is very different from the biomedical understanding of malaria. When local understandings of how illness occurs do not reflect the biomedical approaches that inform the actions of clinicians, NGOs and public health agencies, the result is a clash of values and beliefs that can stand in the way of effective control efforts. Furthermore, people's decision-making processes and health-seeking behavior are influenced by far more than just an understanding of disease. Kamat used a holistic approach that contextualized the socio-economic world of the residents of Mbande to understand the barriers and facilitators associated with accessing care. He describes the political manner in which the village came to exist (a consequence of relocation and then campaigning by a local leader to create a township distinct from already existing ones), the development of an all-weather road that brought in waves of migrants from Northern Tanzania and led to a resulting shortage of land, the ethnic identification of the people in the village, and, finally, the economic activities of its citizens.

While these factors are not necessarily *directly* related to malaria control, they nevertheless affect the access to and delivery of services, such as the availability of medicines, the distance that citizens have to travel to reach the municipal dispensary, the number of trained medical officers and nurses and their availability, the number of traditional healers and local pharmacies and their availability, and the number of people that these health clinics, both biomedical and traditional, must serve. As a great number of children infected with malaria die because they do not get prompt medical attention, these factors have a substantial impact on malaria control efforts (Kamat 2009).

Kamat concludes that even if more efficacious anti-malarial treatments were readily available in Mbande, mothers would continue to delay bringing their children to a health facility because they believe they are dealing with an "ordinary" illness that does not require medical attention immediately. To facilitate early treatment, Kamat suggests that local dispensary staff must be able to effectively communicate the severity of the symptoms of malaria and the importance of early treatment to mothers. This is a conclusion shared by other anthropologists conducting malaria research. Hausmann-Muela and her colleagues (1998) illustrate that in some areas where there is fairly good access to biomedical clinics, a recurring bout of malaria after an individual has received biomedical care is often interpreted as the result of witchcraft or sorcery. While information, education, and communication campaigns can be effective in changing local knowledge about malaria symptoms and treatments, this does not necessarily translate into changed behavior (Hausmann-Muela & Muela-Ribera 2003). Despite the fact that knowledge regarding malaria symptoms and treatment of these symptoms was well known by members of the community where Hausmann-Muela and her associates conducted their fieldwork, they repeatedly witnessed individuals acting in a way that seemed to contradict the scientific knowledge they had so recently learned.

Simply expecting that knowledge produced in a context far removed from everyday realities will immediately lead to changed behavior neglects the power of culture in informing worldviews and values. Recognizing the importance of local knowledge regarding health, illness, and treatment, and the manner in which this knowledge interacts with biomedical approaches, can lead to a better understanding of how best to target behaviors that may have an impact on malaria prevention and treatment strategies. Evidence gained through anthropological studies can provide the much-needed context and perspective that will increase the effectiveness of technical and biomedical approaches to health.

Economic Aid and Development

Since the 1970s, anthropologists have studied the institutions and organizations involved in economic development initiatives with the intent of having an impact on how development takes place. The unequal distribution of wealth among the world's nations, and the post-colonial legacy of political turmoil and economic uncertainty that characterizes much of the world's poorest nations, have led to attempts by aid and development organizations to generate economic activity and improve political stability with the hope that increased and more effective social services will follow. While many of these development initiatives are presented on humanitarian grounds, the motivations for these projects are often entrenched in political and economic issues. In the late 1990s, agencies such as the World Bank came under extreme criticism for failing to assist the poor in the receiving countries to implement policies to improve economic security. Instead, it was the economically developed nations that appeared to benefit from this arrangement, as their business investments resulted in profitable returns and thousands of jobs for the people in their employment, while those in the receiving countries struggled to adapt to strict economic policies.

Large-scale development institutions can roughly be divided into two groups: multilateral organizations, such as the United Nations and the World Bank, which have several donor nations; and bilateral organizations, such as the Canadian International Development Agency (CIDA) and the United States Agency for International Development (USAID), which are characterized by a relationship between the donor and recipient countries. These organizations have particular ways of going about their lending: they may offer loans or grants that are "tied" to certain projects, or they may allow the receiving country to do what it wishes with the money, what are called "untied" contributions. However, the structures and organizing principles of development and aid initiatives are not the focus of this section; rather, we will focus on the role of the anthropologist in working as a link between a donor organization and local people to design and implement a project that will bring the desired effect—an improved quality of life for those in need.

The job of the anthropologist in the early years of development projects was to make things operate as smoothly and efficiently as possible. As anthropologists were *employed* by these organizations, their loyalties were not to the local people but to the organizations themselves, who often had different objectives than the residents. Many of these development schemes had disastrous effects on the local people and their environment, and it wasn't long before the ethical involvement of anthropologists was called into question. This awareness of the negative impact of supposedly positive development schemes led to a shift in the role that the anthropologist assumed: "The question is not: What can we do to make this project successful? Instead,

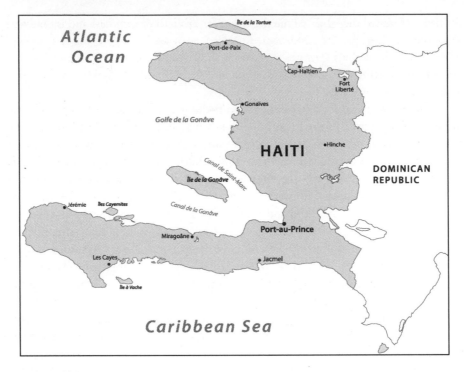

MAP 2.3 Haiti

the anthropologist asks: Is this is a good project from the perspective of the target population?" (Miller, Van Esterik, & Van Esterik 2001: 421). (Indeed, the role of anthropology in development is a contentious and hot topic. For an in-depth and fascinating discussion of some of the difficulties associated with conducting fieldwork in the development and aid world, see the work of anthropologist David Mosse [2005; 2011], who has written extensively on the subject.)

Perhaps one of the best-known examples of an anthropologist playing an *effective* role in a development project is that of Gerald Murray (1987) in Haiti. While this example is now over 25 years old, it is an excellent case study to illustrate how anthropological knowledge can lead to the development of a more successful initiative, for both the organization supplying the funds and the local people. Murray exposed components of a multi-million-dollar reforestation project that were not compatible with the everyday realities of the farmers who were ultimately responsible for the success of the project.

Haiti is one of the poorest nations in the Western hemisphere. It is located on the Caribbean island of Hispaniola, which it shares with the Dominican Republic. It has a long history of colonial rule in which both the French and the

Spanish deforested the island to sell the wood for profit and plant cash crops that were in demand in Europe. After independence, foreign-owned lumber companies cleared most of the island of its valuable hardwoods. Haiti is now essentially deforested, and an increase in population has led to pressure on the land and a high demand for wood and charcoal in the cities.

Reforestation projects were failing miserably, in particular the USAID project that eventually employed Murray, an anthropologist who had just completed his dissertation on "the manner in which Haitian peasant land tenure had evolved in response to internal population growth" (Murray 1987: 225). The problem with the USAID approach lay in its inability to present a project that would allow the peasant farmers control of their land and of the trees that were being planted on it—as farmers, they were dependent on cleared land to plant cash crops and graze their goats. It did not make economic sense to plant the fruit trees that USAID supplied, as they were not meant to be cut down, thus further limiting the already scarce land available. It also made little economic sense to wait for an economic return on trees that would take years to mature. USAID was presenting the project from an ecological perspective— the intent was to aid in soil regeneration, not to offer farmers immediate economic profit. To the farmers who were trying to feed their families and maintain their land, however, the promise of improved conditions years down the road rang hollow in their ears.

After analyzing the shortcomings of the USAID project, Murray stated that it was not the attitudes of the peasants that were causing the project to fail, but instead one or two major flaws in the project plans. He jokingly stated that if he were given a jeep and access to a $50,000 checking account, he would be able to implement a program that would produce more trees in the ground than the current multi-million-dollar "charade" (Murray 1987: 226). Murray packed up his bags and left Haiti, only to receive a startling phone call some time later: "To my great disbelief, as I was correcting Anthro 101 exams some two years later, one of the program officers still in Haiti called to say that an Agroforestry Outreach Project (AOP) had been approved chapter and verse as I had recommended it; and that if I was interested in putting my life where my mouth had been and would leave the ivory tower to direct the project, my project bank account would have, not $50,000, but $4 million" (Murray 1987: 226).

Murray had suggested that, rather than providing fruit trees that were not to be cut, farmers be supplied with fast-growing trees, such as eucalyptus, that could be cut as early as four years after planting. The farmers were given full control over the trees— they could allow their goats to eat them (which is what had happened with the fruit tree seedlings), in which case they would not receive any more seedlings from the project; they could allow the trees to grow for four years and then clear the land and sell the wood for lumber and charcoal; or they could allow the trees to mature and provide coverage for their crops. The choice was theirs.

Initially, Murray had cautiously estimated that three million trees would be planted on the land of six thousand farmers at the end of four years. By the end of the fourth year (by which time another anthropologist had taken over as director), the project had planted *20 million trees on the land of 75,000 farmers*. The project was an astounding success, primarily due to the compatibility of the project aims and the needs of the farmers themselves. The input of anthropological methods and theories greatly influenced the project throughout each stage of planning and implantation: "We are dealing, not with an ongoing project affected by anthropological input, but with a project whose very existence was rooted in anthropological research and whose very character was determined by ongoing anthropological direction and anthropologically informed managerial prodding" (Murray 1987: 235).

Unfortunately, the tumultuous political situation in Haiti has negated much of the positive benefits of the project. A military coup in 1986 disrupted civil society, including the cutting down of trees as an attempt by the military to exert power over the rural population. Since then, Haiti has seen two more military coups, the invasion and occupation by the United States in 1994 and again in 2004, extreme civil unrest, and the country's first democratically elected president, René Préval (b. 1943), who was elected both in 1996 and again in 2006. Perhaps most devastating, however, was the earthquake that struck on January 12, 2010. More than 220,000 people were killed, 300,000 injured, and more than one million made homeless. Three years later, the United Nations estimated that over 1 million people were still in need of humanitarian assistance.

Conclusion

In this chapter we have introduced two prominent approaches, the British and American Schools, that were influential in establishing anthropology as an academic discipline. These approaches brought the concept of culture to center stage and were instrumental in dismantling racist discourse concerning the abilities of the non-white population. Through the work of Franz Boas and his famous student Margaret Mead, we explored how this new approach was applied in ethnographic research and how it has shaped the discipline into its current state. Today, anthropology inhabits an interesting position within academia as a result of its diverse methodological and theoretical approaches. While debate continues about the best approach to understanding the social world, at the same time anthropologists have been busy, applying their skills and analysis to the fields of medicine and economic development. In the next chapter we will explore the discipline's colonial history, and the theoretical and methodological approaches taken by early anthropologists as they set out to create meaning out of the vast jumble of culture and society that was being introduced by way of explorers' journal accounts.

Notes

1   Anthropometry is the study of the human body using quantitative measurements and statistics, such as the "cephalic index," which considered the ratio between the maximum length of the skull to its maximum width. These techniques are now seen as being too inexact to tell us anything useful about genetic relationships between populations, and are no longer used.
2   For World Health Organization information on malaria, see http://www.who.int/malaria/en/ and http://www.who.int/mediacentre/factsheets/fs094/en/.

Study Questions

1   Compare and contrast the British and the American Schools of anthropology using examples from the work of Malinowski, Richards, Boas, and Mead.
2   Explain the *structural functionalism* approach to anthropology by discussing the work of Audrey Richards among the Bemba in what is now Zambia.
3   Explain Boas's anthropological approach, and identify how it is different from that of evolutionary anthropologists.
4   Describe Margaret Mead's theoretical and methodological approach to studying adolescent girls in Samoa.
5   Describe how Mead's findings from Samoa influenced the discipline of anthropology and our understanding of human diversity.
6   Summarize the criticism of Mead's work from a contemporary perspective.
7   Identify some of the professions in which anthropologists can apply their knowledge and skills, and list three challenges that they may encounter.
8   Identify some of the criticisms leveled at economic agencies involved in economic aid and development in the 1990s.
9   Using the example of malaria and *degedege*, explain why implementing a public health initiative is so complex, and how anthropological research may assist in this endeavor.
10 Outline the problems facing the failed USAID reforestation program in Haiti and explain how Gerald Murray used an anthropological approach to craft a successful program.

Discussion Questions

1   How did Boas's approach to understanding human diversity help to dispel quasi-scientific biological explanations concerning the superiority of the white race? How does Boas's work inform your current understanding of race and diversity?

2   Considering the origins of anthropology, discuss the role of anthropologists in the "developing world," and how this role has changed since the work of Richards and Mead. What contribution can anthropologists today make to international development and global health?

3   The nature versus nurture debate rages on today. Given what you've learned about the role anthropology has played in framing the debate, discuss the issue using examples from this text and your other areas of experience and knowledge.

4   What is the relationship between the individual and the wider society? How do our social circumstances affect who we are as people? Consider the person you are today; do you think you would be different if you had grown up in a different place, among different people, or even in a different environment?

PART II

CLASSIC QUESTIONS IN ANTHROPOLOGY

CHAPTER 3

//

Historical Beginnings

LEARNING OBJECTIVES

After reading this chapter, students should be able to

- outline how Darwin's experiences with the people of Tierra del Fuego were central to his understanding of social progress;
- describe the "myth of the savage," and its influence on eighteenth-century anthropology, including its biblical origins, and interpretations by the philosophers Hobbes and Rousseau;
- explain how Locke's concept of private property informed the work of nineteenth-century anthropologists;
- discuss how social theorists used observations of peoples such as the Aboriginals of Australia and the Fuegians to illustrate social evolutionism; and
- summarize the work of Lewis Henry Morgan and explain what differentiates his theory of social evolutionism from other social evolutionists.

KEY TERMS

paradigm	state of nature	totemism

Introduction

In the introduction and Chapter 1, we described a number of first-contact situations, introduced a few concepts, and indicated what kind of anthropology we're dealing with here. Now we must consider the history of the subject. A few more concepts will emerge along the way.

Many years separate Christopher Columbus, James Cook, and Simon Fraser from Bronislaw Malinowski, Elizabeth Fernea, and Cathy Small. Anthropology as we understand it today took shape in the intervening period, and this chapter initiates an account of how that came about. One way of presenting this story is in a more or less linear fashion: what happened and when, how anthropology became an identifiable discipline, and who its important figures are. Another possibility is in terms of dominant themes—questions that recur throughout the history of our subject and the theoretical approaches that have emerged to address them.

We'll use both, but we should point out that we've been selective in our approach to this short chapter. This book is not meant to be a history of anthropology—there are other works that explore this in depth (we attach a short list at the end of this chapter). Instead we will offer a brief look in narrative form at some influential figures and approaches to understanding culture and society.

Charles Darwin: An Anthropologist?

Perhaps you don't think of Charles Darwin (1809–82) as an anthropologist, and yet he was preoccupied throughout his life with questions about the nature of the human species—and not just about our biological place in the scheme of things. He also reflected on culture, psychology, and history. In the conclusion to *On the Origin of Species* (1859), he speculated about where his theory of evolution might lead: "In the distant future I see open fields for far more important researches. Psychology will be based on a new foundation, that of the necessary acquirement of each mental power and capacity by gradation. Light will be thrown on the origin of man and his history" (1979: 458).

This is the only place in his world-changing book that he mentions humankind at all, and yet it's clear that this was a topic that had been on his mind all along. It was already present when in 1832 he encountered the native peoples of Tierra del Fuego in South America during the famous voyage of the HMS *Beagle*—peoples who were, at 55° south latitude, "the most southern aborigines on the globe" (Fitzroy 1966, v.2: 142–43). Darwin's reflections on the Fuegians are of interest in themselves, but they also bring to focus a number of fundamental anthropological questions:

- Is there a basic and universal "human nature"? Or is much of what we take to be human nature actually the product of culture and circumstance?

- What are the evolutionary roots of our social capacities?
- What was the driving force of historical change and social evolution, and what was the ideological role of the "savage" in Western intellectual history?

In 1826 the British Admiralty dispatched two ships—the *Adventure* and the *Beagle*—to survey "the Southern Coasts of the Peninsula of South America." This first voyage of the *Beagle* lasted four years and is a story in its own right. But what concerns us here is that they returned home with four native Fuegians on board, three young men and a girl. Other travelers had encountered Fuegians before, and had formed an unfavorable opinion of them. These hunter-gatherers lived in small and sometimes mutually hostile bands, and subsisted off the products of both sea and land. Robert Fitzroy, captain of the *Beagle*, described them as "… wrapped in rough skins, with their hair hanging down on all sides, like old thatch, and their skins of a reddish brown colour, smeared over with oil, and very dirty. Naturally petulant and quarrelsome, they are also ever intent upon mischief; fear of punishment alone restraining them; their extremely dirty black hair half hides yet heightens a villainous expression of the worst description of savage features" (Fitzroy 1966, v.1: 216, 319; v.2: 137).

PLATE 3.1 Charles Darwin

Nevertheless he reflected that, "unwilling as we may be to consider ourselves even remotely descended from human beings in such a state … [Julius] Caesar found the Britons painted and clothed in skins like these Fuegians" (Fitzroy 1966, v.2: 121). After another incident involving the theft of a boat, the British picked up the four Fuegians as hostages, but found it impossible to drop them off again. Robert Fitzroy assumed personal responsibility for their welfare, and vowed to return them on a subsequent trip. His views on their abilities changed for the better with greater familiarity: "During the time which elapsed before we reached England, I had time to see much of my Fuegian companions; and daily became more interested about them as I attained a further acquaintance with their abilities and natural inclinations. Far, very far indeed, were three of the number from deserving to be called savages [he wasn't so sure about the fourth who, in any event, died of smallpox in England]. They look forward with pleasure to seeing our country, as well as to returning to their own" (Fitzroy 1966, v.2: 1–2, 6).

In the end he became quite fond of his four guests and saw them as possible cultural ambassadors; they were even introduced to King William (Victoria's predecessor) at the monarch's own request. Fitzroy was true to his word, and the remaining Fuegians were returned on the second expedition; this time a 22-year-old Charles Darwin rode along as expedition naturalist on a five-year journey around the world. The role of that trip in the development of Darwin's theory of evolution through natural selection is well known, and we will return to it. The immediate product was his famous travel narrative, *The Voyage of the Beagle* (originally

PLATE 3.2 Robert Fitzroy

PLATE 3.3 A Fuegian

volume 3 of the official report of the expedition, published in 1839). On Christmas Day, 1832, he first encountered the "savage" Fuegians:

> The astonishment which I felt on first seeing a party of Fuegians on a wild and broken shore will never be forgotten by me, for the reflection at once rushed into my mind—such were our ancestors. These men were absolutely naked and bedaubed with paint, their long hair was tangled, their mouths frothed with excitement, and their expression was wild, startled, and distrustful. They possessed hardly any arts, and like wild animals lived on what they could catch; they had no government, and were merciless to every one not of their own small tribe. (Darwin 1966: 642)

> Viewing such men, one can hardly make oneself believe they are fellow-creatures, and inhabitants of the same world.... The tribes have no government or head, yet each is surrounded by other hostile ones, speaking different dialects; and the cause of their warfare would appear to be the means of subsistence.... Whilst beholding these savages, one asks, whence have they come? What could have tempted, or what change compelled a tribe of men to leave the fine regions of the north, to travel down ... the backbone of America, to invent and build canoes, and then to enter on one of the most inhospitable countries within the limits of the globe? (Darwin 1966: 235–37)

PLATE 3.4 Aboriginals

But Darwin was also shipmate with the Fuegians whom Fitzroy had adopted, and that gave him occasion to reflect on racial difference and the nature of civilization. This concern stayed with him throughout his life, and he returned to the theme 30 years later in his 1871 book *The Descent of Man*: "The Fuegians rank amongst the lowest barbarians; but I was continually struck with surprise how closely the three natives on board H.M.S. 'Beagle,' who had lived some years in England, and could talk a little English, resembled us in disposition and in most of our mental faculties" (Darwin 1998: 66).

Having read widely in the anthropology of his day, Darwin made the jump from his comparison between Fuegians and the English to all human "races." He concluded that, no matter how different local varieties of humankind may seem on the surface, "the close similarity between the men of all races in tastes, dispositions and habits" shows that all humanity is a single species with similar psychological qualities. That was exactly what one should expect if—as his evolutionary theory implied—we are all descendants from a relatively recent common ancestor (Darwin 1998: 185). Robert Fitzroy also thought so; but, as a devout Christian, he looked to Adam and Eve for our common parents, and—like Columbus—traced the subsequent settlement of the earth back to the events described in Genesis 9–10. Leaving the truth of the biblical narrative aside, what he was trying to get at remains a problem today: the nature and timing of human settlement in the Americas (Fitzroy 1966, v.2: 640–66).

The Myth of "The Savage"

European observers tended to judge "primitive" peoples in terms of what they lacked. For Columbus it was religion and law; for Darwin it was orderly government and private property. The Fuegians, for example, appeared to be communistic, and tended to go naked as well. We noted above that the concept of the "savage" can function as an inverted image of the Europeans themselves. How they evaluated primitive peoples is therefore a reflection of how they regarded the worth of their own societies.

Such reactions were shaped by the myth of the Garden of Eden, where the parents of humankind are said to have lived as equals off the fruit of the trees, without clothing or social distinction. When Adam and Eve fell from favor from God by attaining knowledge of good and evil, their punishment was childbirth, work, death, and patriarchy. History begins with the Fall; there can be no history where nothing ever changes. The question boils down to whether you see "civilization" as a blessing or a curse. Consider James Cook's description of the Aboriginal Australians he encountered while exploring the coastline of what became New South Wales:

> The Natives of this country … are of a very dark brown or Chocolate Colour with lank black hair, they are under the common size and seem to be a timorous inoffensive race of Men…. Men women and children go wholly naked. It is said of our first Parents that after they had eat of the forbidden fruit they

saw themselves naked and were ashamed; these people are Naked and are not ashame'd; they live chiefly on Fish and wild Fowl and such other articles as the land naturly produceth, for they do not cultivate one foot of it. These people may truly be said to be in the pure state of Nature, and may appear to some to be the most wretched upon Earth: but in reality they are far more happier than … we Europeans. They live in a Tranquility which is not disturb'd by the inequality of condition, the Earth and Sea of their own accord furnishes them with all things necessary for life. (Cook 1968, v.1: 508–9)

Of course, Cook (1728–79) had no idea of what these people were really like, and the phrase "**state of nature**" gives him away. He was, after all, an eighteenth-century man, and speculation about the original condition of humankind was widespread in his day. This concept is associated with the Swiss philosopher Jean-Jacques Rousseau (1712–78), who used it in order to separate what is artificial from what is natural in the human condition—what is due to the influence of culture, what due to human nature itself. "In order to form a proper judgment of our present state," he imagined a time before people lived in societies, and speculated about what a being raised in such a condition would be like (Rousseau 1992: 13). He thought that compassion and pity are intrinsic features of human nature, and as such they contribute "to the mutual preservation of the entire species." They are the basis for the Golden Rule: "Do unto others as you would have them do unto you"—the foundation of all collective morality (1992: 37). These ideas served him as a baseline for a political philosophy, and he used them as a weapon. According to Rousseau, "When human society is considered with calm and disinterested attention, it seems to show at first only the violence of powerful men and the oppression of the weak" (1992: 15). But he concluded that, if people appear to be wicked, it is only because they live in wicked societies based on gross inequalities of wealth and status. That position had revolutionary implications. The myth of the "savage" was used to imagine what a just society would be like if we were free to go back and start again from scratch—to form a democratic social contract based on human sympathy and rational self-interest. The Americans, then the French, and later the Russians took a crack at it.

Rousseau was arguing against a very different view of human nature associated with the seventeenth-century English political theorist Thomas Hobbes (1588–1679), whose image of the "savage" was one of self-centered violence, of a war of all against all. For Hobbes this was a very real issue, since he was writing in the wake of the English Civil War of the 1640s, during which the foundations of society had been seriously shaken. He took events of that sort to be the modern equivalent of the violence supposedly typical of primitive society, and summed it all up in a passage that echoes down to our own day:

[In the State of Nature] there is no place for industry; because the fruit thereof is uncertain: and consequently no culture of the earth; no navigation; no commodious building; no knowledge of the face of the earth; no account of time; no arts; no letters; no society; and which is worst of all, continual fear, and danger of violent death and the life of man, solitary, poor, nasty, brutish, and short. (Hobbes 1962: 100)

The fundamental role of government is therefore to protect us from one another through the rule of law, backed up by the threat of force; only with that assurance is there any possibility of social progress. This contrast between Hobbes and Rousseau shows that the myth of the savage can be used for exactly opposite ends. Examples from the real world can be found to support either position, and both have had an influence on the development of anthropology and social thought more generally. Each can be found reflected in the political divisions of our own time (progressive vs. conservative), and each suggests that the "comparative method" should be used with caution (Evans-Pritchard 1963).

Private Property and Social Progress

Darwin saw that the ancestors of all humanity must have been hunter-gatherers and surmised that our social capacities evolved in that context as a survival mechanism. Anthropological studies of modern hunter-gatherers—for example, the San ("Bushmen") of southern Africa—have therefore been projected backward into the past in order to understand the circumstances in which humankind first arose.

As we've seen, seventeenth- and eighteenth-century thinkers used the image of the savage as a standard against which to measure other societies. By Darwin's time it had become commonplace to situate such peoples at the root of an evolutionary tree that classified societies on a scale from most simple to most complex, from lower to higher. This idea turns up in his reference to the Fuegians being "amongst the lowest barbarians." Such language was everyday currency in those days, and the idea of evolutionary progress was a dominant **paradigm** of the Victorian age (Burrow 1968). But how is relative complexity to be judged? What standard are we to use? And, if we imagine that hunting-gathering is the original human condition, what historical forces led some societies to leave that condition while others, like the Aboriginal Australians, remained behind?

Darwin thought the answer was the presence or absence of private property and the social hierarchy to which it gives rise. As he said of the Fuegians: "The perfect equality among the individuals composing these tribes, must for a long time retard their civilization.... In Tierra del Fuego, until some chief shall arise with power sufficient to secure any acquired advantages, such as the domesticated animals or other valuable presents, it seems scarcely possible that the political state of the country can be improved" (Darwin 1989: 183–84). Here Darwin is virtually quoting John Locke (1632–1704), another English social-contract theorist who wrote very influential works on the nature, origin, and purpose of government. As for the latter, he thought its fundamental role is the protection of individual "property"—which he defined broadly to include people's "lives, liberties, and estates" (2002: 57). Locke looked back over world history and what he knew of the native peoples of the Americas to construct a social-evolutionary scheme beginning when the human population was small. He imagined what happened as it grew larger and the land started to fill up.

The emergence of private property as we understand it was one result, accompanied by the invention of money to facilitate exchange and to make possible the storage of wealth in symbolic form. Locke thought that the current condition of the American Indians resembled closely what things had been like in the "first ages in Asia and Europe whilst the inhabitants were too few for the country, and want of people and money gave men no temptation to enlarge their possession of land, or contest for wider extent of ground" (2002: 49). As he said, "in the beginning all the world was America."

Seen this way, the Fuegians were held back because their population was small and there was nothing worth owning; hence there was no basis for social distinctions within their societies, no internal forces that might lead to their "improvement." Such arguments have often been used as a justification for private enterprise as opposed to socialist collectivism. Perfect equality was seen to equal stagnation, and here we have one possible criterion for the classification of societies along an evolutionary axis: how rights are distributed over those things locally considered valuable, especially access to the means of subsistence—agricultural land or irrigation water, fishing sites or hunting territories, control of pasturage for herds, whatever it may be. But who exercises these rights? How is labor distributed in relation to the fundamental tasks of society? How are the products of labor allocated? Is there a surplus? What about trade? Is there anything resembling money as a medium of exchange? In short, what is the economic system like and what are the environmental, cultural, and sociological factors that constrain and shape it?

Answers to questions such as these require knowledge of the wider social order—in particular, local ideas concerning relatedness and reciprocity, who is an insider and who is not. If Cook and Darwin had been able to get beyond their perceptions of these peoples as naked savages, they might have discovered that the Aboriginal Australians and the Fuegians lived in complex social and spiritual worlds, in which kin relations were a central organizational principle. As you will see in Chapter 4, the study of kinship was for a long time a central anthropological concern. This makes sense, since in "tribal" societies the economic, kinship, and political systems are inseparably wrapped up with one another.

As the Europeans gained deeper knowledge of the indigenous Australians, it became apparent that these peoples have intricate and surprising ways of classifying one another into relationship groups. These practices—embedded in language and enacted in ritual—defined who belonged to what group, who had rights to which hunting territories and water-holes, and who could or should marry with whom. Not only this, but these rules were also seen as having been instituted by the Dawn Beings at the beginning of the world when order was brought out of chaos—a common mythological theme. In the course of their travels these Beings determined the shape of the landscape and established the social practices that make a civilized life possible.

The land itself is therefore a manifestation of the sacred, and contemporary struggles over Aboriginal land rights in Australia—as in Canada and the United States—often invoke this powerful image (Goodall 1996).

The Australian peoples divided themselves up into intermarrying clans, each one symbolized by an animal or bird occupying some significant place in the myths of the Dream Time. The term **totemism** (which is actually of Native American origin) has been commonly applied to practices of this sort, which were once thought of as a distinct phase of social evolution. These systems of classification brought virtually all the people one was likely to meet into networks of affiliation, each grouping having mutual obligations and rights with respect to every other. Not that all was peace and love, because it wasn't; but it wasn't anarchy either, and very far indeed from a Hobbesian nightmare, or for that matter a Rousseauian utopia.

The same can be said for the Fuegians, among whom the property concept proved to be "surprisingly clearly marked." Though their social organization was not as elaborate as that of the Aboriginal Australians, they nevertheless had clear-cut notions of kinship and marriage, and these ideas were in turn linked to control of the land: "Each such band controlled a fixed area which usually extended from the mountains to sea and thus embraced a diversified food-supply." These groups bore collective responsibility for the activities of their individual members, and so "it is quite natural that kinship should be a matter of exact knowledge and that every relative should be designated by an exact term" (Lothrop 1928: 84). With the coming of European settlers, possession of the land became a central issue. As a missionary anthropologist was told in the 1920s, "This land belongs to us. The Europeans are thieves and murderers, they drove our people from this property and anyone who resisted was murdered by them!" (Gusinde 1971: 601). The Fuegians are gone now, another casualty of the colonial order.

With peoples like the Australians and the Fuegians as their baseline, social theorists constructed evolutionary sequences leading from what they considered the simplest societies upwards toward their own. Examples were chosen from around the world and across historical time to illustrate one or another phase of this imagined sequence—from small patriarchal band, to tribe, to tribal confederacy, to small-scale chiefdom, to centralized kingdom, to empires such as Rome and China, and eventually to the modern nation-state. A similar approach was applied to the structure of the family, economic life, and religious belief: human mating practices were supposed to have evolved from general promiscuity (which never actually existed) to Victorian bourgeois marriage; economic life evolved from collectivism and barter toward money-based exchange and contractual relationships; beliefs about the natural order evolved from magic through religion toward science—thus marking the decline of superstition and the advance of universal reason (Kuper 1988).

As Las Casas, Fitzroy, and Darwin realized, the Europeans were once "savages" themselves. In trying to get a grip on what brings about historical change, it was found that one question naturally leads to another, and that soon we end up attempting to comprehend the organization of society—any society—as a whole. This is the task that anthropology set for itself, a task that grew out of eighteenth- and nineteenth-century evolutionary speculation, increasingly enhanced by ethnography, linguistics, archaeology, and the historical record. Anthropology was becoming less speculative and more based on empirical field research. At this point a more concrete example of the evolutionary style of reasoning—and one of great significance in the development of anthropology—will be helpful.

Lewis Henry Morgan

Lewis Henry Morgan (1818–81) was one of the most original social theorists of his time (Trautmann 1987). Not only did he advance a comprehensive evolutionary scheme to explain the advance of civilization, but he is now seen as having initiated the anthropological study of kinship. Morgan was not an academic or a man of letters, but rather a lawyer in the upstate New York town of Rochester. The crucial influence that led to his research was his interest in the Iroquois Indians and his close friendship with a number of them—one of whom, Eli Parker (1828–95), rose to high

PLATE 3.5 Lewis Henry Morgan

rank in the Union Army as an aide to Ulysses S. Grant during the American Civil War. The Iroquois, of course, were already well known because of their pivotal role in the struggle between Great Britain and France for control of North America. But, by Morgan's time, their power had been broken and the population divided between the United States and Canada. Nevertheless, memory lived on, as did many social practices, which in sum led Morgan to reflect on the differences between Indian society and his own.

The first product of Morgan's labors was a very sympathetic historical and ethnographic study entitled *The League of the Ho-Dé-No-Sau-Nee, or Iroquois* (1851). As Morgan noted, "Among the Indian nations whose ancient seats were within the limits of our republic, the Iroquois have long continued to occupy the most conspicuous position. They achieved for themselves a more remarkable civil organization, and acquired a higher degree of influence, than any other race of Indian lineage, except those of Mexico and Peru" (1851: 3). In historical times the Iroquois had grown into the powerful Six Nations confederacy, and Morgan came to see this process as analogous to similar events in the early history of Israel, Greece, and Rome. He had read widely in history and political theory, and by 1851 he was already thinking of the Iroquois in terms of the classical Greeks and their republican city-states.

PLATE 3.6 Joseph Brant: Mohawk Leader

Morgan was also well aware of the great diversity of social organization and social complexity among native peoples themselves, and so he had what appeared to be an evolutionary sequence laid out before him—a sequence leading in specific stages from savagery to civilization, with the Iroquois somewhere in between. Morgan assumed that the Iroquois of recent times were as the Europeans once had been:

> Since mankind were one in origin, their career has been essentially one, running in different but uniform channels upon all continents, and very similarly in all the tribes and nations of mankind down the same status of advancement. It follows that the history and experience of the American Indian tribes represent, more or less nearly, the history and experience of our own remote ancestors when in corresponding conditions. Forming a part of the human record, their institutions, arts, inventions and practical experience possess a high and special value reaching far beyond the Indian race itself. (1877: vii)

The Iroquois were therefore taken to illustrate a particular stage in the development of the human spirit. We've seen such notions before. However, Morgan's scheme was based on what turned out to be a very fruitful and more complex idea: that the various aspects of a society at a given stage of its development *cohere* together as a package: "Each of these periods has a distinct culture and exhibits a mode of life more or less special and peculiar to itself. This ... renders it possible to treat a particular society according to its condition of relative advancement, and to make it a subject of independent study and discussion" (1877: 13).

In his 1851 book Morgan showed how Iroquois social institutions and economic practices are related to one another as parts of a whole. He came to see this problem in broadly theoretical terms and, in his classic work *Ancient Society* (1877), generalized these notions to the entire world by dividing human history up into what he called "ethnical periods." The major periods were Savagery, Barbarism, and Civilization, each having internal gradations (lower, middle, upper) characterized by *technological* innovations, particularly those related to food production. These terms seem quaint to us now, but Morgan had a precise idea of what they were supposed to mean and, as we've said, they were the common currency of his day.

He envisioned intellectual progress as a feedback loop, the brain and mind expanding "with the production of inventions and discoveries" (1877: 37). Where a people ended up on the social evolutionary scale depended on local circumstances, and so, given the wide variation in local conditions, every position on it save one was represented by "tribes still existing." The only exception was the "lower status of savagery," when "mankind were then living in their original restricted habitat, and subsisting upon fruits and nuts" (1877: 10)—Morgan's equivalent to the Garden of Eden. The "middle status of savagery" was represented by the Aboriginal Australians, who had fire but not much else, and so on up the scale.

The Iroquois were placed in the "lower status of barbarism," having acquired agriculture, the bow and arrow, and pottery. For our purposes the most important part of his theory was how he correlated a given stage of evolutionary progression with particular modes of kinship and political organization. When the Iroquois were still a free people, they depended on maize cultivation and hunting. Like many tribes of eastern North America they were matrilineal, meaning they traced inheritance through the mother's side of the family, lived in communal long-houses, followed complex religious practices, and had a council form of government—ruled by what were known among the Iroquois as *sachems*. These were hereditary office holders, but they could hold their titles only if judged by their peers to be fit for the job (Morgan 1851: 62–63). As Morgan saw it, the Iroquois had an essentially *republican* social order based upon relative equality of status, not unlike the United States itself. Tendencies to despotism were thwarted because power was distributed among the *sachems* and the tribes of the Confederacy. Descent and group membership followed the female line, and we will have more to say about this in Chapter 4.

Morgan thought that the place of a given society as more or less advanced along the evolutionary scale reflected increasing individualism and erosion of group identities, which in turn was correlated with the rise of individual property rights and patriarchal authority. Therefore the broad sweep of history demonstrates a transition from clan-based societies based on personal relationship to state structures "founded upon territory and upon property" (1877: 7). Tribal confederations such as the Iroquois represent a stage in this upward movement. Though Morgan was not a socialist, Karl Marx (1818–83) and Friedrich Engels (1820–85) thought highly of his "materialistic" evolutionary scheme and adopted it in their analysis of the social processes at work in pre-capitalist societies.

Conclusion

There is nothing unreasonable about Morgan's questions, though some of his speculative conclusions were certainly misguided. All societies are derived from their predecessors, and the ancestors of all societies now existing—no matter how complex—must have once been hunter-gatherers. The questions asked by the evolutionists are important ones, including the one that Darwin raised about evolutionary psychology. Archaeologists are often engaged in tracing the remains of bygone societies back to earlier forms, and the relationship between culture and social complexity remains an ongoing issue. But, most importantly, these earlier anthropologists were beginning to think in terms of social *systems*. The Victorian social evolutionists therefore set the stage for what anthropology would become in the twentieth century, and that is our next topic.

Study Questions

1 What changes in society did Charles Darwin believe were necessary for social progress? Give an example.

2 Compare and contrast the political beliefs of Hobbes and Rousseau and explain how the "myth of the savage" can be applied to both extreme understandings of human nature.

3 How does Cook apply Rousseau's concept of the "state of nature" when describing the Aboriginal peoples of Australia?

4 Explain how Locke's perspectives on private property informed Darwin's interpretation of the Fuegians' "savagery."

5 Summarize what Cook and Darwin failed to observe about the complex societies of Aboriginals in Australia and the people of Tierra del Fuego. Explain how the "myth of the savage" interfered with their understanding of these peoples.

6 Describe the Iroquois people from the perspective of Lewis Henry Morgan's ethnographic findings.

7 Explain Lewis Henry Morgan's approach to anthropology. What aspect of the social world was he most interested in? Why?

Discussion Questions

1 Discuss the concept of human nature. Given your understanding of human diversity thus far, do you think there is a basic and universal "human nature"? Or is much of what we take to be human nature actually the product of culture and circumstance? Use examples from what you've learned to illustrate your argument.

2 Human curiosity has always been the motive behind anthropology. As the world becomes more accessible through the Internet and affordable travel, we are aware as never before of the diversity that makes up humankind. How might anthropology help in understanding this new world? What future roles do you see for anthropology in the global community?

3 It's easy for us to analyze the failings of early anthropological theory: Cook and Darwin failed to see the complexity of the societies they observed; Mead believed the Samoan people to be primitive before she began her work. Social context always creates a bias for the observer. How do you think future anthropologists will contextualize the work of today? What biases do you think you might hold in the field?

CHAPTER 4

//

Kinship

LEARNING OBJECTIVES

After reading this chapter, students should be able to

- understand the concept of kinship and the role kinship systems play in anthropology;
- understand how in-vitro fertilization highlights Euro-American social and cultural beliefs about kinship;
- discuss the myth of the family in Western culture and understand its biblical origins;
- explain the role of marriage in society and the concepts of endogamy, polygyny, bridewealth, bride-service, and dowry;
- explain the meaning of descent and identify the differences between matrilineal and patrilineal systems; and
- understand the difference between genetic identity and social/cultural identity as it relates to kinship.

KEY TERMS

bride-service	endogamy	matrilineage
bridewealth	kinship	patrilineage
descent	kinship systems	polygyny
dowry	marriage	rite of passage

Introduction

The cross-cultural study of "**kinship**" and "**kinship systems**" has been a central anthropological topic at least since the time of Lewis Henry Morgan. Why is this so? The primary reason is because early anthropology chose to concentrate on "primitive" societies. Many of these lacked the social institutions—bureaucratic government, money-based economies, formal law, etc.—that western observers were accustomed to. It came to be perceived that, where such institutions are lacking, "kinship" serves as an integrating force, an all-purpose social glue: "blood kinship" provides the basis for the formation of cohesive groups, marriage establishes cross-generational connections between them, and bonds of affection and complex economic relationships hold it all together. These perceptions were coupled with the evolutionary assumption that "the family" must have been the earliest form of human association, from which all later forms are derived.

Anthropologists and social historians have documented the worldwide range of practices relating to kinship, marriage, and the family. As always, the first impulse was to collect and classify, and then to interpret what was found—as Morgan did— in evolutionary terms. We saw in Chapter 2 that this impulse gave way to detailed ethnographic studies of social systems in their own terms, how they function on the ground.[1] But, given all the diversity that was revealed, even *defining* "kinship" and "the family" proves a difficult order.

The anthropological study of kinship is a game that nearly everyone can play, since most of us have known kin. We invite you, therefore, to think about your own family and its history in light of the discussion to follow. In this chapter we will identify certain key questions that have emerged from these efforts, look back on the history of the subject, and examine how the study of kinship is unfolding in our own rapidly changing world.

We start with an example from our own time that explores the social implications of revolutionary developments in reproductive technology—the role of genetic, social, and cultural factors in shaping who we think we are. We then turn to the ancient world and the biblical saga of Abraham, Sarah, Hagar, Ishmael, and Isaac, which is a tale about preserving the continuity of a family under threat of extinction. This old story is historically important and contains elements that have been widely observed by anthropologists in the field. It has implications for Jewish and Arab identity and for the Palestinian/Israeli conflict that echo down to our own day.

These examples lead to some general remarks on social structure and the nature of kinship. Finally we bring all this together by describing an important case recently argued before the US Supreme Court concerning the adoption of a Native American child by Euro-American foster parents. Once more the issue is social identity and cultural integrity. As you will see, it's all very political.

What Is "The Family"?

The first baby created through in vitro fertilization (IVF) was born in 1978, accompanied by media hype about "test tube babies" and a good deal of public hand-wringing over doctors "playing God." This outcome was the result of the long and patient efforts of an English doctor, Robert Edwards (1925–2013), to find a way to fertilize a human egg outside of the body and then to implant it successfully in the uterus. In 2010 his efforts were rewarded with a Nobel Prize in Medicine. At the Nobel ceremony a colleague celebrated him for "transforming the intellectual landscape not just of gynaecology, but also of ethics and social anthropology."[2] The mention of "social anthropology" in this context is interesting. The speaker was referring to the fact that anthropologists can now be found working in IVF clinics and other medical locales, attempting to understand the implications of these new technologies at a local and personal level (Franklin and McKinnon 2001). Consider the following situation that Dr. Edwards's work made possible.

In 2013 a story entitled "What Makes a Jewish Mother" appeared in the *New York Times*. A Jewish couple decided rather late in life that they wished to have a child. The prospective mother, Caren Chesler, was 42 at the time, but she reported that, "three years later, I finally accepted that it wasn't going to happen naturally. We narrowed our options to two: use eggs donated by another woman, or adopt."[3] They opted for the former, which meant they would follow the IVF procedure, using eggs from an anonymous donor fertilized with the husband's sperm. "A year and a half later … I gave birth to our son, Eddie. Weighing 7 pounds, 7 ounces, he was the spit and image of my husband. Some said he had my eyes, but I knew that couldn't be true. He has none of my genetic material. It bothered me, but I told myself nature is only half the equation. I would contribute greatly on the nurture front. And of course our baby would be Jewish, given that I am. Under Jewish law, a baby's religious identity is determined by his mother. Or so I thought…."

Experts on Jewish family law were divided on the issue. The fact that the egg came from an unknown donor raised problems about whether Eddie was "really" Jewish or would have to go through a ritual conversion to Judaism. So here we have a complex debate, rooted in a deep religious tradition, about the relation between *social identity* and *genetic identity*. Which do we think is more important in determining who a person *really* is? This is a tricky problem that could not have arisen in this form before the emergence of modern genetics and the invention of IVF. How puzzling it can become is seen in the case of the older women who, with the help of IVF and hormone treatments, become surrogate mothers for their infertile daughters, thus becoming the birth mothers of their own grandchildren.

Such questions go beyond these particular cases. For example, conflicts have arisen over whether persons conceived through anonymous sperm donation have a natural *right* to know who their genetic "father" is. Likewise, some adoptees find it impossible to rest easy until they learn who their *real* parents are. Hidden within such debates are cultural assumptions concerning the nature of kinship.

In the 1960s, anthropologist David Schneider and his colleagues undertook an extensive ethnographic study of American ideas about relatedness. They found that kinship "by blood" was seen as being of paramount importance in defining relationship:

> In American cultural conception, kinship is defined as biogenetic. This definition says that kinship is whatever the biogenetic relationship is. If science discovers new facts about biogenetic relationship, then that is what kinship is and was all along, although it may not have been known at the time. Hence, the real, true, verifiable facts of nature are what the cultural formulation is. And the real, true, objective facts of science ... are that each parent provides one-half of his child's biogenetic constitution. The relationship which is "real" or "true" or "blood" or "by birth" can never severed, whatever its legal position. Legal rights may be lost but the blood relationship cannot be lost. It is culturally defined as being an objective fact of nature, of fundamental significance and capable of having profound effects, and its nature cannot be terminated or changed. (Schneider 1980: 23–24; see also Schneider 1984: 72)

Schneider already had experience of another society—the Yap Islanders in the western Pacific—with a very different take on what constitutes "kinship" (Schneider 1984). He had found that some key relationships, such as that between "father" and "child," were not defined by "blood," but by the services that people do for one another—an exchange relationship and not a blood relationship (1984: 72, 121). There are societies in which what we think of as "kinship" is defined by the sharing of food—by "common belonging" (Sahlins 2013: 6, 22). In these cases "kinship" is created in practice, not laid down in advance by some essential quality that people are thought to share.

Schneider knew that in many societies the two biological parents are held to have an unequal role in procreation, and to contribute quite *different* psychological and physical qualities to their offspring: for example, the man the bone and the woman the blood. There are cases in which the male is thought to have little or nothing to do with conception, and others in which the woman is seen as merely an incubator for the husband's seed. These notions reflect broader structural features and cultural assumptions of the societies concerned.

From his comparative perspective David Schneider was able to speak to fellow Americans about a usually taken-for-granted reality as though it were actually foreign and exotic. A more recent study of British attitudes about the social implications of IVF arrived at similar conclusions by similar means:

> The priority that Euro-Americans ... put on the bodily process of procreation is rather special to them. Indeed, a point of debate in anthropology is that

while everywhere social arrangements attend to the production and rearing of children, it is not the case that everywhere the facts of procreation are taken to be of prime significance. Where they are, then the circumstances of birth confer an identity on the child. For Euro-Americans there is no getting around the tie that exists with those persons whose genetic substances combined at the child's conception. This is taken as a fact of life. (Strathern 1992: 14)

We would add that the circumstances of conception also confer an identity on the early-stage embryo, even if it hasn't yet been implanted. This problem is evident in political attempts in the United States to get fetuses defined as "persons" in a legal sense, and hence abortion classified as murder. That question extends to what should be done with frozen embryos in IVF clinics that could—in principle—become full human beings. In other words, do embryos have "rights"? In an odd legal case early in the days of IVF it was debated whether an embryo stored in an Australian clinic whose American "parents" had been killed in a plane crash would have inheritance rights if it were brought to term through a surrogate mother.[4] As IVF has become more widely used, issues have also arisen over "orphan" embryos—surplus frozen embryos abandoned by their creators and left behind in the storage vaults of IVF clinics without instructions about what to do with them.

Questions such as these have no obvious answers, and their outcomes arise from complex interactions between culture, religion, politics, the legal system, and perceptions of what best serves the common good.

Returning to Caren Chesler's problem, the matrilineal inheritance of identity is surprising at first sight given the patriarchal values so evident in the Hebrew Bible, and the fact that the scriptures mention a number of Jewish men having children by non-Jewish women, children who went on to become important figures in ancient Israel. The reasons for this change are obscure but in the early days may have had something to do the consequences of intermarriage between Jewish women and non-Jewish men; in any event, this practice is not found in all branches of Judaism, but its implications were of concern to Ms. Chesler. Faced with this dilemma, she relied on her heart: "The other night, I was making dinner and my husband had taken our son for a walk. After about half an hour, I heard our screen door opening and the patter of toddler feet running toward the kitchen. 'Muh-MAH!' Eddie said as he ran into my arms. I should have just asked my son who his mother is. He's known all along."[5]

The Power of Myth

Our second example is also about social identity, but in a quite different context. The story of Abraham's family comes from the biblical book of Genesis; it has parallels with the findings of modern anthropological research on family structure, inheritance, and group formation.

For those unfamiliar with the Bible, the Genesis narrative is the first in a group of five texts that outline the formation of the Jewish people and the revealing of laws to govern them. Thinking back to his fieldwork in the Trobriand Islands, Bronislaw Malinowski observed that "myth … in its living form, is not merely a story told but a reality lived … believed to have once happened in primeval times, and continuing ever since to influence the world and human destinies. The story of origin literally contains the legal charter of the community" (1954: 100, 116). The Genesis narrative is a story of just this kind.

You are no doubt familiar with the story of Noah. One of Noah's sons was Shem, the ancestor of Abraham. God singled Abraham out for a special destiny and promised, "I will make of you a great nation, and I will bless you … and in you all the families of the earth shall be blessed" (Gen. 12: 2–3). However, Abraham's wife, Sarah, was barren—a terrible fate for both of them. But Sarah saw a way out: she had an Egyptian slave-girl named Hagar, and she told her husband, "you see that the Lord has prevented me from bearing children; go in to my slave-girl; it may be that I shall obtain children by her' … and gave her to her husband Abraham as a wife" (Gen. 16: 2–3).[6] This was a surrogacy relationship; Hagar was to bear Abraham's children in Sarah's name so that the family line could carry on.

Hagar conceived, but she held Sarah in low esteem because of her infertility. Sarah perceived this and abused Hagar, who fled into the wilderness where she encountered the Lord, who promised that she too would be the mother of a great nation: "Hagar bore Abraham a son; and Abraham named his son, whom Hagar bore, Ishmael" (Gen. 16: 15). In the passages that follow, the Lord makes a "covenant" with Abraham, a kind of legal contract in which all good things are promised to them if Abraham and his descendants follow the Lord faithfully. The sign of the covenant is to be male circumcision. The text does not explain why that particular mark was chosen (other references indicate an association with purity), but this ceremony remains a central feature of male Jewish identity and is also the majority practice among Muslims. It is a pivotal "**rite of passage**"—a sign of incorporation into the community and identification with it: "Any uncircumcised male who is not circumcised in the flesh of his foreskin shall be cut off from his people; he has broken my covenant" (Gen. 17: 14).

But Abraham still did not have a legitimate son of his own; the Lord promised him that Sarah—in spite of advancing age—would bear one, and that he should be called Isaac. Abraham asked that Ishmael not be forgotten, and the Lord replied, "I have heard you; I will bless him and make him fruitful and exceedingly numerous…. But my covenant I will establish with Isaac." There were further adventures, and Sarah eventually produced a son. But tension remained high between Hagar and Sarah, who demanded that her husband "cast out this slave woman with her son; for the son of this slave woman shall not inherit along with my son Isaac." Abraham was conflicted, but he was reassured by the Lord that the descendants of Ishmael would also prosper.

So Hagar and her son were sent off, and again they wandered in the wilderness (always a sign of transitional status) where they nearly died of thirst. Hagar prayed,

"Do not let me look on the death of the child," and a well of water was revealed to her. "God was with the boy, and he grew up; he lived in the wilderness, and became an expert with the bow. He lived in the wilderness of Paran; and his mother got a wife for him from the land of Egypt" (Gen. 21: 20–21).

We are told that when Abraham died, Ishmael and Isaac laid him to rest in "the cave of Machpelah" where Sarah was also interred. Ishmael's part in this story concludes with an account of what groups descended from him. The Hebrew writings then go silent about him save for the occasional mention of "Ishmaelites," desert peoples, presumably the ancestors of the migratory Bedouin Arab tribes. The main narrative shifts its attention to Isaac and his descendants, from whom the Jewish people are derived.

Arab tradition has quite a different emphasis. Ishmael and Hagar are here seen as instrumental in finding the holy spring that became the site of Mecca; Ishmael himself is regarded as an ancestor of the Prophet Muhammad. Whether Isaac or Ishmael was Abraham's favored son became and remains a matter of debate.

Continuing the Family Line

A number of themes run through this story, most obviously the stress on family continuity—a problem that comes up a number of times in the Hebrew writings. It has also been widely noted by anthropologists who have worked in lineage-based societies. Inheritance is a central factor. What happens when a family is in danger of dying out or the property is in danger of being lost to outsiders because there is no legitimate heir? The early Hebrews got around this by marrying *within* the family— "**endogamous**" marriages—preferably with a father's brother's child.[7]

This may seem rather close to incest, but it has the virtue of keeping property within the broader political and economic group—the **patrilineage** as a whole.[8] The Hebrew scriptures attribute this practice to a ruling of the prophet Moses: "Every daughter who possesses an inheritance in any tribe of the Israelites shall marry one from the clan of her father's tribe, so that all Israelites may continue to possess their ancestral inheritance" (Numbers 36: 8).

Similar practices remain widespread in many Middle Eastern, North African, and West Asian societies—among them the Iraqi Arabs with whom Robert and Cathy Fernea worked (see Chapter 1). Arranged parallel-cousin marriage is reported among British Pakistanis; the intent of such alliances is to sustain and strengthen ties between the branches of the family in Britain and Pakistan. The family of the Prophet Muhammad also exhibits such a pattern: his daughter, Fatima, married her paternal cousin, Ali—Muhammad's father's brother's son. The descendants of this marriage proved to be extraordinarily important in the history of Islam, and disagreements over their status are at the root of the current divisions in the Muslim world between the Sunni and Shi'a branches of the faith. Marriage between a daughter and a male cousin was also not uncommon in Victorian England when property issues were involved. Moreover, cousin marriage was virtually the norm among European royalty.

PLATE 4.1 Cave of the Patriarchs

When one sees how the characters in the Genesis story interacted, it is easy to identify with the real-world dilemmas that they faced. Our own soap operas explore similar
themes. But there's more to it than this superficial level. The story of the parentage and
separation of Isaac and Ishmael also accounts for the origin of major political, cultural,
and geographical groupings. It's an example of our earlier discussion of the processes
of family life being mapped onto an interpretation of history.

The family grows and divides along natural lines of tension. For example, co-wives
in a **polygynous** household—a household in which there is one husband and multiple
wives—may suspect one another of witchcraft. Half-brothers descended from the same
father but different mothers may be rivals for the father's inheritance, which leads to
quarreling and dispersal of the family. Such tales account for perceived similarities and
differences—and political distance—between the groups held to be descended from
the founding ancestor. It is impossible to judge their historical truth, and from our
point of view it doesn't matter. These "genealogical charters" serve to validate claims to
land, power, status, or anything else of social value. Such ancient narratives have been
used to back up rival claims in the modern Middle East.

Old stories can have a long afterlife. "The cave of Machpelah"—where Abraham,
Sarah, and other biblical figures were said to be buried—is now contained in the Cave
of the Patriarchs, which is in the city of Hebron in the West Bank, an area administered
by the Palestinian Authority. It has been fought over in various conflicts and is currently
maintained by the organization responsible for Muslim holy sites. The site is honored by
both Jews and Muslims, who nevertheless must use separate entrances. How we think
about kinship has an impact on how we understand history itself and our place in it.

The Nature of Kinship Systems

Social practices like those described above direct our attention toward the "structural" factors involved in the study of kinship. What do we mean by "structure"? Generally the term refers to a larger whole made up of interdependent parts; it could be the "structure" of a language, a body, a building, an economy, or a society. Much anthropological effort has been devoted to unpacking the structure of kinship systems. But all one sees in the field is what people do, or say they do, along with the physical contexts in which they do it. We need to keep in mind that "structures" and "systems" are abstract concepts used to organize and interpret the complex information produced in the course of ethnographic fieldwork.

British social anthropologist A.R. Radcliffe-Brown (see Chapter 2) had a considerable role in the development of kinship studies (see Fortes 1969).

PLATE 4.2 A.R. Radcliffe-Brown

He worked up from the smallest and most local parts of a system toward a consideration of the greater whole, a "tribe," perhaps, or some other higher-level social formation: "… a complex unity, an organized whole" (Radcliffe-Brown 1952: 53). As we've seen, this way of thinking led to a large ethnographic literature, much of it on Africa, which attempted to show how the parts of such systems work in an integrated fashion and result in a more or less orderly society. Audrey Richards's writings on the Bemba (see also Chapter 2) are an example. Radcliffe-Brown put it this way in his introduction to an influential collection of essays entitled *African Systems of Kinship and Marriage* (1950):

> A system of kinship and marriage can be looked at as an arrangement which enables persons to live together and co-operate with one another in an orderly social life. For any particular system as it exists at a certain time we can make a study of how it works. To do this we have to consider how it links persons together by convergence of interest and sentiment and how it controls and limits those conflicts that are always possible as the result of divergence of sentiment or interest. In reference to any feature of a system we can ask how it contributes to the working of the system. This is what is meant by speaking of its social function. (3)

In these African societies and many others, ties of kinship and marriage served to form and bind together politically significant groups. Kinship, economics, and politics were entangled with one another, which made it possible to think about these relationships in functional terms.[9] For example, if conflict were to arise between descent groups, ties of marriage between them might serve to damp it down, thus contributing to overall social stability. This approach would not be directly relevant in Euro-North American society, where kin groups such as lineages and clans do not generally function in a political capacity. For the most part we live in much more "individualized" societies.

Kinship and the Gift

Ties of kinship are also ties of moral and economic obligation. There are many formal and informal ways of establishing such bonds: adoption, surrogacy, common-law relationships, and—of course—marriage.

Marriage is a classic rite of passage, often involving complex ceremonies and intricate economic transactions. In North America, marriage is now largely a matter of personal choice theoretically based on "love." It's not as popular as it once was; currently in the US and Canada only about 50 per cent of adults are married, and less traditional arrangements are on the rise. In other societies marriage remains a profoundly social act—an affair between groups, not individuals. The ties established between groups by marriage are both political and economic and can span generations. Gift giving of one kind or another is a common feature of these relationships. It is an aspect of what the French ethnologist Marcel Mauss (1872–1950), in his well-known essay *The Gift*, called a "total social phenomenon"—in which "all kinds of institutions are given expression at one and the same time—religious, juridical, and moral, which relate to both politics and the family ... production and consumption" (Mauss 1990: 3).

Exchanges involving **bridewealth**, **bride-service**, or **dowry** are frequently found in these contexts. In the case of bridewealth, valuable property is transferred from the family of the man to that of his prospective bride. The Nuer people of South Sudan were put on the anthropological map by the work of another British social anthropologist, E.E. Evans-Pritchard (1902–73).[10] They are a patrilineal society economically based on cattle herding, similar to ancient Israel in some respects. Marriage establishes bonds between lineages that are defined by the transfer of bridewealth in the form of cattle and with definite but negotiable rules about who should get what. Marriage ceremonies are "important public events in Nuer life. A whole district attends them, the mere coming together of so many people making marriage a memorable event. Neighbours thus bear witness to the creation of new social ties and by their presence sanction them" (Evans-Pritchard 1951: 59). Dances are held, speeches are made, and a lot of beer is drunk. You may well have attended large and expensive formal weddings of just this sort!

But what happens if a man dies childless? One option is "ghost marriage." A relative of the dead man may act in his place, and marry a wife to the dead man's name, with bridewealth being transferred in the usual way. The relative takes on the normal role of husband but "the legal husband is the ghost in whose name the bridewealth was paid and the ritual of matrimony was performed." It is the ghost's name that will be remembered in the family genealogy, not that of the biological father. "The woman is ... the wife of a ghost, and her children are ... children of a ghost" (1951: 110). Genealogies are thus not always what they seem.

The principle of bride-service is simple enough: a man works for his in-laws in return for their daughter. We've mentioned the case of the Bemba, but there is another striking example of this practice in the Hebrew writings. The story of Jacob, son of Isaac, continues the narrative we've outlined above.

Isaac wishes to maintain the integrity of the family line through cousin-marriage, and instructs Jacob to journey to the home of his mother's brother, Laban. He encounters Laban's daughter, Rachel, and is much charmed by her. Laban agrees to a marriage if Jacob agrees to work for him for seven years. This he does, and a marriage takes place. However, after it's consummated it turns out that his father-in-law has played a trick on him and in the dark substituted Rachel's older sister, Leah. Laban explains that he did this because in his country the senior sister should marry first. But he promises that, if Jacob works for him another seven years, he can have Rachel as well. Jacob finally ends up married to two sisters who are also his maternal cousins, and who, along with Jacob, become the ancestors of the tribes of Israel. These tribes are unified into one nation because of their common father, but are divided from each other because of descent from different mothers. As myth often does, this kind of story explains large-scale structural arrangements through the recounting of an intimate family drama.

Dowry refers to property that accompanies a woman into the marriage relationship—a kind of pre-inheritance that in an ideal world would be passed on to her offspring (Goody & Tambiah 1973). How much property is involved depends on the status and importance of the marriage. Getting together a considerable dowry is one way for the bride's family to move up in the world, and a good deal of public display may be involved in bringing it off. Such practices are well known in India, and to some extent among migrant Indian communities elsewhere. Indeed, families with high-value professional-class sons may hold out for a considerable dowry before they will agree to a marriage:

> In India, almost all marriages are arranged. Even among the educated middle classes in modern, urban India, marriage is as much a concern of the families as it is of the individuals. So customary is the practice of arranged marriage that there is a special name for a marriage which is not arranged: It is called a "love match." Dowry, which although illegal, has become a more pressing issue in the consumer conscious society of contemporary urban India. In many cases, where a groom's family is not satisfied with the amount of dowry a bride brings to her marriage, the young bride will be constantly harassed to get her parents to give more. (Nanda 2000: 196; 203–4)

But that's not the only side of the story. At the beginning of her fieldwork in India, American anthropologist Serena Nanda at first found herself baffled by the readiness of many middle-class Indians to accept a marital choice negotiated by their families. However,

> … during months of meeting many young Indian people, both male and female … I saw arranged marriages in a different light. I also saw the importance of the family in Indian life and realized that a couple who took their marriage into their own hands was taking a big risk, particularly if their families were irreconcilably opposed to the match. In a country where every important resource in life—a job, a house, a social circle—is gained through family connections, it seems foolhardy to cut oneself off from a supportive social network and depend solely on one person for happiness and success. (Nanda 2000: 198)

India, of course, is large and diverse, as are Africa and North America. There are great differences of class, religion, and ethnicity in all three. There is no single pattern of marriage and family life that applies universally to any of them. Social institutions such as these depend on history, cultural context, and economics, and simple formulations are always going to be misleading if applied too loosely.

Descent

In the course of his extensive research among Native American peoples, Lewis Henry Morgan had found that

> the American Indians always speak to each other, when related, by the term of relationship, and never by the personal name of the individual addressed. In familiar intercourse, and in formal salutation, they invariably address each other by the exact relationship of consanguinity [kinship by blood] or affinity [kinship through marriage] in which they stand related. I have put the question direct to native Indians of more than fifty different nations, in most cases at their villages or encampments, and the affirmance of this usage has been the same in every instance. Over and over again it has been confirmed by personal observation. (1871: 132)

Clearly these relationship terms were of great social importance, and Morgan aimed at working out the details of the systems in use by the various North American tribes. His approach was influenced by his early experience with the Iroquois, where he found that their way of classifying relationships was quite different from that of Euro-Americans and was an aspect of their **matrilineal** social order: "Not the least remarkable among their institutions, was that which confined the transmission of all titles, rights and property in the female line to the exclusion of the male. It is strangely unlike the canons of descent adopted by civilized nations ..." (1851: 84).

Early-seventeenth-century European explorers and settlers in North America soon became aware of this unfamiliar way of reckoning kinship among the eastern tribes. The Virginia Colony was the first permanent English settlement in the New World, and Captain John Smith (of Pocahontas fame; see Chapter 8 for more on this episode) took careful note of the native inhabitants and geography in the vicinity of the Jamestown settlement. He found that these people had a paramount chief named Powhatan, and a number of dependent sub-chiefs in surrounding villages. Smith described their dwellings, their religious practices, and their mode of **descent**. Powhatan's "kingdoms descend not to his sonnes nor children, but first to his brethren, whereof he hath 3... and after their decease to his sisters. First to the eldest sister, and to the rest, and after them to the heires male or female of the eldest sister, but never to the heires of the males" (1624: 38).

Matrilineal descent was the norm over a vast area: from Lake Huron in the north, to Florida in the south, and west to the Mississippi. He may have exaggerated a bit, but a Catholic missionary writing in New France in 1724 noted the extraordinarily high status of women among the Iroquois:

> It is they who really maintain the tribe, the nobility of blood, the genealogical tree, the order of generations and conservation of the families. In them resides

all the real authority: the lands, fields and all their harvest belong to them.... They arrange the marriages; the children are under their authority; and the order of succession is founded on their blood. The men, on the contrary, are entirely isolated and limited to themselves. Their children are strangers to them. Everything perishes with them. A woman alone gives continuity to the household. (Lafitau 1974: 69)

The discovery of such practices came as a great surprise. Everything then known to the Europeans suggested that a patriarchal form of inheritance and family life was the natural human condition. And yet the Iroquois, Huron, and kindred peoples in eastern North America were divided up into matrilineal totemic clans—going under names such as Wolf, Bear, Turtle, and Heron. Office-holders inherited their titles, not from their fathers, but from their mother's brothers, or equivalent relatives on the maternal side. Iroquois clans, and those of numerous other peoples, were divided up into two opposed hereditary groups; members of one grouping of clans (Bear, Wolf, Beaver, Turtle) intermarried with the members of the other group (Deer, Snipe, Heron, Hawk), but they could not marry within their own (Morgan 1877: 90).[11] There were other complementary relationships of this sort between the two halves of the tribe, expressed in ritual and accounted for by myth.

Morgan and others came to believe that matrilineality was the *earliest* form of human kinship organization; this became the collective wisdom of their day concerning the evolution of the family. The reason they thought so is simple: you generally know who your biological mother is, but paternity is more uncertain. Morgan also came to realize that Native American kinship systems differ considerably from one another. He wondered if the distribution of such systems could be used to chart the global history of ethnic migration. Following this logic, similar systems should imply a common historical origin. The result of those labors was an innovative book with an impressive title: *Systems of Consanguinity and Affinity of the Human Family* (1871). It is based on his own research and information provided by foreign correspondents.

The method was straightforward. Morgan asked his informants about terms in the local languages that correspond to English kin-terms such as "mother," "father," "cousin," "aunt," "uncle," "grandfather," "grandmother," and so on. It was found, for example, that Iroquois terminology distinguishes the mother's from the father's side of the family in a way that English does not. In English the siblings of one's mother and father are "aunts" and "uncles" regardless of which side of the family they are on; likewise all their children are lumped together as "cousins," *whatever their sex*. On the other hand, the Iroquois terms equate mother with mother's sisters, and father with father's brothers; their children are referred to by the same terms as one's own siblings. Thus a mother's sister's daughter is referred to by the same term as one's own sister. Mother's brothers and father's sisters are referred to by different terms than mother's sisters and father's brothers. What we call "cousins" are *distinguished by sex*.

These linguistic practices reflect a generalized principle whereby all the members of one's own matrilineal clan and of one's own generation could be spoken of using the same terms as those used for "brothers" and "sisters"—in other words, it expresses a collective identity reckoned through women. A diagram will make this clearer:

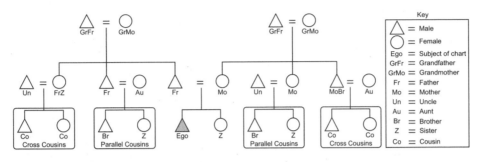

FIGURE 4.1 Iroquois Kinship Diagram

Given facts of this kind, Morgan made a speculative leap and concluded that if entire groups referred to one another as brothers and sisters, this reflected a bygone practice of group-marriage. The idea was that, if one calls entire collections of people by the same terms as one's own biological siblings, then this is a linguistic relic of a time in which groups of siblings in the parental generation married (and could have sex with) one another collectively. Morgan's mistake was simple: he projected western ideas about *biological* kinship onto the quite different systems of kin classification that his comparative research was turning up.

In time, in fact, some of Morgan's other theories came to be seen as misguided. He had indeed determined that many societies classify relatives as "marriageable" or "unmarriageable." But marriageability certainly doesn't correlate to group sex, and never did. Terms like these reflect group identities of individuals as members of clans and lineages—in other words, they reflect local social structure. As the earlier preoccupation with social evolution faded away, anthropologists became more concerned with analyzing such systems on the ground, and produced a large literature in doing so. Kinship systems were classified into types, and much effort went into investigating relationships between the elements in such systems. Works such as Radcliffe-Brown's *African Systems of Kinship and Marriage* are an expression of this endeavor.

For example, the question of how mode of descent affects relations between the genders and between generations has been long been an anthropological theme—a classical application of the comparative method. If a male child doesn't inherit anything worthwhile from his father, and instead inherits from his mother's brother, how does this affect the authority patterns and emotional tone of family life? How do these factors affect who lives with whom and relationships between family groups? What are relations like between same- and opposite-sex siblings? How does marriage work in societies of different types? Do women fare better in matrilineal societies?[12]

Specialized anthropological works on kinship go into more detail about this kind of thing, and as you see it's a vast topic. But we'll now move on to explore in a little more detail the relationship between kinship and politically charged issues concerning social identity.

Defining Kin: Legal Implications

The case with which we began this chapter pertained to who is regarded as "really" Jewish. As Caren Chesler found out, there may be no clear-cut answer to a question like that. We'd broaden the question to ask: Who is really *anything*? What determines how people get categorized, including the slots we place *ourselves* in—say on a census form that asks for our race or ethnicity? Of course the application of kinship terminology is one way of doing this; after all, it's a scheme of social classification. But anthropological research has shown that how such schemes work in practice can be a slippery business—in other words, it may depend on social context and relate to pragmatic interests such as claims to resources. "Kinship" imposes moral and practical burdens on us, which sometimes can weigh very heavily and which we'd rather avoid if possible. Some relatives get remembered, but many more are eventually forgotten or ignored. Genealogical memory is highly selective.

During the Nazi period in Germany, the answer to the question "Who is a Jew?" could have fatal consequences. This problem was particularly evident in cases of mixed marriages—in which the social identity of the offspring was at issue. Just how "Jewish" did one have to be before racially discriminatory legislation kicked in? Relative proportions of Jewish "blood" also determined who could and couldn't marry. Legal criteria for deciding these things were laid out in the 1935 "Law for the Protection of German Blood and German Honor," which "was designed to separate Jews from non-Jews in the sphere of reproductive and familial relations" (Proctor 1988: 132). These measures were based on the belief that Jews are a "race" with unchangeable and inferior moral characteristics relative to those of Aryan Germans.

The other side of this story is the question of who has an automatic right to citizenship in the State of Israel. When Israel was created in 1948, its founders wanted to make it a refuge and secure home for Jews everywhere, and to do that the question of "Who is a Jew?" was answered in very broad terms by the 1950 "Law of Return." The criteria were social and historical, not racial, and only religious in a secondary way: "For the purposes of this Law, 'Jew' means a person who was born of a Jewish mother or has become converted to Judaism and who is not a member of another religion."[13] By this definition, one could be an atheist and not engage in Jewish ritual life at all, and still be certifiably Jewish. However, the application of the Law has led to a lot of problems in particular cases. Specific answers to the identity question can have serious practical implications.

The same is true elsewhere, such as deciding just *who* is an American Indian, a native Hawaiian, an Aboriginal Australian, or a member of a Canadian First Nation. As in the Israeli case, the answer determines who has legal rights to a particular political identity and access to significant resources. Canada, the United States, and Australia have parallel histories with regard to the treatment of native peoples. Similar moral, political, and economic issues have arisen as a result. All three went to considerable lengths to induce or compel indigenous peoples to become "civilized" and assimilate to the European-derived mainstreams. Pressures of this sort existed in any event, in that native peoples ended up as relatively small and powerless minorities in what had once been their own countries.[14]

Governments, churches, and private agencies all bent themselves to the task of converting the local "savages" to "civilization." Their methods focused on religion, language, economics, education, and family life. Since civilization was associated with private property, tribal peoples had to be decoupled from the communal economies that had historically sustained them (see Chapter 2). More radical approaches involved segregating them from their families and their languages altogether. In Canada this led to the rise of the residential school system, run by the churches and still the focus of grievance on the part of First Nations, who call what the state was trying to do to them "cultural genocide" (see Miller 1996).

In the United States the most radical social experiment was the removal of many Native American groups from their original homes and their forced resettlement in Indian Territory, which eventually became the state of Oklahoma. The intent was to settle the Indians down, teach them how to farm, and give them agricultural land in the form of private allotments. This was supposed to teach personal responsibility and how to function as responsible progressive citizens. Schooling was also part of the mix. Over time, significant numbers of Indian children were taken from their families as well, and adopted by white foster parents. The picture in Australia was much the same, and those treated in this manner are now known as "The Stolen Generation." In 2008 the Government of Australia apologized to Aboriginal peoples for the treatment they had received. But our topic is kinship, and a recent case argued before the Supreme Court of the United States brings together a number of the themes in this chapter.

Baby Veronica

It is known as the "Baby Veronica" case, the name of a child caught up in a complex custody dispute in South Carolina. It "has stirred powerful emotional responses from child welfare groups, adoptive parents and Indian tribes."[15] The basic facts are as follows.

Veronica's biological mother and father were residents of Oklahoma. They had not married, though they had intended to. However, the relationship ended before this happened, and the mother (who is of Hispanic descent) decided to put her child up for adoption through a private agency. A couple in South Carolina was chosen as adoptive parents. The biological father, who was a Native American, had relinquished his parental rights, but he later claimed that he was unaware that the child was going to be put up for adoption rather than being raised by her birth mother. He then sued in South Carolina for possession of the child, citing the 1978 Federal Indian Child Welfare Act, which states that "it is the policy of this Nation to protect the best interests of Indian children and to promote the stability and security of Indian tribes and families by the establishment of minimum Federal standards for the removal of Indian children from their families and the placement of such children in foster or adoptive homes which will reflect the unique values of Indian culture."[16]

The Supreme Court of South Carolina decided that, even though the father had never had possession of the child, the Federal act applies here, since he is in fact a registered member of the Cherokee Nation and desired to raise the child himself.[17] He also took and passed a genetic paternity test. Baby Veronica was therefore given over to him and they went back to Oklahoma. But the decision was highly controversial and on appeal made its way up to the US Supreme Court, which reversed the South Carolina decision and ordered the return of the child to her adoptive parents. The preamble to the US Supreme Court decision summarized the view of the majority of Justices: "This case is about a little girl [Veronica] who is classified as an Indian because she is 1.2% (3/256) Cherokee. Because [she] is classified in this way, the South Carolina Supreme Court held that certain provisions of the federal Indian Child Welfare Act of 1978 required her to be taken, at the age of 27 months, from the only parents she had ever known [who are non-Indian] and handed over to her biological father, who had attempted to relinquish his parental rights and who had no prior contact with the child."[18]

As always in anthropology, we have to consider the overall context that frames events such as these. There are three key elements involved in this one: the relation of this case to the Indian Child Welfare Act, the status of the biological father and his child as members of the Cherokee Nation, and the troubled history of Indian/White relations that we mentioned in the previous section.

The Cherokee are by origin a matrilineal southeastern people, first encountered by the Europeans in what are now North Carolina, Georgia, Alabama, and Tennessee. They were organized under a government of their own during the British colonial period and the early years of the American Republic. Encroachment on their territory by white settlers led to political pressures for their removal from the region, and in 1838–39 they were "induced" to relocate to Indian Territory. Some 16,000 of them made the trek, along what is remembered as "The Trail of Tears": "It was not a friendly removal. It was ugly and unwarranted. For too many Cherokees, it was deadly.... It also meant the continued loss of tribal knowledge and traditions. It is important that we never forget what happened to our people on the Trail of Tears. It was indeed our holocaust" (Perdue & Green 2005: 184, 185; see also Perdue & Green 2007).

Relations between the Cherokee and the colonial powers were defined by treaty. The United States regarded the Cherokee as a separate though dependent nation

PLATE 4.3 Trail of Tears

until 1907, when Indian Territory became Oklahoma. The Cherokee tribal government was then dissolved and tribal lands allotted to Cherokee individuals as their personal property. These holdings were recorded name by name on a document known as the Dawes Roll. However, in 1976 the Supreme Court decided that the status of the Cherokee as a sovereign nation had *not* in fact been terminated at the time of the allotment. The tribal government was reconstituted, and Veronica's father is currently a member in good standing of the Cherokee Nation, which, like Israel, defines eligibility broadly: "To be eligible for Cherokee Nation citizenship, individuals must provide documents connecting them to an enrolled direct ancestor who is listed on the Dawes Roll with a blood degree. Tribal Citizenship is traced through natural parents."[19]

The proportion of Cherokee "blood" doesn't matter, as long as there is a proven connection to a lineal male or female relative on the Dawes Roll (a great-grandfather or grandmother, say). Given this liberal definition, the original 16,000 Cherokee settlers in Indian Territory have grown into about 320,000 Cherokees today—the largest Indian tribe in the United States. In the US, the criteria for tribal membership are established by the tribes themselves, although not all are as liberal as the Cherokee. The same is true for First Nations bands in Canada, and for Aboriginal Australians as well.[20] If economic issues are involved—such as income from tribal enterprises—the more citizens or band members there are, the less there is to go around, and so a more restrictive definition may seem the best course. Deciding who's in and who's out can get very political.

Note that the US Supreme Court decision emphasizes how *little* Indian ancestry Baby Veronica has (3/256th). It was also pointed out that neither biological parent had ever lived on a reservation. The implication is that—in the majority view—she and her father have minimal Indian cultural heritage and therefore that the Cherokee Nation has little to lose through her adoption. The Court did not dispute that Veronica and her father are tribal members; but the majority of justices concluded that the welfare of the child and the unusual circumstances of the case outweighed the rights of the biological father and fall outside the limits of what the Indian Child Welfare Act had intended.

It was a split decision (5 to 4). A dissenting Justice cited previous Supreme Court cases in support of the rights of Veronica's biological father: "A natural parent's desire for and right to the companionship, care, custody, and management of his or her children is an interest far more precious than any property right." The dissenter also cited the Indian Child Welfare Act: "there is no resource that is more vital to the continued existence and integrity of Indian tribes than their children."

This affair has already come before the Cherokee Tribal Court, which *also* claims jurisdiction in such matters. Temporary custody was granted to the paternal grandparents and the father's present wife; Veronica went to live with them on tribal land. The adoptive parents tried to regain the child, and South Carolina was helping them do it. She was returned to her adoptive parents in September, 2013. As one observer put it, "from a legal point of view, this case is just a mess."[21] Perhaps, but it's an interesting mess!

Conclusion

It should be apparent by now that there's nothing self-evident about concepts such as kinship, marriage, family, and blood relationship. These are all cultural constructs that have to be understood in their own terms and in relation to local circumstances. There is always the danger of projecting one's own sense of what is natural and proper onto the ways of others.

Consider the factors highlighted by the Baby Veronica case and our other examples above:

- Kinship is not a fact of nature, but a matter of social convention, and there are many ways of defining it.
- Kinship systems are flexible schemes of social classification intimately related to the structure and history of the wider society.
- Our case studies reveal complex tensions between *social* and *genetic identity*.
- They suggest the various ways in which community boundaries are created and maintained, and the challenges that can arise in ambiguous situations.
- Each case also involves controversies over "rights": to inheritance, to children, to group membership, to life itself.
- And each shows how political the whole business can be. What are the local ideas about the nature of conception, gestation, and childbirth? What are the respective roles of male and female seen to be?
- The nature of marriage and other types of union is also brought into question. How are male and female brought together for the purpose of legitimate procreation? What kinds of relationships arise between their respective families? Are exchange and gift-giving involved (bridewealth, dowry, bride-service, etc.)? What ceremonies mark such events?
- A lot of anthropological ink has been spilled on the "incest taboo." What principles govern who can marry or have sex with whom? What kinds of persons are included, and what kind excluded from this sort of relationship?
- Children are also an important consideration. What wider groups do children belong to by virtue of who their parents are? What "rights" do they have (to nourishment, to love, to inheritance, etc.)? What obligations do they have in return?
- And finally, the very nature of "kin" and "family" are subject to debate. Who counts as kin, and what kind of kin? What broader structural arrangements are these families a part of, how is the family defined, and what ritual practices sustain a sense of collective identity?

All of these questions can be asked of the world right around us. As mentioned in the introduction to this chapter, we invite you to think about your own circumstances in light of this discussion.

Notes

1   See Fox (1967) for a useful overview.
2   See http://www.nobelprize.org/nobel_prizes/medicine/laureates/2010/edwards_lecture.pdf.

3   See http://well.blogs.nytimes.com/2013/06/03/what-makes-a-jewish-mother/.

4   See http://www.nytimes.com/1984/06/21/us/new-issue-in-embryo-case-raised
    -over-use-of-donor.html. At the time there were only about 500 people worldwide
    who had been conceived through IVF; now there are an estimated five million.

5   See n.3, above.

6   Biblical quotations are from the *New Oxford Annotated Bible*, 3rd ed. (New
    York: Oxford University Press, 1991).

7   The technical term for this arrangement is "patrilateral parallel cousin mar-
    riage." Parallel cousins are the children of parents' siblings of the same sex as
    the parent: i.e., mother's sister's children and father's brother's children. "Cross
    cousins" are children of parents' siblings of the opposite sex: mother's brothers
    and father's sisters.

8   There are indications in the text that Sarah was in fact Abraham's half-sister.
    First-cousin marriage is banned or restricted in a number of US states, but not
    in Canada or Europe.

9   Radcliffe-Brown also had an influence on the development of North American
    anthropology through his teaching at the University of Chicago. See Eggan
    (1955).

10 See Evans-Pritchard (1940). You will meet him again in Chapter 5 via his re-
    search on witchcraft. As for the Nuer, they are currently caught up in a complex
    ethnic and political dispute in the newly formed Republic of South Sudan.

11 We prefer to avoid professional jargon, but should mention that the Iroquois
    clans practiced what is termed exogamy. In other words marriage had to take
    place *outside* of one's own group; the opposite would be endogamy, in which
    there is a requirement or at least a preference to marry *within*. The division of
    the clans into *two* complementary sections is known as a moiety system and has
    been found in various parts of the world.

12 For a comparative study of matrilineal kinship systems in relation to other
    types, see Schneider & Gough (1962). See also Richards (1950).

13 See http://www.mfa.gov.il/mfa/mfa-archive/1950-1959/pages/law%20of%20
    return%205710-1950.aspx.

14 The question of "ownership" is a big one, and we will examine it in Chapter 6.

15 See http://www.nytimes.com/2013/06/26/us/justices-order-return-of-indian-child
    -to-adoptive-parents.html.

16 See http://www.nicwa.org/Indian_Child_Welfare_Act/ICWA.pdf.

17 In the United States, Indian affairs are exclusively a federal matter.

18 For the decision, see http://www.supremecourt.gov/opinions/12pdf/12-399
    _q86b.pdf.

19 See http://www.cherokee.org/Services/TribalCitizenship.aspx. There are also
    criteria for cases of adoption within the Tribe.

20 "An Aboriginal or Torres Strait Islander is a person of Aboriginal or Torres Strait
    Islander descent who identifies as an Aboriginal or Torres Strait Islander and is

accepted as such by the community in which he [or she] lives" (http://www.alrc .gov.au/publications/36-kinship-and-identity/legal-definitions-aboriginality). In Canada, unlike the United States, the term "First Nations" has replaced "Indians" in commonly accepted usage. First Nations are distinguished from Inuit and Métis; the former were previously known as "Eskimos," and the latter are the descendants of early relationships between European men and indigenous women. Each of the three groups has a special status under Canadian law.

21 See http://www.tulsaworld.com/archives/biological-father-of-baby-veronica-files-appeal-with-oklahoma-supreme/article_389a51b1-567a-56c8-ae89-d2585ef82342.html.

Study Questions

1 Using the example of Caren Chesler and her family, explain the tension between social identity and genetic identity.

2 Summarize the concepts of family structure, endogamy, inheritance, and group formation using the biblical stories of Sarah and Hagar and Rachel and Leah as examples.

3 Describe Radcliffe-Brown's approach to studying kinship and outline his contribution to anthropology.

4 Explain the concept of marriage and its role within kinship systems from the perspective of "the gift" and descent.

5 Outline the matrilineal form of descent amongst the tribes of North America. Explain how Europeans interpreted these kinship systems and why Morgan's Western ideas about biological kinship were inappropriate in this context.

6 Using the example of Baby Veronica, compare and contrast the genetic and social understandings of kinship and explain how cultural beliefs impact whom one identifies as kin.

Discussion Questions

1 Why was kinship deemed such an important area of study by early anthropologists? Do you think kinship remains an important area of study?

2 Consider the paired terms matrilineal vs. patrilineal and matriarchy vs. patriarchy. What is the difference between *matrilineal* and *matriarchal*? Discuss why matrilineal societies can still be considered patriarchal.

3 Given what you've learned about kinship systems, discuss why marriage is becoming less common in the Western world.

4 Think about your family in terms of kinship. How does your "family" define who counts as "kin" and what kind of kin? What ritual practices sustain a sense of collective identity?

CHAPTER 5

//

Symbol, Myth, and Meaning

LEARNING OBJECTIVES

After reading this chapter, students should be able to

- discuss the concept of culture as a system of meaning and understand why the definition of culture is so disputed;
- define the term *habitus* and explain the relationship between culture and bodily techniques as discussed by Mauss;
- summarize the work of Benedict and her perception of culture and cultural patterns;
- discuss how the understanding of culture is related to an understanding of language;
- outline the study of witchcraft by Evans-Pritchard and how his work illustrates the concept of paradigm;
- discuss Durkheim's work and his use of the term *mana*; and
- summarize Luhrmann's ethnographic work on the American evangelical community.

KEY TERMS

culture	*habitus*	paradigm
epistemology	*mana*	sociocentric theory
ethnology		

Introduction

Culture Is Human Nature

Try to imagine what it would be like for a child to grow up without other human beings around. Would such a child really be very human at all? Accounts of "wild children"—even of children raised by wolves—have turned up from time to time, though the facts are usually in dispute. For example, one such child—who came to be known as "The Wild Boy of Aveyron"—was discovered in southern France in the early years of the nineteenth century. Until his capture, he had been wandering around the forest, occasionally stealing food from farmers. The doctor who was granted legal custody of this boy was particularly interested in his ability to acquire language, which turned out to be very limited (the renowned French director François Truffaut made a film in 1970 called *L'enfant sauvage—The Wild Child* about the episode).

This case and a handful of others that have emerged over the last century were of great interest to the general public because they seemed to cast light on what human nature might be like "in the raw." As mentioned in Chapter 1, so much of our cultural knowledge passes as ordinary common sense that we usually don't think much about it. Only when we are faced with different ways of doing things do we become conscious of the rules of the game, particularly the ones we don't understand properly. Learning another language is a good example. Some of you probably know very well, or your parents know, what it's like when you move from a place where a different language is spoken into the world of English-speaking Canada or the US. A language is a form of life. And it's not only the language: our interactions with people of different cultures may also be based on quite different assumptions about how to act and what kind of person to be.

As the French anthropologist Claude Lévi-Strauss (1908–2009) put it, society is the natural human condition (1969). We need society to become fully human. It is a biological necessity: our nervous system will not develop properly without social stimulation. But we are also cultural beings, living in a world full of meaning. Just how much of what we are is cultural in nature can be seen if we use the well-known definition of **culture** formulated by the nineteenth-century British anthropologist Edward Burnett Tylor (1832–1917): "Culture or civilization, in its wide ethnographic sense, is that complex whole which includes knowledge, belief, art, morals, law, custom, and any other capabilities and habits acquired by man as a member of society" (Tylor 1903: 1).

If culture is a system of meaning, then on some level there *must* be rules and conventions or else social life would be chaotic. Of course, sometimes it does seem chaotic, and we shouldn't conceive of cultural rules as rigid—cultures are not clearly defined objects with perfectly clear outlines. Cultures are sets of practices and attitudes that are very complex, particularly in this day of mass media and migration, and the notion that specific cultures are associated with specific geographical locations is no longer entirely relevant.

Reconsidering the Culture Concept

Despite the centrality of the concept of culture to anthropology there continues to be much debate over developing a definition. The word has been described as one of the two or three most complex in the English language. As of the early 1950s, there existed over 150 definitions (Wright 1998)! Some view culture as rules that help govern people's actions and beliefs and unite them as a community or a society, while others view culture as the material things that are specific to particular areas. You might think of food, language, dress, family relationships, mourning rituals, or any other actions and beliefs that dictate a way of life for a group of people. Most recent definitions of culture seem to favor an approach that focuses on the sharing of ideals and values, and how people interpret experience and behaviors. Terre Satterfield, an anthropologist whose ethnography we will consider in the next chapter, considers culture as a "multi-origined and multi-faceted resource" from which individuals draw—it is not a force that directs an individual's behavior, but a collection of ideas, behaviors, and beliefs that inform the way an individual lives (2002: 6). These cultural resources, such as symbols and meanings, manifest themselves in the everyday actions of groups who share a cultural identity. These definitions of culture, as well as the one given by Tylor and the hundreds that came after it, are necessarily broad and extremely general. In the following section we will not spend much time discussing what is or is not cultural, or what the best way to define it might be. Rather, we will examine some of the issues and concerns that have emerged as a result of the use of the word to define certain people, objects, and beliefs.

Cultural anthropologists are interested in examining the local and specific situations of a group of people. Implicit in this interest is a desire to learn about the individual—that is, what they actually do, say, and believe rather than what they *say* they do, say or believe. Of course, all of this is a matter of interpretation, and it is up to the researcher to make clear how their own beliefs or experiences might influence their interpretation of an event or a group of people. What fascinates anthropologists is considering how people act within their own social world—while it is true that there are social rules and regulations that influence how people act and what they believe, it is important that we consider the agency, or power, of the individual to behave in a way that may contradict the social rules and norms of their society. Culture does not bind individuals but rather provides "a network of choices" in which the individual chooses, subconsciously or not, how they will believe or act (Yengoyan 1986: 396). Cultural symbols and traditions are extremely powerful and relevant to understanding the world. What is essential, however, is that we pay attention to the diversity that exists *within* these communities, groups, or locales so that we do not assume that generalizations are factual representations of people.

Determining a definition of culture might seem very theoretical and irrelevant to your daily life—in fact, what purpose does defining a concept serve? The reality is that the way we view culture has many political and social consequences, as we will see repeatedly throughout the book. How we define culture affects people at all levels of society—from the local context of the family and the community to the realms of national and international politics. In this chapter we explore some of the ways in which anthropologists have engaged that topic. First we will show that our everyday lives are full of symbolic significance, much of which—like the air we breathe—we're totally unconscious of until forced to think about it. How do we go about interpreting complex cultural phenomena?

As discussed in Chapter 2, Ruth Benedict was one of Franz Boas's early students, a close friend of Margaret Mead, and author of the anthropological bestseller *Patterns of Culture* (1934; see Benedict 1959)—"probably the most popular book in anthropology ever published" (Geertz 1973). We will briefly look at her role in establishing and popularizing the modern culture concept. We'll then explore the idea that culture can be thought of as an open arena in which meaning is dynamically created in the flow of life and therefore can be studied objectively "in the field." As examples we will use a "classic" study of witchcraft beliefs in action, as well as a recent account of the process of religious conversion. In conclusion we briefly revisit the death of Captain James Cook. Just why did he die? How are we to make sense of a fatal encounter between an eighteenth-century British explorer and native Hawaiians in the midst of one of their religious festivals? The Hawaiian episode raises questions about the relation between culture, myth, history, and the interpretive process.

We should also say what we're *not* going to do. Our topic is vast, and there are many ways of approaching it. The formal study of language is certainly an important aspect of the subject, and a vital part of anthropology, but given our ethnographic focus we will have little to say about language as such. On the other hand, culture is often seen as being *like* a language—elements set in meaningful relationship with one another—and this a metaphor well worth exploring.

Nor will we be dealing to any great degree with the analysis of "myth." This too is an important area, and we should at least take note of an anthropological movement known as structuralism (not to be confused with British structural-functionalism). It is associated with the French anthropologist Claude Lévi-Strauss, mentioned above; one of the central features of this approach, which is based on linguistic theory, is an attempt to unpack the formal logical structure of myth in order to get at underlying universal properties of human thought.

Comprehending Others

If understanding those around us, and even ourselves, can be difficult, then other cultures and times present an even more formidable problem. It has been said that "the past is a foreign country: they do things differently there." Reality doesn't come to us straight on: the world is always understood from a human point of view, and that is always partial. How could it be otherwise? We may try to imagine what it's like to be a dog, a bee, or an extraterrestrial being, but our own standpoint is where we must begin. This is an issue that anthropology has always faced—that of translation between different cultural worlds. Meaning is embedded in language, but also in behavior, and that is where we start.

You are probably aware of the condition known as "autism spectrum disorder." It is evident at an early age, and it is defined by the psychiatric community as "persistent deficits in social communication and social interaction. Deficits in nonverbal communicative behaviors used for social interaction, ranging, for example, from poorly integrated verbal and nonverbal communication; to abnormalities in eye contact and body language or deficits in understanding and use of gestures; to a total lack of facial expressions and nonverbal communication" (American Psychiatric Association 2013). Psychologists and philosophers believe that one of the things lacking in this disorder is a "theory of mind"—the ability to perceive other people as *real* and like oneself. In other words, there is some kind of impairment in the capacity to function as a social being.

Oliver Sacks (b. 1933) is a neurologist and best-selling science writer; the central feature of his work is the attempt to understand neuropsychiatric disorder from *within*—to know as best we can what it's like to *live in* such a world.[1] One of his best-known essays is about Temple Grandin, a well-known figure who has been very successful in educating the public about autism through the telling of her own story (in 2010 a film was made about her life starring actor Claire Danes). She finds animals easier to understand than human beings, has had a successful career as a Professor of Animal Science, and is an advocate for both animal and autistic rights. Sacks met with Grandin and heard her story firsthand. He learned that she has trouble understanding the nuances of personal interaction. These difficulties "seemed to arise from her failure to empathize ... to follow the intricate play of motive and intention. She said that she could understand 'simple, strong, universal' emotions but was stumped by more complex emotions and the games people play. 'Much of the time,' she said, 'I feel like an anthropologist on Mars'" (Sacks 1995: 259).

For Grandin, "normal" people are the Martians. One thinks of Commander Data in the *Star Trek: The Next Generation* TV series. He is an artificial entity—an android—and incapable of experiencing feeling. To get along with real people, he has to learn how to imitate their behavior and act as though he were actually one of them. He has to deal with a world of gesture, emotion, and nuance that he has no built-in capacity to understand. Problems such as this are compounded when cultural differences are factored in. Therefore it's an anthropological issue as well. We live in a social world in which much goes unspoken and usually remains at the fringes of consciousness. And yet it clearly is meaningful; just imagine what you would think if you were talking to someone whose face was devoid of expression and who did not use body language. Try it yourself and see how long you can hold out! Another sign of autism spectrum disorder is "difficulties adjusting behavior to suit various social contexts." We will have more to say about meaning and context in the sections below.

Techniques of the Body

Marcel Mauss (1872–1950) was a French **ethnologist** and nephew of the great social theorist Émile Durkheim (1858–1917), to whom we'll return shortly. Though an armchair scholar and not an ethnographer, Mauss was a keen observer of the world around him and ranged widely in the search for common denominators underlying the diversity of human customs. He is principally remembered for *The Gift* (1924; see Mauss 2006), an anthropological classic on the nature of gift exchange as a moral phenomenon—the obligation to give and receive in comparative perspective (see Chapter 4). Another thing that caught his attention was cross-cultural difference in bodily style and deportment. He called these "the techniques of the body": "A kind of revelation came to me in hospital. I was ill in New York. I wondered where previously I had seen girls walking as my nurses walked. I had the time to think about it. At last I realized that it was at the cinema. Returning to France, I noticed how common this gait was, especially in Paris: the girls were French and they too were walking in this way. In fact, American walking fashions had begun to arrive over here, thanks to the cinema. This was an idea I could generalize" (Mauss 2006: 80).

And generalize it he did. Mauss had been in the French army in World War I and had served with English and Australian troops. He noted differences in bodily style between the English and Australians, and between both of them and the French. He wondered how this had come about, and so he was led to reflect on the cultural history of the societies in question and on the social situations in which particular bodily

PLATE 5.1 Marcel Mauss (center)

mannerisms are called for. In 1935 he asked a lecture audience to "look for a moment at ourselves. Everything in us all is under command. I am a lecturer for you: you can tell it from my sitting posture and my voice, and you are listening to me seated an in silence. We have a set of permissible or impermissible, natural or unnatural attitudes. Thus we should attribute different values to the act of staring fixedly: a symbol of politeness in the army, and of rudeness in everyday life" (Mauss 2006: 83).

Mauss went through a long list of bodily techniques: gender and age differences in deportment, variations in athletic styles, use of the hands, eating, sexual positions, ways of giving birth and holding infants, marching, sleeping, dancing, being at rest, etc. Some peoples squat, others sit, some stand on one leg: "the whole of Nilotic Africa … is populated by men who rest in the fields like storks. Some manage to rest on one foot without a pole, others lean on a stick. These resting techniques form real characteristics of civilisations, common to a large number of them, to whole families of peoples" (2006: 88).

Mauss used a Latin term—*habitus*—to cover the meaningful yet unconscious activity that pervades our daily lives (see Hall 1959, 1966). You don't have to look far to find it in your own. Just think about "table" manners, but bear in mind that

PLATE 5.2 A Dinka Man: South Sudan

not everyone uses tables, and some may eat with their hands (probably only the *right* hand) rather than with forks or chopsticks. The point of much childhood education is to make all of this "second nature." Anthropological and historical studies of *habitus* seek to restore that lost world to consciousness and expose the hidden processes behind it (see Hall 1959, 1969). Audrey Richards's study of the Bemba (see Chapter 2) touches on this theme, as well as that of "the gift"—the ritual significance of preparing, giving, and receiving food.[2]

Etiquette is another word for this kind of thing, and in North America the "bible" of etiquette has long been Emily Post's book of the same name, first published in 1922 and now in its 18th edition:

> Etiquette must, if it is to be of more than trifling use, include ethics as well as manners. Certainly what one is, is of far greater importance than what one appears to be. A knowledge of etiquette is of course essential to one's decent behavior, just as clothing is essential to one's decent appearance; and precisely as one wears the latter without being self-conscious of having on shoes and perhaps gloves, one who has good manners is equally unself-conscious in the observance of etiquette, the precepts of which must be so thoroughly absorbed as to make their observance a matter of instinct rather than of conscious obedience. (Post 1922: 8)[3]

Marcel Mauss couldn't have put it better. But he was well aware of how culturally relative this whole business is, and Post was not. The sub-text of her book is social class and the gender relations that go with it. The evolution of Western table manners and other aspects of *proper* behavior is a story about the democratization of European aristocratic values—part of the unconscious background to the way in which many of us in North America behave every day. China has its own history in this regard, as do Japan and other parts of the world.

The message here is that culture and history are mixed up in everything we do: how we act; how we dress; how we evaluate personal appearance; our preferred colors; notions of hygiene; the foods we eat (and don't); ideas about age, ethnicity, race, gender, and physical disability; health, illness, and healing; and much else besides. The challenge is learning how to read the code.

Culture Goes Public

The term "culture" suggests something—my culture, your culture—that is our unique and valuable heritage. In fact, this way of looking at things owes a great deal to the influence of early-twentieth-century cultural anthropology, and most particularly to the influence of Franz Boas (1858–1942) and his students. As mentioned above, Ruth Benedict (1887–1948) was one of these students, and her *Patterns of Culture* is a foundational work of North American anthropology. It was this book,

PLATE 5.3 Ruth Benedict

more than any other, that popularized the modern culture concept. Her aim—like Margaret Mead's—was to get her largely American readership to think more clearly about their own society by presenting examples of very different ways of doing things. Throughout her career she was, like other Boasians, also a critic of racism and the race concept.

Benedict was a published poet herself and conceived of culture in terms of form, theme, configuration, and pattern—as being made up of related elements in much the same way as language itself is, or a poem, or an artistic style. She compared cultural traits with the fundamental meaningful units of a spoken language (phonemes): the human vocal apparatus can produce an indefinite number of sounds, but a given language selects only a few of them and places them in a particular order in relation to one another. Meaningful speech is the result. It's the same, Benedict thought, with culture: "It is in cultural life as it is in speech; selection is the prime necessity" (1959: 23). Out of a vast range of possibility, a given culture selects only some elements for emphasis (see Darnell 2001: 191–200).

As a more recent anthropologist put it, the analysis of culture is "not an experimental science in search of law, but an interpretive one in search of meaning" (Geertz 1973: 5). However, that assertion leaves hanging the problem of validity. How are we to decide whether a particular interpretation is satisfying, that it fits the evidence and feels "right"? Interpretation involves the search for relationships between cultural elements. Benedict believed that so-called "primitive" cultures allow such patterns to be seen with greater clarity than in complex modern societies: "They are a laboratory in which we may study the diversity of human institutions. With their comparative isolation, many primitive regions have had centuries in which to elaborate the cultural themes they have made their own.... It is the only laboratory of social forms that we have or shall have" (1959: 17). She thought that, if a society has been left in relative isolation for long enough, it would tend to assume a more or less stable and integrated form, and to impress itself upon the very psyches of the people who share it: "A culture, like an individual, is a more or less consistent pattern of thought and action" (1959: 46). Following this logic, along with a given cultural pattern there should also be a preferred personality type.

It was also recognized that some people just don't fit in, and Benedict had a good deal to say about their fate. The deviant "is the representative of that arc of human capacities that is not capitalized in his culture. In proportion as his civilization has committed itself to a direction alien to him, he will be the sufferer" (1959: 25). She had "homosexuals" particularly in mind, but she noted that how sexuality is regarded varies considerably from society to society along that great "arc" of human possibility (Benedict 1959: 262–65; see also Foucault 1988, 1990). For example, some native North American societies had an honored role for the *berdache*—cross-dressing men. Benedict was also familiar with the highly elaborate artistic traditions, myths, and formal ritual practices of the town-dwelling Puebloan peoples of the American Southwest. She thought that they are all connected together as expressions of an underlying pattern that turns up in every facet of life: a culture "whose delight is in formality and whose way of life is the way of measure and of sobriety" (1959: 129).

The other case studies in *Patterns of Culture* receive similar treatment, but Benedict's most satisfying study of a cultural pattern came in her last major work, *The Chrysanthemum and the Sword* (1946), which wasn't about a "primitive" society at all, but about Japan. It was written during World War II and had been commissioned by the government to help Americans understand their exotic adversary. Since Benedict couldn't actually visit Japan, she used published historical and ethnographic sources, novels, memoirs, local informants in New York, and Japanese art—particularly cinema—to get at the inner logic of Japanese culture. She saw the way the Japanese conducted their war not "as a military problem but as a cultural problem" (2005: 5). Japanese soldiers would rather die than surrender.

She found that she had to consider history, religion, family life, and fundamental concepts governing social relationships, particularly concepts relating to indebtedness and social hierarchy—what we owe to others and what they owe to us: "righteousness in Japan depends upon recognition of one's place in the great network of mutual indebtedness that embraces both one's forebears and one's contemporaries" (2005: 98–99). It is as if the Japanese had taken the principle of reciprocity to its greatest

PLATE 5.4 President Obama and Emperor Akihito

extreme: each person calculating the favor given and received and being deeply anxious about whether there is an even balance. Failure results in loss of face and in deep shame that in some cases can only be counterbalanced by suicide.

Benedict placed one Japanese word—*on*—at the core of her analysis. She impressionistically defined the word as "a load, an indebtedness, a burden, which one carries as best one may" (2005: 99). In her view, the Japanese saw no gift as free, and therefore they went to great lengths to avoid situations that might create imbalance. An elaborate and formal code of manners suppresses self-assertion for the sake of smooth social relations. Bowing correctly is an element in this pattern of etiquette—of *habitus*. Respect has degrees, and getting it right is as important as it is difficult. The truly successful person is one who knows how to balance all the obligations that emerge in social life, in addition to those that one is born with, such as obligations to one's parents: "The tensions that are thus generated are enormous, and they express themselves in a high level of aspiration which has made Japan … a great power in the world. But these tensions are a heavy strain upon the individual" (2005: 293).

Patterns of Culture and *The Chrysanthemum and the Sword* were not based on Benedict's own fieldwork; her examples have a static quality and have been criticized for it. We see what Benedict takes to be the patterns, but not the living societies themselves, actual people in real situations. These works are quite old now; both anthropology and the world have moved on. Nevertheless, her books provided an important example of how to go about engaging in cultural analysis. But it should be remembered that "cultures" are abstractions and never reveal themselves directly; their contents and themes are a matter of interpretation. The culture concept, as we now understand it, arose out of the study of relatively isolated tribal societies. But what about vast "multicultural" societies such as Canada, the United States, and the globalized world of the Internet? Social formations like these are of a different order entirely. Anthropologists work in local contexts, while keeping in mind the global processes that surround them. You will learn more about the current status of the culture concept in our next chapter. Meanwhile, we will consider the importance of context itself.

Meaning in Context

We've said that culture is sometimes compared to language. Of course, language itself is an *aspect* of culture, but this analogy has much broader implications. Any ordinary language has a lexicon and a grammar: a vocabulary and some general and usually unconscious principles that guide the formation of meaningful utterances. From this point of view culture and history are behind everything that we say, or even *can* say. But there's more to it than this. "Meaning" is context-dependent: if you want to know about what someone *really means* by what they say or do, the overall situation must be taken into account. Meaning, in other words, has a sociological dimension.

Bronislaw Malinowski (1884–1942) was very interested in language and collected many native texts during his fieldwork in the southwest Pacific; many of these related to magical practices and were very obscure, metaphorical, and difficult to translate. In keeping with his brand of functionalism, he focused on what such utterances were aimed at actually accomplishing: getting yams to grow, canoes to sail successfully, enemies kept at bay, etc. As he put it, "a statement, spoken in real life, is never detached from the situation in which it has been uttered. For each verbal statement ... has the aim and function of expressing some thought or feeling actual at that moment and in that situation" (Malinowski 1947: 307). It is part of the ongoing flow of social life, and its meaning depends on where it stands in relation both to local circumstances and to the wider cultural pattern. That is all a bit abstract, so a couple of examples will help to illustrate the principle.

Who's the Witch?

Sir Edward Evans-Pritchard (1902–73) was a contemporary of Audrey Richards and, like her, had been a student at the London School of Economics, where he inevitably came under Malinowski's influence. E-P (as he was known) didn't much like Malinowski; nevertheless, he applied a contextual approach to the understanding of witchcraft beliefs

PLATE 5.5 Sir Edward Evans-Pritchard

among the Azande, a people who overlap the borders of what are now the Republic of South Sudan, the Central African Republic, and the Republic of the Congo. The product of this research was his classic study *Witchcraft, Oracles and Magic among the Azande* (1937). In addition to an ethnographic contribution to what had been a neglected subject, the book is philosophically important because of the **epistemological** questions it raises—questions about social experience and the limits of knowledge.

It's fair to say that E-P wrote *the* book on witchcraft; after him the entire subject appeared in a different light. What was earlier dismissed as primitive superstition could now be viewed as a rational approach to the world, once the underlying premises were understood (see Wilson 1970). Evans-Pritchard presented the Azande as not all that different from ourselves. He said that his interpretations emerged from what Zande people did and thought about the difficult situations they frequently found themselves in—chronic illness, the problems of getting by in economically marginal conditions, the envy, jealousy, and petty quarrels of village life: matters of life and death to them. Underlying all of this was the assumption that most misfortune can be accounted for by human ill-will. However, E-P stressed that this does not mean that the Azande have no clue about natural causes, but merely that they add another element—witchcraft—to their explanation of misfortune. This doesn't mean that Zande beliefs about witchcraft were *true*, but they were reasonable under the circumstances. This is true of all anthropological studies of religion or belief—the aim is to understand both what these beliefs mean to the people who value them, and what role they play in society.

In 1937, Zande witchcraft was held to be due to an intrinsic "mystical" power that some people had, perhaps even without knowing it. Where we might see fate or bad luck, the Azande suspected the hostility of those close by—neighbors, even family members: "In a study of Zande witchcraft, we must bear in mind, firstly, that the notion is a function of situations of misfortune, and, secondly, that it is a function of personal relations" (Evans-Pritchard 1937: 106). In other words, it is a function of context. Unlike earlier times in Europe where there was a well-developed theology of witchcraft, in Zandeland in the 1930s there was only the application of specific ideas in specific circumstances, such as particular cases of illness or crop failure; they had no Devil, no general principle of "evil" to explain witchcraft, and not much of an idea about God either. In Europe the presence of absolute concepts such as "good" and "evil," or God and the Devil, helped to account for the ferocity of witchcraft prosecutions; witches violated the cosmic order itself. Azande were only interested in sniffing out particular witches. Nevertheless, even without such concepts, Zande witchcraft beliefs contained an implicit moral philosophy—about what kind of person it's good to be, about the circumstances that generate ill-will, and about what it takes to maintain or restore social balance. They had a **sociocentric theory** of why bad things happen: looking for causes internal to society, rather than to impersonal notions such as fate or physical causality.

Coping with misfortune therefore involves determining *who* is behind it and bringing the matter out into the open. That is where Zande "oracles" came in. These were technical procedures that could sniff out the truth, most famously the "poison oracle," which worked by putting poison down a chicken's gullet and posing yes-or-no questions to it, for example: "if X is innocent chicken live, if X is guilty chicken die," and so on. The poison itself, extracted from a forest plant, was regarded as an impartial judge: "If you press a Zande to explain how the poison oracle can see far-off things he will say that its *mbisimo*, its soul, sees them." However, "in saying that the poison oracle has a *mbisimo* Zande means little more than 'it does something' or, as we could say, 'it is dynamic.' You ask them how it works and they reply, 'It has a soul.' If you were to ask them how they know it has a 'soul,' they would reply that they know because it works" (1937: 320–21).

Evans-Pritchard filled his notebooks with observations like these from everyday life; he also sought out the experts—so-called witch doctors and the oracle specialists. He used his observations to ask some profound questions about different systems of thought and how to bridge them. As he said, we are:

> not content to know bare facts but seek to discover uniformities in them and to relate one fact to another. Only by so doing can we understand Zande beliefs and compare them with our own. Is Zande thought so different from ours that we can only describe their speech and actions without comprehending them, or is it essentially like our own though expressed in an idiom to which we are unaccustomed? What are the motives of Zande behavior? What are their notions of reality? How are these motives and notions expressed in custom? … I have always asked myself "How?" rather than "Why?" I have tried to explain a fact by citing other facts from the same culture and by noting interdependencies between facts.… My interpretations are contained in the facts themselves, for I have described the facts in such a way that the interpretations emerge as part of the description. (1937: 4 5)

So let us take a particular case. Someone is suspected of witchcraft; this possibility is based on the assumption that witchcraft is *real* and operates in a certain way, perhaps even as an expression of *unconscious* hostility. When put together systematically, such facts indicate patterns of stress in the community and point toward the *kinds* of people likely to come under suspicion (which could be either men or women). Suspicion is one thing, proof another, and so we turn to an oracle to settle the matter. If the answer seems straightforward, then an accusation is made and the supposedly guilty party is warned to back off and make compensation. However, no one freely *admits* to witchcraft, and so it's all really a question of perspective and always contains an element of ambiguity. Such events reveal the sociological dynamics of the society in question, and historians have used that insight to explore witchcraft in the European past, using records of court proceedings and other written sources.

Evans-Pritchard approached his problem "by noting interdependencies between facts." These facts emerged in particular situations or in response to specific questions. As noted above, there was no theology of witchcraft; no Zande could put things together in the way E-P did in his book, or for that matter in any other way. They had a tendency to reason in a circle when challenged to explain their worldview. Their approach was practical, not theoretical. Is witchcraft at work? If yes, what do we do about it? It proved difficult to get them to consider, much less question, the assumptions that guided their day-to-day activities.

And here's the philosophical issue. We talk today about "thinking outside the box." What we mean by this is getting beyond our conventional way of doing things and acting in an innovative and creative manner. But what if we don't know that we're *in* a box? The situation that Evans-Pritchard describes is something like that. He stood outside the Zande world looking in; witchcraft was real enough for the Azande, but *for him* witchcraft did not and could not exist in some ultimately real sense. The universe as he understood it just doesn't work that way; it doesn't have forces that operate in the same way that witchcraft operates, though it has invisible forces of other kinds (gravity, electricity, etc).

Why couldn't the Azande see the flaws in their own reasoning? Their oracles sometimes contradicted each other; a verdict of witchcraft might be given, accepted by the accused, rituals performed, and the patient died anyway; medicines and magic were used to alleviate suffering, but the suffering continued. On the other hand, sometimes such measures seemed to work. As with us, most illness episodes ended with the patient getting better, no matter what was done about it in the meantime. Success counts much more than failure. Failure could be explained away, but *success* always validated the Zande way of doing things:

> Witchcraft, oracles, and magic form an intellectually coherent system. Each explains and proves the other. Death is proof of witchcraft. It is avenged by magic. The achievement of vengeance-magic is proved by the poison oracle.... Azande often observe that a medicine is unsuccessful, but they do not generalize their observations. Contradictions between their beliefs are not noticed by the Azande because the beliefs are not all present at the same time but function in different situations. They are therefore not brought into opposition. (1937: 475)

The Azande appear to have been stuck inside a particular worldview, a **paradigm** full of unconscious assumptions about how the world works. We owe the popularity of this concept to the historian and philosopher of science Thomas Kuhn (1922–96), who—in his famous book *The Structure of Scientific Revolutions* (1962; see Kuhn 1970)—examined how scientific theories constrain and shape knowledge. But, as his title implies, he was also interested in analyzing the circumstances that lead to thinking *outside* the box—resulting in a *paradigm shift*. He suggested that after such a thing happens there is a sense in which we now live in a *different world* than we did before. The outlines of the box have changed. With the onset of colonial rule, missionaries and British government servants made it their business to change the outlines of the Zande world, in order, among other things, to convince these people that witchcraft is unreal.

Belief Is the Least of It

It's not easy to see a process that is usually evident only after the fact; but anthropologists are sometimes in a position to witness and even experience something like this personally. The missionaries of various faiths are professional paradigm shifters. They aim to change people and the societies of which they are a part for the sake of some greater good—personal salvation, social justice, political assimilation, or whatever it might be. There have been anthropological studies of missionaries themselves, which only seems fair. However, what we're concerned with here is how one process—the conversion experience—plays out in individual lives. Our example comes from a contemporary anthropologist, Tanya Luhrmann (b. 1959), who has worked among American evangelical Christians in order to understand what conversion is like, how it comes about, and what changes it leads to. But first some background.

In 1912 the great French sociologist Émile Durkheim published a highly influential book concerning the origin and nature of religion. It was called *The Elementary Forms of Religious Life*,[4] and it is one of the foundational works of social anthropology. The title is significant: by "elementary forms" Durkheim meant the most basic, the common denominator underlying *all* religious belief and practice ("primitive" in the sense of "original"). His method was anthropological. He reasoned that, if we could examine the "simplest" human society now known and study its religion, insight could be gained into the nature of religion in general. His example was Aboriginal Australia.

PLATE 5.6 Émile Durkheim

Like Lewis Henry Morgan (1818–81) and many others of that time, Durkheim was a social evolutionist. And, like others, he believed that the Australians were at the bottom of the social evolutionary scale. He correlated social structure with religious practice. As we've mentioned, the Aboriginal peoples were organized into totemic clans, each clan being symbolically identified with a living creature. In those days, a clan-based social system was seen as the structurally simplest form of human society, all others having evolved out of this basic form. Likewise totemism was seen as the simplest religion. But Australian clans were not isolated entities; they were parts of wider societies based on precise marriage rules and elaborate ceremonials. Durkheim found that the Aboriginal peoples used their own social life to provide a model for the universe in general. Human groups, animal species, and the natural landscape were brought together into a unified symbolic system of belief and practice, and all accounted for in stories about the journeys of the Dawn Beings (Durkheim & Mauss 1965).

Throughout his sociological career Durkheim pursued one consistent theme: the nature of the moral bond that ties people together into communities. His focus was not on *belief* but on religious *practice*, and he found the answer to the problem of religious origins to lie in religious *feeling*. It is essentially a social-psychological theory: the psychology of crowds. By 1912 there was already a good deal of ethnographic material available on Aboriginal Australian religion and ritual (Stocking 1995: 84–98). The early ethnographers had seen that much Aboriginal ritual was accompanied by great emotional displays. Durkheim maintained that when people act collectively in groups, they feel the presence of a life-enhancing power that is experienced as originating outside themselves (think of emotionally charged religious rituals, political rallies, rock concerts, etc.). Following this logic, the sense of transcendental power doesn't come from beyond the world at all, but from within us as members of society.

But this is a sociological perspective, and "primitive" peoples (like most of us, most of the time) aren't in a position to see things this way; instead they *project* the emotions they experience in collective ritual onto their totemic symbols. Those symbols are then experienced as the *source* of the power their worshippers feel. Durkheim appropriated a Polynesian word—**mana**—to characterize this free-floating power, which he found to be "the distinguishing characteristic of any sacred being" (1995: 59). Something like this power is present no matter whether the object in question is a totem, the flag of a modern nation state, or any other symbol that inspires and articulates collective action. Living persons can also seem to contain such power: Polynesian royalty, the Queen, the Dalai Lama, the Pope—any charismatic source of spiritual authority.

As Durkheim said, "the whole social world seems populated with forces that in reality exist only in our minds. We know what the flag is for the soldier, but in itself it is only a bit of cloth" (1995: 228). Likewise, the totem symbol is the flag of the clan, even though to an outsider it's only a carved stick. For Durkheim these are all constructs of our collective imagination and—as a sociologist—he wanted to know how they arise and what gives them their power. But there's a problem here: since he was concerned with group dynamics and religious expression, Durkheim did not really consider the "insiders' perspective": that of the Aboriginal Australians themselves. Of course, he was an armchair scholar and the sources he consulted didn't consider this perspective either. Even though the sources are often good on a descriptive level, they are from the perspective of an outsider looking in. The problem boils down to the question of what it is like to actually *live* in an Aboriginal world in which "man, society and nature, and past, present and future, are at one together within a unitary system" (see Stanner 1979).

Much more could be said about Durkheim, but let's return to Tanya Luhrmann, who did indeed try to see the evangelical world from within. When discussing her work we are not referring to a distant land or time, but to something around us that is of great present-day social and personal importance. According to a respected survey of religious affiliation, 26 per cent of the American adult population identify themselves as evangelical Christians; they are followed by Roman Catholics (24 per cent), "mainline Protestants" (18 per cent), "unaffiliated" (16 per cent), and other smaller groups—Jews, Muslims, etc. (Pew Forum 2008). The evangelical component in the Canadian religious scene is less prominent, but still significant.

As we have seen, anthropology is engaged in mediating between cultural worlds. In this case, Luhrmann set out to bridge a cultural divide—an "abyss" as she sees it—between evangelicals and those who know little about them. This divide is often seen in terms of the so-called "culture wars"—"conservatives" on one side and "liberals" on the other. The debate is fueled by hot-button political and moral issues such as gay marriage, abortion, and evolution vs. divine creation. Luhrmann's intent was to get beneath the stereotypes and find out what the evangelical world looks like from within:

> The tool of an anthropologists' trade is careful observation—participant observation, a kind of naturalist's craft in which one watches what people do and listens to what they say and infers from that how they come to see and know their world.... I watched and I listened, and I tried to understand as an outsider how an insider to this evangelical world was able to experience God as real. Members of these churches became my friends and confidants. I liked them. I thought they liked me. They knew I was an anthropologist, and as they came to know me, they became comfortable talking with me at length about God. I have sought to understand what they said. (2012: xx)

The outcome was her 2012 book *When God Talks Back: Understanding the American Evangelical Relationship with God.* She recognized that the evangelical community is huge and diverse, so she focused on one rapidly growing segment of it that emphasizes establishing a personal relationship with God—not as judge but as a friend and companion, though one who sometimes dishes out tough love: "God answers every prayer, but sometimes the answer is no" (2012: 270). Her fieldwork took place in a number of churches in Chicago and Southern California, where her informants often expressed "an intense desire to experience personally a God who is as present now as when Christ walked among his followers in Galilee" (2012: 13).

Evangelical Christianity is *experiential*: feeling should accompany belief. The roots of this religious tradition go back to the Protestant Reformation and, before that, to the earliest days of the Church. Conversion experiences are actively sought, and the imagery is that of *rebirth*: "Very truly I tell you, no one can see the kingdom of God unless they are born again.... The wind blows wherever it pleases. You hear its sound, but you cannot tell where it comes from or where it is going. So it is with everyone born of the Spirit" (John 3: 3–8). Luhrmann therefore didn't think it was enough just to understand what her informants were telling her, but to also make an attempt to feel what they felt (see Luhrmann 2013). It's an unusual stance, because strictly speaking she wasn't a believer at all. This is where Durkheim enters the story. As discussed above, he gave priority to religious practice and placed belief in a secondary role. Such a view is the reverse of how we usually think about such things, but it is consistent with Durkheim's emphasis on ritual and the emotional bonds of community life.

Luhrmann followed Durkheim's lead and investigated the social contexts in which church members develop the sense that divine power is at work among and within them (2012: 279). Of course, they had to profess belief in certain things as well, particularly the truth of the Christian Bible. The focus of their practice was making the stories in the Bible come alive in their own lives—bringing past and present together in real time. They did this through Bible readings, spiritual retreats, Christian-oriented self-help books, testifying before one another in church, and above all in prayer. It could become very emotional: "people often talk about the Holy Spirit as if it is substance, as if it flows through the body like water through a chute.... People describe feeling a great surge of power running through their bodies" (2012: 12, 146). Indeed, Luhrmann found herself weeping when the people around her wept. Church members learned to interpret some subjective experiences as God speaking back to them, and certain events as being due to God's direct intervention in worldly events. As one informant put it, "patterns and coincidences are not random.... A huge part of hearing God, for me, is just being able to recognize patterns" (2012: 56–57). Correlation becomes cause; you pray and something significant happens; your prayer is seen as helping to bring the event about—this is evidence that God was listening, and that becomes a story worth telling to others. Experience reinforces belief, and vice versa.

Certain experiences seemed to come from "somewhere else":[5] "The central principle was identifying the 'not-me' experience: a thought or image or sensation that one felt was not one's own. If a thought felt spontaneous and unsought, it was more likely to be identified as God's". (2012: 67). Luhrmann suspended whatever disbelief she may have felt, and followed along with her informants/friends in all of this. In the end she found herself somewhere between cultural worlds: "I began to understand parts of the church teaching not just as so many intellectual doctrinal commitments but as having an emotional logic of their own" (2012: 325). "For these Christians, religion is not about explaining reality but about transforming it: making it possible to trust that the world is good, despite ample evidence to the contrary" (2012: 295):

> Knowing God involves training, and it involves interpretation. Each faith … forms its own culture, its own way of seeing the world, and as people acquire the knowledge and the practices through which they come to know that God, the most intimate aspects of the way they experience their everyday world change. Those who learn to take God seriously do not simply interpret the world differently from those who have not done so. They have different evidence for what is true. In some deep and fundamental way, as a result of their practices, they live in different worlds. (2012: 226)

The Dying and Reborn God

Luhrmann's informants sought to incorporate the teachings of an ancient text into their daily lives. This occurred on an individual psychological level, and also within the rituals of their communities. Much anthropological effort has gone into exploring processes of this sort.

When we go back and examine what happened to Captain Cook (see Introduction), it's evident that the Hawaiians interpreted his arrival in terms of their own mythic under-standings about the world. Cook's ships arrived from the Bering Sea in late 1778 during the Hawaiian New Year festival, the time after the winter solstice when the rains come to the Big Island and the days start to grow longer. His presence was associated with the god Lono, and he was honored accordingly. When the *Resolution* and *Discovery* appeared off the north end of the island, the image of Lono was being carried around the island in a clockwise direction, stopping at each coastal community along the way: "The season of Lono's passage, period of winter rains, is the transition from 'the dying time of the year' to the time when 'bearing things become fruitful'" (Sahlins 1985: 115). Cook's ships followed the same course and finally ended up at Kealakekua Bay where the king was also in residence. Everything seemed to fit the association of Cook with Lono.

He and his crew were treated royally, and—as we see from Lt. King's account—Cook himself went along with the role he was assigned. In a sense Cook *became* the god: "a form of the god who makes the earth bear fruit for mankind: a seminal god, patron of the peaceful and agricultural arts" (Sahlins 1985: 131). The British soon left to resume their explorations on the Northwest Coast. That was also an appropri-ate moment—close to the same time that the king of Hawai'i was to ceremonially open the agricultural year, accompanied by human sacrifice. Cook's movements still corresponded with the ritual cycle, but the weather intervened, the foremast on the *Resolution* was broken, and the ships returned to the Bay. That was not an opportune time at all: "Unlike his arrival, his return was generally unintelligible and unwanted…. And things fell apart" (Sahlins 1995: 79).

After the fight on the beach, Cook's body was dismembered, only some of the parts recovered for burial at sea. Before they left for a second time, the British were mystified by questions the Hawaiians asked about whether Lono would return again the following year. Evidently the idea of a dying and reborn god was a familiar notion to them. Missionaries later reported that "the relics of Cook were ... worshipped in a temple of Rono ... of whom the people had a notion that the British navigator was the representative, if not the incarnation of him" (Sahlins 1985: 102). In his history of the Hawaiian Islands, Daws writes, "It was a curious fate for him to have suffered.... Natives at Kealakekua Bay and elsewhere looked back on Cook's death with a mixture of genuine sorrow and mournful relish, the kind of feeling shared by people who have survived a great catastrophe and cannot stop talking about it. Even as late as [the mid-nineteenth century,] old Hawaiians would claim to have seen Cook killed, and even after that, storytellers could command fascinated audiences for their tales of the return of Lono long ago ..." (1968: 24).

In 1820 the first missionaries—Protestants from New England—arrived in Hawai'i, stimulated by what they had heard of the Islands and by native Hawaiians whom they had met in Boston. They went about preaching the gospel, and by 1822 they had built a church in Kailua on the Big Island, which stands to this day. They were particularly concerned about sexual immorality, especially the famous *hula* dance that had been such a part of the celebrations surrounding the god Lono. The Kingdom of Hawaii became officially Christian and the old taboos were abolished; in time the native Hawaiian population came to be greatly outnumbered by immigrants from many parts of the world, and the Kingdom itself was overthrown by the Americans. This illustrates that history can shift its meaning depending on one's perspective. In the Introduction we mentioned the Hawaiian gentleman who was giving out pamphlets protesting what he took to be the illegal American occupation of the islands. Recall that on his t-shirt were the words "My People Killed Captain Cook!" Here Cook was no longer considered a god, but rather associated with the beginnings of foreign domination.

Conclusion

It's good to keep in mind the very broad definition of "culture" advanced by Edward Burnett Tylor in the 1870s: "Culture or civilization, in its wide ethnographic sense, is that complex whole which includes knowledge, belief, art, morals, law, custom, and any other capabilities and habits acquired by man as a member of society." His definition points to the truth of Lévi-Strauss's comment that society is the natural human condition. Subtract all of the things in Tylor's list and ask yourself what would be left over? Seen in this way, *all* human societies are "civilized," no matter how different they may appear on the surface.

Of course Tylor's definition is too broad to be of practical use. It does, however, call attention to the wide range of phenomena that anthropologists have been concerned with. But when we focus in more closely we need sharper concepts, and this chapter has explored some of the ways in which the culture concept has been applied to specific problems—from "techniques of the body" to Japanese etiquette, Zande witchcraft, and the death of Captain Cook.

The next chapter continues this discussion and expands it to look at other aspects of what the culture concept is used for—both by anthropologists and in society at large. After all, though anthropologists are largely responsible for its development and elaboration, this notion is now public property. And it's not a *neutral* concept, some kind of disembodied abstraction. The culture concept evolved in response to particular circumstances of time and place, and in large measure this had a political aim—to show that all human beings are in this world together, that we are all civilized beings, and—as Darwin thought—that we are all one species under the skin. We'll now take a close look at several cases in which the culture concept has been used politically.

Notes

1   One of Sacks's essays, *Awakenings*, was used as the basis for a 1990 film with Robert de Niro, Robin Williams, and Julie Kavner. It tells the story of what happens when a patient in a catatonic state is restored to consciousness after years "away."

2   The French anthropologist Pierre Bourdieu (1930–2002) made much use of the concept of *habitus*, which he regarded as an "embodied competence" that becomes manifest in the flow of social life and in the context of particular situations (1977).

3   There is an entertaining YouTube video of Miss Post speaking on this subject in 1947, along with examples of what and what not to do at the dinner table: http://www.youtube.com/watch?v=HAPcnZAJanE.

4   *Les Formes élémentaires de la vie religieuse.* The term "sociology" was invented by the French philosopher and historian of science Auguste Comte (1798–1857). Durkheim's brand of sociology included what we now think of as socio-cultural anthropology.

5   Experiences that seem to come from outside the conscious self led Sigmund Freud (1856–1939) to invent psychoanalysis. It is a method of symbolic interpretation, finding meaning beneath what often seems like nonsense. Dreams are one example, as are delusions and hallucinations at the other end of the spectrum. There is also a considerable anthropological literature on spirit-possession phenomena in which a person may seemingly be "taken over" by an external being. Anthropologists have looked into the social circumstances of the possessed, and the procedures that lead to the identification of the troubling spirit.

Study Questions

1 Summarize the various definitions of culture referenced in this chapter.
2 Temple Grandin once said that she feels like an "anthropologist on Mars." Explain how autism spectrum disorder might lead her to use this metaphor.
3 What did Mauss mean by the terms *bodily techniques* and *habitus*? Use examples from the text and from your own culture to illustrate these terms.
4 Explain how etiquette and the concept of "the gift" are related to Mauss's concept of *habitus*, using examples from the text.
5 Outline Benedict's perspective on cultural patterns and explain why she believed so-called primitive societies were central to understanding cultural patterns.
6 Explain how our understanding of language can be used to understand culture as a system of meaning.
7 Summarize Evans-Pritchard's findings on Zande witchcraft and oracles. Explain how this worldview is considered sociocentric.
8 Outline Durkheim's study of religious practice. Why did he focus on religious *practice* rather than *belief*? What is meant by the term *mana*?
9 How did Luhrmann's study of American Evangelicals differ from other anthropological studies of religion? Compare and contrast her methods and findings with those of Evans-Pritchard and Durkheim.

Discussion Questions

1 Why is defining culture important to society? Why is it such a difficult concept to define? What is meant by the phrase "society is the natural human condition"?
2 Benedict's major works were not based on fieldwork. Evans-Pritchard and Durkheim studied culture from the position of outsiders. Luhrmann became a member of the community she studied, but was not a true believer. How valid and accurate can an outsider's portrait of a culture be? Can we ever really define, describe, or explain another culture fully, or even our own?
3 Consider the assertion that with the advancement of science and technology, the place of religion and religious beliefs will gradually fade away. Do you think this is the case? Why or why not?

PART III

CONTEMPORARY ANTHROPOLOGICAL ISSUES

CHAPTER 6

//

The Politics of Culture

LEARNING OBJECTIVES

After reading this chapter, students should be able to

- understand the modern concept of culture and anthropology's role in developing it;
- discuss culture in terms of ownership and define the terms *cultural nationalism* and *revitalization movement*;
- discuss the Handsome Lake Religion, the Whaler's Shrine, and the Makah whale hunt within the context of cultural ownership and revitalization;
- summarize Sproat's experience of the First Nations he helped to displace and his observations on private property and the potlatch;
- understand the circumstances that surrounded the First Nations land claims in British Columbia and the significance of oral tradition in the Skeena River Valley case; and
- outline Satterfield's work on the culture of activism and her findings on the dispute over the old-growth logging in Oregon.

KEY TERMS

activism	oral traditions	savage beast
essentialism	potlatch	treaty
noble savage	revitalization movement	

Introduction

The concept of "culture" in its modern form is probably anthropology's greatest contribution to human self-understanding, and is certainly its greatest contribution to the English language. As we've seen, it's also a notion that has political implications. As discussed in Chapter 4, the 1978 US Indian Child Welfare Act speaks of protecting "the unique values of Indian culture." Like all ideas, this particular concept has a history—and that takes us back once more to Franz Boas and his students.

Ruth Benedict declared that it's not race or common blood that binds people together; "what really binds men together is their culture,—the ideas and the standards they have in common" (Benedict 1959: 14)—different ideas and standards, and therefore different cultures, each with its "unique values." As we explored in the last chapter, cultural identity is a truly complex thing. To us this may seem almost self-evident, which suggests how successful the Boasians were in getting this perspective across to the general public. It's a tolerant, relativistic, and hopeful worldview.

But that doesn't really tell us what culture itself is and how we should think about it. Benedict's approach was one possibility—by envisioning culture in terms of patterns, how its elements relate to one another. These patterns are to be seen as a product of history, and therefore subject to change. Similarly, Margaret Mead's *Coming of Age in Samoa* was an attempt to change North American attitudes about adolescence and sexuality.

That vision owes much to Boas, and it reflects his own German heritage. Germany as we know it today is a relatively new country, first unified in 1870. Before that it was divided into states and principalities of greater or lesser size. But already there was a sense of emerging unity. Philosophers, geographers, historians, linguists, and folklorists attempted to articulate it, and they discerned a common Germanic culture rooted in a common language, geographic locale, and historical experience. This called for seeing things holistically—in the round—motivated by "the desire to understand the phenomena and history of a country or of the whole earth" (Boas 1996: 16). Boas brought this attitude with him to North America, where it became a central feature of his anthropological research and teaching: "The culture of any given tribe ... can be fully explained only when we take into consideration its inner growth" (Boas 1963: 157).

Thus "culture" itself—which even Boas himself called "a vague term"—took shape as a distinct object, something good to "think with" (Boas 1963: 145). Indigenous peoples, who had been the traditional objects of anthropological research, began to see themselves in these terms as well. It became possible to speak about a culture in general terms, something to be preserved and defended—a site of resistance against colonial oppression. This process is related to the rise of advocacy groups that seek to speak for their peoples in relation to national or regional governments. From this point of view, the colonial encounter is what made Aboriginal identity possible. Michael Brown, an anthropologist who has studied the "cultural property" issue, observes that the culture concept originated as "a useful analytical device and nothing more. But in promoting the concept of culture anthropologists inadvertently spawned a creature that now has a life of its own. In public discourse, culture and such related concepts as 'tradition' and 'heritage' have become resources that groups own and defend from competing interests" (2003: 4).

Anthropologists have sometimes been seen as exploiters themselves, alien visitors engaged in cultural theft. This is a recipe for distrust and anger by the subjects of anthropological research, and then for self-examination by anthropologists themselves. In this chapter, we'll look at two episodes in which these issues came to the fore in controversies over land, identity, and cultural property. They are from the Pacific Northwest, an area of central importance in the development of North American anthropology. It also happens that we (your authors) live here and have a certain attachment to the region.

The first case study considers the controversy over possession of the "Whaler's Shrine," once an important ritual object among the Nootka (Nuu-chah-nulth) of western Vancouver Island, where Captain Cook made landfall in 1778. The shrine was purchased in 1904 by Franz Boas's ethnographic assistant, George Hunt, for the American Museum of Natural History in New York. The circumstances of that purchase are disputed, but—whatever the truth of the matter—the Muchalaht band of the Nuu-chah-nulth want it back. The question has arisen over whether whaling should be brought back as well, as it has been among the related Makah people of Washington state. The second example is an important Canadian land-claims case, in which anthropologists became advocates for the native cause. It began in British Columbia but made its way to the Supreme Court of Canada. The arguments turned on the validity of oral tradition and a confrontation between radically opposed visions about what pre-European native society was actually like. Old controversies about savagery and civilization took a new form, shaped by the adversarial nature of the legal system. In a third and somewhat different example we consider the culture of environmental activism, and how two opposing groups engage with political discourse in ways that stand to engender support for their positions.

The Concept of Ownership

If culture is an important aspect of identity and self-respect, then a threat to it cuts very deep indeed. We've mentioned the forced immigration of the Cherokee to Oklahoma along the Trail of Tears, and their "continued loss of tribal knowledge and traditions." Anthropologists have long been concerned about what happens to a people under this kind of stress. Social and psychological breakdown is one possibility. Rebellion is another option, but the law of the stronger generally prevails. Effective resistance or accommodation may have to take another form.

Anthony F.C. Wallace (b. 1923), a Canadian-American anthropologist and historian, became interested in the psychological issues arising as a result of colonial domination. He charted the fate of the Iroquois from their position of strength in the early eighteenth century to their decline and fall as an independent people following the American Revolution (Wallace 1972). They were squeezed into small landhold-ings surrounded by ever-growing American settlements; their religious and political institutions were undercut by missionaries; alcoholism and other symptoms of social disintegration became widespread. Subsequently, an early-nineteenth-century Iroquois prophet—Handsome Lake (1735–1815)—preached a message that promised to lead his people back out of the cultural wilderness through a revival of native practices, accompanied by a new moral code stressing order and self-discipline. His followers became known as "The People of the Longhouse"—the traditional structure in which their rituals are held. Stories were told of the coming of Columbus to the new world and of the "swarms" of white men who came afterwards bringing gambling, frivolous entertainment, and rum that would "turn their minds to foolishness and they will barter their country for baubles; then will this secret poison eat the life from their blood and crumble their bones" (Parker 1913). So the Creator took pity on his people and sent them prophets with instructions on how to set things right again.

The Handsome Lake religion is still practiced by some Iroquois on both sides of the US/Canada border. Wallace found the Handsome Lake religion as it was practiced in the 1950s to be a nostalgic "identification with Indianness itself, with the group of 'real' Iroquois people, as opposed to identification with white men and white-dominated organizations" (1972: 336–37). He generalized his findings to other colo-nial situations and hit on the term "**revitalization movement**" for what Handsome Lake and those like him had accomplished (Wallace 1956). This idea is central to the United Nations Declaration on the Rights of Indigenous Peoples, passed by the UN General Assembly in 2007:

> Indigenous peoples and individuals have the right not to be subjected to forced assimilation or destruction of their culture. Indigenous peoples have the right to practise and revitalize their cultural traditions and customs. This includes the right to maintain, protect and develop the past, present and future manifestations of their cultures, such as archaeological and historical sites, artefacts, designs, ceremonies, technologies and visual and performing arts and literature.
>
> States shall provide redress through effective mechanisms, which may in-clude restitution, developed in conjunction with indigenous peoples, with respect to their cultural, intellectual, religious and spiritual property taken without their free, prior and informed consent or in violation of their laws, traditions and customs. (United Nations 2007)

One outcome of the tendencies expressed in the UN Declaration is the rise of what might be called "cultural nationalism." That said, we return to Vancouver Island and ask what became of the Whaler's Shrine.

HMS *Resolution* arrived off what is now Nootka Sound on Vancouver Island in March 1778. Captain Cook wrote that "we no sooner drew near the inlet than we

PLATE 6.1 Nootka Village

found the coast to be inhabited and the people came off to the Ships in Canoes without showing the least mark of fear or distrust" (Cook 1967: 295). They began to trade with the English at once and kept at it vigorously until the visitors' departure a month later. Cook noted a tendency to theft, but relations between the parties were generally cordial. As always, he was a keen and generally sympathetic observer of the peoples he encountered, noting their great cedar-log canoes, their method of building houses of planks, and their extraordinary ceremonial masks.

Cook observed that, "at the upper end of many apartments, were two large images, or statues placed abreast of each other and 3 or 4 feet asunder, they bore some resemblance to the human figure, but monsterous large. The men on some occasions wore Masks of which they have many and of various sorts such as the human face, the head of birds and other Animals, the most of them both well designed and executed" (1967: 314, 319). He also commented on their concepts of ownership, and early observations like his would play an important role in twentieth-century land-claims disputes: "I must observe that I have no where met with Indians who had such high notions of every thing the Country produced being their exclusive property as these; the very wood and water we took on board they at first wanted us to pay for" (1967: 306).

In the years that followed Cook's visit, the British, the Spanish, the Americans, and the Russians jostled for control and commercial advantage along the Northwest Coast.

PLATE 6.2 Nootka House

Cook's account of his voyage stimulated the trade in fur seal and sea-otter pelts. British settlement on Vancouver Island was stimulated by a desire to keep the Americans out (Johnston 1996). Native peoples were essential players in these early days, and that relationship had inevitable consequences.

Gilbert Malcolm Sproat (1834–1913) documented and lamented some of these changes. He was a Scot in the logging business, and in 1860 he established a camp at Port Alberni, which lies at the head of a long fiord leading into the interior of Vancouver Island from the sea. The British had declared themselves sovereign in the region and sold logging rights to Sproat's company. The local First Nations, of course, knew nothing of this and were not pleased to hear about it: "These were the first savages I had ever seen, and they were probably at that time less known than any aboriginal people under British dominion" (1868: 4). In his memoirs, Sproat recounts his initial conversation with a local chief:

> [I] explained to him that his tribe must move their encampment, as we had bought all the surrounding land from the Queen of England, and wished to occupy the site of the village…. He replied that the land belonged to themselves. "We do not wish to sell our land nor our water; let your friends stay in their own country. We don't care to do as the white men wish." Whether or not," said I, "the white men will come. All your people know that they are your superiors." "We do not want the white man. He steals what we have. We wish to live as we are." (Sproat 1868: 2, 4)

Sproat and his well-armed loggers moved in anyway. But he was curious about the people they were displacing, and over time he developed a greater sympathy for their predicament. He confirmed from his own experience what Cook had said 80 years earlier:

> While ... private property in land is not fully recognized among these people, each tribe maintains the exclusive right of its members to the tribal territory— including all lands periodically or occasionally occupied and used, sites for summer and winter encampments, fishing and hunting grounds and spots for burial—and would strongly resist encroachment upon these places. They believe that their villages existed and were occupied by birds and beasts even before the Indians themselves took human form. What Captain Cook said of this people ... is quite true of these tribes, as tribes. (1868: 80)

He also took note of the **potlatch**—a form of ceremonial gift-giving marking notable occasions such as a marriage, inheriting an important title, or erecting a totem pole: "The principal use ... of an accumulation of personal chattels is to distribute them periodically among invited guests, each of whom is expected to return the compliment by equivalent presents on like occasions" (Sproat 1868: 211). The etiquette of the potlatch—who sits where, who receives what and in what order—is quite elaborate and determined by the rank of the participants and the history of past exchanges (Adams 1973: 51–78).

In his famous essay *The Gift* (see Chapter 4), the French ethnologist Marcel Mauss used the ethnographical methods of Franz Boas and others to examine the potlatch and similar exchange systems.[1] The basic question he asked was, "How do such exchanges create and reinforce a moral bond between those engaged in them?" As noted above, in Chapter 4, Mauss had said that, "in these 'total' social phenomena, as we propose calling them, all kinds of institutions are given expression at one and the same time—religious, juridical, and moral, which relate to both politics and the family; likewise economic ones, which suppose special forms of production and consumption ..." (Mauss 1990: 3).

Even though he was broadly sympathetic to native society, Sproat later came to think that the potlatch had undergone a kind of inflationary process that led to "thriftlessness ... inconsistent with all progress. It is not possible that the Indians can acquire property, or can become industrious with any good result, while under the influence of this mania" (quoted in Cole & Chaikin 1990: 15; see also LaViolette 1961). He encouraged the Canadian government to put a stop to it, and the potlatch was banned in 1884. This measure was a radical attempt to undermine an important social institution in order to set the natives on the path to assimilation—to redirect their local economies from communal redistribution to individual accumulation (Loo 1992). The potlatch went underground, and native people went to jail for practicing it. The ban was ended only in 1951.

Gilbert Sproat looked with some regret on the European seizure of Aboriginal land and reflected on what gave them the right to do it:

> The whole question of the right of any people to intrude on another, and to dispossess them of their country, is one of those questions to which the answer is practically always the same.... The practical answer is given by the determination of intruders under any circumstances to keep what they have obtained; and this, without discussion, is what we, on the west coast of Vancouver Island, were all prepared to do. (1868: 8)

He documented some of the effects of this intrusion. Disease spread outward from the white settlements into native communities. Missions were established but, in his opinion, accomplished little: "Their hunting and fishing places are intruded upon, their social customs disregarded, and their freedom curtailed, by the unwelcome presence, and often unseemly bearing, of those who are stronger than themselves. [The Indian] began soon to disregard his old pursuits, and tribal practices and ceremonies" (Sproat 1868: 278, 289). Sproat leaves us with a picture of a society caught between the old world and the new, fading away because it had lost the will to live. "There is, in my mind, little doubt that colonization on a large scale, by English colonists, practically means the displacing and extinction of the savage native population" (1868: 273).

That caught Charles Darwin's attention. He was in the process of finishing *The Descent of Man* (1871) when he came across Sproat's memoir. Extinction was an important topic, since Darwin was attempting to apply the insights he had developed in *On the Origin of Species* to humanity itself. The subtitle of *The Origin* is "the preservation of favored races in the struggle for life." Given the astonishing human adaptability to all sorts of environmental conditions, Darwin concluded in *The Descent of Man* that "extinction follows chiefly from the competition of tribe with tribe, and race with race" (1998: 189). The Vancouver Islanders were among the many who had lost out, and it looked to him like the Hawaiians were going to share their fate—a regrettable fact, but a fact nevertheless.

Whaler's Shrine

But this isn't what actually happened. As the British and Canadians consolidated their hold over what would become British Columbia, native peoples were allotted land for reserves.[2] On the coast this often meant just the areas around their permanent villages. Most of the rest of the province was declared publicly owned "Crown Land"—which could be leased to logging and mining interests. The way in which this allotment was carried out led to constitutional problems that we'll discuss shortly.

Franz Boas arrived in British Columbia in 1886, having already developed something of a reputation in Germany because of his ethnographic and geographical research on Baffin Island in the Canadian High Arctic. He had also become interested in Northwest Coast art and culture, and that would shape both his career and the general direction of anthropology in the United States and Canada (Cole 1999). His own ethnographic research was mainly among the Kwakiutl (Kwakwaka'wakw) people around Fort Rupert at the northeastern end of Vancouver Island. Ruth Benedict tapped his findings for the Northwest Coast chapter in *Patterns of Culture*, in which she stressed the dramatic nature of the Kwakiutl potlatch ceremonials.

Boas was involved with museums from the start. In 1896 he became Assistant Curator of Ethnology at the American Museum of Natural History in New York. Collecting native artifacts and designing their display spaces became an important element in his career. He documented the ethnographic context of each item, often placing them in their natural settings, using realistic human figures in lifelike poses doing everyday things. The American Museum is proud of its Northwest Coast collection.[3] He traveled widely while conducting his linguistic and ethnographic research, and he employed research assistants to carry on in his absence. One of these was George Hunt (1854–1933), the son of an English Hudson's Bay Company employee and his Alaskan Tlingit wife. Hunt himself married into a Kwakiutl family, was proficient in the language, and became Boas's principal associate. It was this insider status that led him to the Nootka Whaler's Shrine.

Such shrines belonged to high-ranking individuals with a hereditary connection to whaling, a dangerous and highly ritualized activity (Arima & Hoover 2011): "These rituals and the sites in which they were performed were closely guarded secrets known

PLATE 6.3 Yuquot Totem Pole

only to family members" (Jonaitis 1999: 5). They were houses of purification and prayer, in which the ancestors, whose skulls were kept in the shrine, were prayed to for their assistance in the hunt: "A whaler believed that a specific whale gave itself to him, through a mysterious power. Prayer and cleansing the mind and body made the whaler worthy of the great whale's gift of life" (Coté 2010: 34).

Boas had heard of the shrine and wished to acquire it for the American Museum. Though not a Nootka himself, Hunt was able to begin negotiations for purchasing the shrine by virtue of his status as a Kwakiutl shaman and his knowledge of sacred songs. The shrine was in a plank house, and, "as it turned out … the house was filled with human images, some ninety-five, with whale sculptures and human skulls" (Cole 1985: 161). Two chiefs claimed to own the shrine, and they dithered over the asking price (Jonaitis 1999: 62–65). In the end they divided $500, quite a substantial sum in those days: "Hunt had to promise to leave the house alone until all the people were away to the Bering Sea sealery and at the [salmon] canneries in New Westminster. He was to leave Nootka 'so as the Indians think I have not Bought to Keep things Quiet.' The two vendors promised 'that they will work to Bring it out in the night time'" (Cole 1985: 162). However, "the secret was not well kept and … Hunt learned that 'all the Indians is angry about their chief selling it to me.'" Nevertheless the shrine had already been shipped off to the American Museum, where it remains to this day in storage. The place where it once stood is now a Canadian National Historic Site.[4]

By fair means and foul, native artifacts from everywhere made their way into the world's museums and private collections, abetted by a craze for "primitive art" (Price 2001). In fairness to ethnographic collectors like Boas, it should be said that their activities were also driven by the urgent sense that native arts, languages, and cultures must be recorded and preserved before they were gone.

Many indigenous peoples are now keen to defend what they still possess, reclaim what was once theirs, preserve their languages, and revive their artistic traditions. The same applies to human remains, which in the US are covered by the 1990 federal Native American Graves Protection and Repatriation Act. The shelves of American museums are full of Native American bones, dug up over the years by ordinary citizens, archaeologists, and physical anthropologists, including Boas (Cole 1985: 119–21). The Repatriation Act states that they should be returned to native communities if (a) they were found on reservation land and are known to be the lineal ancestors of native people presently living, or (b) claimed by "the Indian tribe that is recognized as aboriginally occupying the area in which the objects were discovered" (US Congress 1990: Sec. 3C-1).[5] If the Whaler's Shrine had been situated in the US, the Act would certainly have applied to it. But this is a cross-border issue, and therefore a question to be settled between the American Museum and the Muchalaht Band. The Museum is unwilling to repatriate the Shrine until the Band has a proper place to safely display it, and the Band is trying to raise the money to build one—in part as an incentive for local tourism. However, "the community itself is divided over whether the shrine should return, and if it does, whether it should be open for public viewing or returned to its original status as a sacred place open only to its owners. Some people say that period in our history is over and we're moving forward. Other people say [the shrine] is very powerful and should come back, and since it left the power of their community has suffered and if it is brought back the power will return" (Lee 2013). The dispute over the Whaler's Shrine was the subject of a 1994 National Film Board of Canada documentary film by anthropologist and filmmaker Hugh Brody. It is called *The Washing of Tears*, and cultural revitalization is the central theme. Brody was also expert witness in an important land-claim case to be discussed below.

The Nuu-chah-nulth have been involved in another repatriation fight, this one over the fate of blood samples that were collected from some of their people in the course of medical genetic research and ended up in England. That issue turns on the meaning of "informed consent," and we'll return to it in Chapter 8.

Traditional Practices, Contemporary Times

The Makah of Washington state are close linguistic and cultural relatives of the Nuu-chah-nulth. They reside around the town of Neah Bay near Cape Flattery at the southern entrance to the Straits of Juan de Fuca, and—like their kin on Vancouver Island—have been traditionally involved in whaling. They were guaranteed that right in the **treaty** they signed with the United States government in 1855 as part of the agreement to move onto their present reservation. Relations with their white neighbors have occasionally been tense, and the Makah have suffered from the same social problems as many other Native American communities.

Anthropologist Elizabeth Colson lived with them in the early 1940s and produced a still relevant ethnography that documents many aspects of their culture as it then was, including their relationship to the land: "For Makah and whites, the features of the landscape may seem to be the same; but so long as ... traditions are repeated and known, the two do not live in the same land; for they do not share a common background of symbolism and each reacts to the land in a different way" (Colson 1953: 49). She speaks of the "latent culture" of the Makah—gone in practice, but still remembered—and the role of oral tradition, which "helps to keep alive a feeling of belonging to a tradition other than the American" (1953: 184). In 1979 the Makah Cultural and Research Center was founded to serve the same end by more formal means—particularly the establishment of a museum:

> The MCRC expresses the Makah sense of continuity between contemporary identity and oral history, songs, objects, and landscape (both land and sea).... The MCRC is an important means for the Makah people to continue to vitalize their ways of knowing. It is also an important means to establish their knowledge as valid in the eyes of outsiders, as part of a self-determination process. The vitalization of their ways of knowing may take the forms of

continuing to remember and honor ancestors … or remembering to care for objects as possessions of ancestors rather than simply as scientific artifacts. (Erikson 1999: 575)

Whaling came to an end in the early twentieth century following the commercial decimation of the whale population. However, the whales have now largely recovered and—with that recovery—the Makah expressed a desire to resume whaling for food and ceremonial purposes. That desire was put into practice in 1999 when—after long deliberation and public controversy—they exercised their treaty rights again and put to sea in a traditional canoe to kill—with a high-powered rifle rather than harpoons—a gray whale. The world's media were treated to the strange spectacle of a whale hunt being conducted in full public view, with the US Coast Guard protecting the Indian hunters from anti-whaling activists, some of them Canadian. Revitalization was a central motivation in bringing back the hunt—restoring the pattern of Makah culture: "Many of our tribal members feel that our health problems result from the loss of our traditional seafood and sea-mammal diet. We would like to restore the meat of the whale to that diet. We also believe that the problems that are troubling our young people stem from lack of discipline and pride and we hope that the restoration of whaling will help restore that. But we also want to fulfill the legacy of our forefathers and restore a part of our culture that was taken from us" (quoted in Erikson

PLATE 6.4 Makah Whaler

1999: 563). Another member of the Makah tribe stated, "Whales are special. And they are wonderful and beautiful. My people do not deny this. And they have remained in our lives and cultures as sacred and respected animals, but they were also once an important food source. Our whaling tradition was and continues to be at the heart of our cultures, our spirituality, and our identities.... When we do harvest a whale, we will not only restore this missing link in our tradition but we will be truly be honoring the spirits of our whaling ancestors" (Coté 2010: 206–7).

And harvest one they did: an adolescent female gray whale. None have been officially hunted since then because of uncertainty over an environmental impact assessment. That story is still being played out. What will happen on Vancouver Island, where there were no treaties, also remains to be seen. Some Nuu-chah-nulth regard what the Makah did as a precedent.

Culture, Law, and the Role of the Anthropologist

The European occupation of North America was a complicated affair: the Spanish in the southeast and southwest, the French along the St. Lawrence River and interior fur-trade routes, the English expanding westward from their first settlements in Virginia and Massachusetts Bay. Given the strength of Indian nations such as the Iroquois, it became British policy to handle relations between them through treaties. The new American government undertook to honor the treaties the British had made, and began negotiating new ones of its own. In Canada the treaty-making process continued westward into what are now the Prairie provinces of Manitoba, Saskatchewan, and Alberta.[6] But there it stopped. British Columbia was settled mainly from the other direction, eastward from the Pacific coast, and there was no organized treaty process at all. Instead, the province allocated reserves to local native people according to its own estimation of what was required for their subsistence. This became a constitutional issue in our own time.

First Nations argued that the precedent established in the east should also have been followed in the far west, and that there is still a lot of unfinished business to do. The provincial government countered that native rights had been "extinguished" when the British Crown declared its sovereignty over the region. Court decisions at the federal level undercut that argument. This led to the initiation of an ongoing treaty process in British Columbia—very difficult and slow (and expensive) three-way negotiations between Canada, the province, and local First Nations bands.[7]

That's the context of the case that concerns us here. In 1987 the Gitksan and Wet'suwet'en peoples launched an action in the Supreme Court of British Columbia seeking to gain title and governing authority over 22,000 square miles of territory surrounding the Skeena River Valley in the north central part of the province.[8] Both are interior groups, living along the Skeena and its tributaries, but both are coastal with regard to artistic traditions and social practices such as potlatching. The countryside above the rivers is remote and rugged.

So what does anthropology have to do with all this? First, the case turned on the relation between oral tradition and historical fact, a subject of long concern to anthropologists, biblical scholars, and folklorists.[9] Second, it involved a debate about concepts of ownership and the nature of government in tribal societies. Third, it revisited controversies that have been around since the seventeenth century about the nature of civilization, savagery, and social progress. and finally, several anthropologists spoke in support of the native claim. This case therefore also involves the role of anthropologists as advocates and the status of anthropology as an objective science.[10]

The success of the Aboriginal case depended on convincing the court of the historical relevance of their **oral traditions**. The most important goal was to demonstrate that they did indeed have definite ideas about land ownership before the Europeans arrived—that tradition pointed to long-standing occupation and uninterrupted use of salmon streams and the resources in the mountains surrounding their river-valley settlements. "Occupation" and "use" are the key words here; proof that they had existed since early times would back up the claim to collective title.

But it's misleading and ethnocentric to think about these matters in exclusively Western legal terms. Pre-European conceptions were aspects of a "total social phenomenon"—involving ecological relations, land, religious conceptions, the arts, social rank, and politically important exchange relationships between groups as expressed in the potlatch. As John Cove, an anthropologist who worked with the Gitksan during the 1970s and 1980s, points out, "A house was deemed to have title to a territory because it had merged its essence with a piece of land. That essence was its stock of supernatural powers acquired by ancestors of the House from spirits who had taken on physical forms to live in the same domain as humans" (1982: 7). These encounters with spirits in animal form, as recited in songs and stories, are what gave a House the right to use specific carved images on its totem pole—symbolizing that group's claim to a particular piece of territory and the mythic stories that went with it. As we've seen, Gilbert Sproat had also remarked on this. Cove continues: "Resources on a House territory were not seen as 'things' merely there for its members use. Rather, a House had a special and exclusive relationship not only to its lands but to everything in or on them. A territory was a House's sacred space which it shared with other beings.... All having similar underlying form, consciousness, and varying degrees of power. Relations to them were not seen as unilateral and exploitative, but rather reciprocal and moral" (1982: 8).

Of course, many things had changed between the early days and the late 1980s when the Delgamuukw case began. Nevertheless, Cove found that "myths, names, crests, songs, feasts and Houses [remain] integral components of contemporary culture; as are traditional patterns of resource exploitation on House territories. Gitksan involvement in the land claims movement can be seen as an attempt to re-establish in a more complete way their relations to these territories" (1982: 14). The potlatch was certainly alive and well into modern times: "That the potlatch survives today in a state of considerable complexity is undoubtedly due to its value in the Natives' eyes

PLATE 6.5 Gitksan Village

as a means of furthering their land claims against the government. But it is also a touchstone of Indian identity in a world increasingly dominated by the Whiteman's values" (Adams 1973: 12). Traditional stories were family property, and the plaintiffs represented them at the trial as an essential part of the rituals validating chiefly titles and hence land-use rights. One Wet'suwet'en elder put it this way: "I always knew that the land that went with the chief's name would come to me some day. It isn't something I could just reach out and grab. It doesn't work that way. It isn't something that was made up. It was given to us and handed down in unwritten records, mouth to mouth. It was drilled into us around the campfires. It was drilled into our forefathers" (Mills 1994a: 119; see also 1994b and 2005).

The trial judge—Allan McEachern (1926–2008), Chief Justice of the BC Supreme Court—viewed such evidence as largely "hearsay"; it also contained mythological elements, and therefore it was seen as an unreliable guide to what went on in real time. The claimants responded that these stories were recited at potlatches, and therefore validated on each occasion that a title was passed on. The community as a whole served as witness. Nevertheless the Justice concluded:

> the plaintiffs have a romantic view of their history which leads them to believe their remote ancestors were always in specific parts of the territory, in perfect

harmony with natural forces, actually doing what the plaintiffs remembered their immediate ancestors were doing in the early years of [the twentieth] century. They believe the lands their grandparents used have been used by their ancestors from the beginning of time. When I come to consider events long past, I am driven to conclude on all the evidence, that much of the plaintiffs' historical evidence is not literally true. I am not able to find that the ancestors of the plaintiffs were using all of the territory for the length of time required for the creation of aboriginal rights. (McEachern 1991: 49)

He had a similar opinion concerning the general nature of pre-colonial native society. A few quotations illustrate the stark contrast between the Gitksan view expressed in their opening statement at the trial and that of the judge in his final decision:

The Aboriginal View (Wa and Delgamuukw 1992)	The Crown's View (McEachern 1991)
"For us, the ownership of territory is a marriage of the Chief and the land. Each Chief has an ancestor who encountered and acknowledged the life of the land. From such encounters come power. The land, the plants, the animals and the people all have spirit—they all must be shown respect. That is the basis of our law."	"Aboriginal life … was far from stable and it stretches credulity to be believe that remote ancestors considered themselves bound to specific territories. They governed themselves in their villages and immediately surrounding areas to the extent necessary for communal living, eking out an aboriginal life."
"By following the law, the power flows from the land to the people through the chief; by using the wealth of the territory, the [matrilineal] House feasts its Chief so he can properly fulfill the law. This cycle has been repeated on my land for thousands of years."	"I am not persuaded their ancestors practiced universal or even uniform customs relating to land outside their villages. It cannot be said that they owned or governed such vast … tracts of land in any sense that would be recognized by the law."
"My power is carried in my House's histories, songs, dances and crests. It is recreated at the Feast when the histories are told, the songs and dances performed, and the crests displayed. With the wealth that comes from respectful use of the territory … the law, the Chief, the territory, and the Feast become one."	"The primitive condition of the natives described by early observers is not impressive. Being of a culture where everyone looked after himself or perished, the Indians knew how to survive (in most years). They became a conquered people, not by force of arms … but by an invading culture and a relentless energy.…"

Looking at these two versions of reality side by side is like contrasting Jean-Jacques Rousseau with Thomas Hobbes (see Chapter 3). Rousseau saw Aboriginal America as more "virtuous" than corrupt old Europe—like the Garden of Eden from which the collective ancestors of the human race were expelled when they ate the forbidden fruit. These, of course, are images—but so were those of the lawyers and witnesses used to defend the province against the native land claim. Justice McEachern believed that concepts of land ownership had once been very vague, but crystallized with the coming of the fur trade and the necessity to control trap-lines. He believed that Aboriginal society was in a state of constant low-level war, and cited Hobbes himself (misspelling Hobbes's name) in his "Reasons for Judgment": "there is no doubt, to quote Hobbs [sic], that aboriginal life in the territory was, at best, 'nasty, brutish and short'" (McEachern 1991: 13).

He spoke about native people living in a "communal" society but also about this being "a culture in which everyone looked after himself or perished." He used the phrase "eking out an aboriginal life," when the evidence shows that in fact these societies were generally capable of sustaining themselves in reasonable comfort and generating enough surplus for their potlatch system. If the native witnesses were inconsistent in their testimony about what lands were actually used, Justice McEachern was inconsistent in his views on the nature of pre-European society.

But the final judgment was unequivocal. The Gitksan/We'suet'en would retain exactly the same rights they had before the case began, and no more—the use of traditional fishing sites, and the right to hunt and gather on otherwise unused Crown Land. To participate in the modern economy, they would have to join it: "The plaintiff's claims for ownership of and jurisdiction over the territory, and for aboriginal rights in the territory are dismissed" (McEachern 1991: 297).[11]

The testimony of the anthropologists serving as expert witnesses for the First Nations got the same treatment. There were three: Antonia Mills and Richard Daly, both of whom had lived and worked with the Gitksan and Wet'suwet'en; the third, Hugh Brody, had worked with groups in the north of the province, mapping trap lines and hunting territories. The result of Brody's research was a notable book—*Maps and Dreams*—that contrasted Western ideas about the land with those of the people he worked with (Brody 1981). As in the present case he found that Euro-Canadian concepts are utilitarian and individualistic; native concepts are spiritual and communal—a mystical relationship.

McEachern dismissed the testimony of all three because of supposed pro-native bias and lack of scientific objectivity. One was singled out because "he made it abundantly plain that he was very much on the side of the plaintiffs" (1991: 50). The statement of professional ethics of the American Anthropological Association became an issue here, and the Justice quoted it: "In research, anthropologists' paramount responsibility is to those they study. When there is a conflict of interest, these individuals must come first. Anthropologists must do everything in their power to protect the physical, social, and psychological welfare and to honor the dignity and privacy of those studied."[12] The implication is that anthropologists can *never* give unbiased testimony if it goes against the interests of the people they've worked with; they must either distort the facts or hold their tongues. Justice McEachern concluded in sorrow that "it is always unfortunate when experts become too close to their clients" (1991: 51).

He expected his decision to be appealed, and it was—eventually making its way to the Supreme Court of Canada. This time there was a radical change in direction. Two major flaws were identified in the original judgment in the light of legal precedents at the federal level: devaluing the use of oral tradition as evidence and restricting Aboriginal economic rights to traditional subsistence practices:

> The factual findings made at trial could not stand because of the trial judge's treatment of the various kinds of oral histories. The oral histories were used in an attempt to establish occupation and use for the disputed territory which is an essential requirement for aboriginal title.... Had the oral histories been correctly assessed, the conclusions on these issues of fact might have been very different.... The courts [must] come to terms with the oral histories of aboriginal societies, which, for many aboriginal nations, are the only record of their past.... Those histories play a crucial role in the litigation of aboriginal rights. (Persky 1998: 84, 75)

On the land issue, the Supreme Court concluded that the First Nations retained Aboriginal title—a right to the land itself, and that its use does not have to be restricted to traditional subsistence practices. Its economic potential can be enhanced, though not in such a way as to "destroy" the land's value to the community as a whole. Such activities could include forestry, mining, and commercial fish farming, if conducted in an ecologically sensitive manner. In the Supreme Court's opinion, the original judgment had hopelessly stacked the deck against the Aboriginal claimants and blocked their chance for economic progress as peoples—condemning them to live in rural ghettoes on the fringes of the white-dominated economy. The matter was sent back to the province for consideration, with the hope that these issues could be resolved through negotiation. This decision formed part of the background to still ongoing treaty negotiations.[13]

Cultural Survival

These are complex tales, typical of our times. They involve new concepts of human rights that have emerged slowly and painfully over the years—sometimes taking the form of declarations of general principles or legislation on a national level. Getting "rights" enshrined in law changes the nature of the debate. In Chapter 4 you saw how the Baby Veronica case has played out, and in this chapter we've described a similar process at work with regard to cultural property and land claims. A lot of money can be at stake, too, since identity issues are also economic issues. In western Canada much of the legal action has been aimed at providing rural First Nations peoples with a viable economic base in the form of natural resources; in urban settings the goal is the acquisition of land for real estate and commercial development.

If we look elsewhere, Australia for example, the same tendencies are at work, and there have been legal actions similar to the ones described above. In the United States there are advantages in having official recognition as an Indian tribe; federal benefits come with that status, as does exemption from local taxes (Clifford 1988). But these developments are all part of a bigger picture—the discourse of cultural survival and renewal. One sign of the times is the founding in 1972 of an organization called Cultural Survival and its journal *Cultural Survival Quarterly* by two Harvard anthropologists who worked in the Amazon region. The initial impetus was the effect of natural resource development on South American tribal peoples, a problem that is even more acute today. Cultural Survival has also become interested in "the much-needed revitalization of critically endangered Native American languages"—a serious concern among Canadian First Nations and Aboriginal Australians as well.[14]

The movement to reclaim cultural property has affected many museums with ethnographic collections, and formal procedures have been adopted to deal with such issues. The Department of Anthropology at the American Museum of Natural History, for example, has an office devoted to this problem.[15] As we have seen with the Whaler's Shrine and the Makah Museum, the establishment of such institutions on native soil is in itself an important aspect of cultural preservation and revitalization.

Those with a skeptical take on such things have suggested that all this makes "culture" into a more solid object than it actually is, more like a brand or trademark (Brown 2003). Questions can also be raised about cultural "authenticity" and about who gets to decide what is authentic or not. And this applies to personal status as well. In the last chapter we raised questions about personal and national identity, and asked who is *really* anything? Who, for example, is *really* an Aboriginal Australian, or eligible for nationally recognized status as First Nations or Native American? In the next and final section of this chapter, we take a look at the culture concept from a slightly different angle. Instead of culture as a thing to possess or an identity one is born into, we consider the culture of activism, an identity that one chooses as a result of circumstance.

Analyzing a Conflict: Activism and Land Use

In this chapter we have considered how cultural symbols and meaning are embodied by things, spaces, and activities. When aspects of one's culture are threatened, the reaction is to push back. This pushback takes many forms, but no matter how we look at it, **activism** also brings people together. There is a common struggle, a perceived wrongdoing, and a motivation to enact change.

Anthropologist Terre Satterfield (2002) explores the culture of activism in the United States through an in-depth, ethnographic study of the intense dispute over old-growth logging and the protection of the northern spotted owl in Oregon's rain forests. Her research participants are two groups of opposing activists: the Forest Community Movement, consisting of small-scale loggers, and the Ancient Forest Movement, consisting of environmentalists. Satterfield explores how each group attempts to achieve its desire for a changed social world by engaging and manipulating political discourses, conceptions of morality, and symbolic tools. Satterfield is not concerned with who is right or wrong in this dispute; rather, she is interested in *how* each group expresses its agenda: "Rather than thinking of conflict as a contest of political, economic, and scientific forces (which it certainly is), I choose as my primary objective to draw attention to how these forces are expressed culturally in the impassioned wrangling of locally situated and politically committed loggers and environmentalists" (2002: 3).

While an individual's cultural identity is related to a host of categories, including ethnicity, gender, and age, an activist *chooses* to organize with others based on shared beliefs and solutions for dealing with a perceived threat or condition. Their shared position may be based on a shared ethnicity, for example, as is the case with First Nations who are actively engaged in movements for cultural repatriation. What sets them apart from others who share their ethnicity but do not identify as activists is their decision to unite and resist. Activists have organized in retaliation to a perceived threat to their right to exist, such as a threat to their livelihood, to their belief system, or to their right to expression. Examining a conflict illuminates how ideas and arguments (or discourse) are interpreted and embodied by the individuals involved. The identity they assume in terms of their activism is only one of many identities that these individuals embody: they are mothers and fathers, they work in the city or in the country, they are men and women, they are university graduates or have technical diplomas—the list goes on.

We are all familiar with the two groups engaged in the conflict, at least superficially. On the one hand are the "timber activists" or loggers—the popular image of these men (for it is almost always men) has changed over the last 50 years, from a wholesome and hard-working profession to one composed of unintelligent and rootless men. Cultural identity is not immune to the influences of changing political and economic forces, and the image of the logger certainly reflects the popularity of conservation. Loggers are rarely thought of as grassroots activists; however, the loggers whom Satterfield encountered strove to be taken seriously as legitimate activists wrongly portrayed in the media. Rather than dumb, careless men unconcerned for the future of the forests, they were men with families to feed and mortgages to pay who were simply trying to make a living in a dangerous, strenuous, and necessary profession. They were not big industry, but small business owners trying to make ends meet. One man described loggers as being "like eggs; tough on the outside, soft on the inside" (2002: 51).

The figure of the environmentalist evokes quite a different image. In contrast to loggers, popular conceptions of the environmentalists portray them as well-educated city dwellers who outfit themselves in Gore-Tex and hiking boots on the weekends. We are very familiar with the environmentalist as activist, for the media have done a great job of documenting Greenpeace activists chaining themselves to trees or circling whaling boats off the coast of Russia. While many of the environmentalists that Satterfield spoke with and observed appeared to be sympathetic toward the loggers' plight (especially those who lived locally and counted the loggers as their neighbors), the protection of the trees and habitat was their primary concern.

PLATE 6.6 Greenpeace Protester

While issues of class and gender are ever present within these two groups, they are not defining characteristics. Instead, it is their individual identities as loggers or environmentalists that unite them collectively. One way of understanding the worldview of each of these groups is to consider the types of discourse used by each to get their point across. Satterfield took note of the various slogans she encountered during her fieldwork. These messages appeared on bumper stickers, on posters, on signs stuck on the side of the road, on lawns, and in stores (keep in mind—this research was pre-Twitter and pre-Facebook!). These slogans provide an effective, if simplistic, summary of each side's position on the conflict. Decorating the side of the Forest Service Road, one sign read, "If environmentalists could have their way, we [timber activists, one assumes] would live from day-to-day. The spotted owl and the seal would thrive, and you and I could not survive" (2002: 42). Another bumper sticker jeered, "Do you have a job or are you an environmentalist?" At a Spirit of the Earth Activist Conference, large slogans adorned the walls. Posters read, "You may not like living with us now, but conservationists make great ancestors" and "We don't inherit the earth from our ancestors, we borrow it from our children" (quoted in Satterfield 2002: 55). Here we see the two sides at work—timber activists embody the here and now. Their struggle has immediate consequences to their lives and those around them. Environmentalists, on the other hand, focus on the future. What we do today will have serious consequences for future generations.

Of particular interest to Satterfield were the ways in which these two opposing groups engaged with language and concerns as if the other group did not exist. She examined popular discussions and debates surrounding nature that both loggers and environmentalists drew from, and the ways in which the arguments and stance of each activist group interacted with one another. Both activist groups challenged and conformed to the dominant ideas of scientific, congressional, economic, or corporate bodies who were able to construct and impose their version of reality as seemingly "natural" (2002: 7). One body of discourse that both groups engaged with, albeit in very different ways, was the assumption of a shared vision of forest management with Aboriginal groups. As we have already encountered during our examination of the Gitksan and Wet'suwet'en peoples' land-claim case and Justice Allan McEachern's ruling, the construction of Aboriginal peoples by European explorers, philosophers, and politicians has not always been accurate or pleasant. Generally, this construction has taken the form of two interpretations: that of the "**noble savage**" and that of the "**savage beast**." Both constructions operate on **essentialist** understandings of Aboriginal peoples' way of life, spirituality, and knowledge forms. The noble-savage construct refers to the notion that "there are simple people, living in an Edenic landscape and gentle climate, whose powers of reason and ability to live in harmony with nature ensure relief from the evils of civilization" (Satterfield 2002: 100). In contrast, the savage-beast construct portrays Aboriginal peoples as living in a constant state of violence, disorganization, and chaos. While these two culturally constructed interpretations are based on outdated and racist understandings of human diversity, their use continues to be accepted by many non-Aboriginals as true understandings of the "nature" of Aboriginal life.

Satterfield explores how the environmentalist movement has appropriated the "noble savage legacy" to legitimize its own cause. For many activists, drawing on Aboriginal practices reflects their continued commitment to protecting the earth and adds a sense of "cultural authenticity to activists' imaginings of future land-use practices" (2002: 120). Because many environmentalists do not live in rural areas, nor do they work in forestry disciplines, their legitimacy is less substantiated than that of the loggers who live and work on the land. Their ability to align themselves with Aboriginal peoples who, many believe, "effortlessly embody principles of Western conservation" adds authenticity to their argument (2002: 134).

Loggers are also in need of a means to validate their "right" to legitimacy over the land, and they often attempt to dismantle the notion of ecological nobility that environmentalists preach is at the heart of Aboriginal relationships to the land. Loggers draw a parallel between Aboriginal land use and knowledge with their own approach to maintaining the land, suggesting that they too deserve a level of public respect similar to what is afforded Aboriginal peoples. Just as Aboriginals claim that their use of the land is part of their "cultural" way of life, loggers argue that their way of life is also cultural. For example, many loggers argue that their way of forest management is simply another method that has evolved over time, and that Aboriginal peoples themselves managed the forest using fire, a comparison that attempts to illustrate that the forest must be managed, and indeed always has been. The voices of the Aboriginal peoples themselves are noticeably absent in both these instances: "Aboriginal peoples are caught up in a pro/anti dialogue not of their own making—a dialogue between competing White activists (loggers and environmentalists) that, at times, is ugly, racist and dehumanizing. It is a dialogue that reduces Aboriginal peoples to unidimensional strategic and counter-strategic implements caught in the crossfire of the struggle over Oregon's forests" (2002: 121).

While you may identify with the loggers, with the environmentalists, or with neither group, you may not find any relevance in this discussion to your own life. Regardless of your opinion, however, one cannot dispute that the environment is a hot political topic that transcends national borders and political parties. Politicians continually talk of their efforts to enact policies that will protect endangered species and vulnerable areas of land, while at the same time forging ahead with economic endeavors that are potentially disastrous for the environment. Celebrities endorse and create TV shows and documentaries that aim to educate and stimulate young people to get involved in protecting the environment. The word "green" has been slapped onto anything that can be recycled, and magazines and newspapers are full of articles about how to minimize your "ecological footprint." So what are the discourses and ideologies that inform these debates? What images are continually relied upon in order to make a lasting and effective argument? How do issues of class, gender, and race come into play? By considering how one debate in a local, specific context was constructed and enacted, we have gained a better understanding of some of the popular discourse that surrounds all environmental debates in North America.

Conclusion

In this chapter we have focused mainly on the politics of culture in the Pacific Northwest, given the relevance of the cases we describe to the history of North American anthropology. However, cultural politics can be found everywhere and is easy enough to spot once you know what you're looking for. The question takes on added levels of complexity in multiethnic/multicultural societies where there are many alternative ways of living, being, and seeing, and it becomes increasingly difficult to find a common denominator among the competing voices. Just look around you.

Notes

1   Another such system was the *kula* exchanges of the Trobriands in the southwest Pacific, where Malinowski worked in the early years of the twentieth century (see Chapter 1).

2   Gilbert Sproat became a central figure in the allotment process in the southern interior of BC. He attempted to allot land sufficient for the economic needs of local First Nations and ran into trouble with white settlers because of it.

3   See http://www.amnh.org/exhibitions/permanent-exhibitions/human-origins-and-cultural-halls/hall-of-northwest-coast-indians.

4   See http://www.historicplaces.ca/en/rep-reg/place-lieu.aspx?id=17981. An overview of the history of the controversy and a detailed examination of the elements in the shrine can be found in Jonaitis 1999. Going back to the late eighteenth century, Jonaitis also looks at the ways in which the shrine has been represented by academic writers and the popular media.

5   This is Public Law 101–601: An Act to Provide for the Protection of Native American Graves. The Law also applies to native Hawaiian remains.

6   Whether these treaties were honored, or even properly understood when first signed, is another matter.

7   For historical background see Tennant 1990.

8   The case is known as "Delgamuukw v. The Queen." "Delgamuukw" is a clan title held by the original plaintiff in the case, a Gitksan elder named Ken Muldoe, who was acting on behalf of the Gitksan and Wet'suwet'en as a whole. "The Queen" means, in this instance, the province of British Columbia.

9   For a general introduction to the topic see Vansina 1985.

10 For the full details of the case and its anthropological relevance see Culhane 1998.

11 The proceedings lasted three years. The "Reasons for Judgment" document is itself 394 pages long, which is an indication of the importance attached to this case.

12 See http://www.aaanet.org/profdev/ethics/ (1971 Statement; amended 1986).

13 There is still no Gitksan treaty. Though one is being negotiated, it looks like the process has some way to go. See http://www.gov.bc.ca/arr/firstnation/gitxsan/.

14 See http://www.culturalsurvival.org/node/10279.

15 See http://anthropology.si.edu/repatriation/. The Canadian Museum of History has a detailed policy to deal with repatriation claims: http://www.civilization.ca/about-us/corporation/about-the-corporation/repatriation-policy.

Study Questions

1   How do Franz Boas and Ruth Benedict define culture?
2   Explain how places, things, and activities embody cultural meaning, using examples from the chapter.
3   Explain why Sproat encouraged the Canadian government to ban the potlatch.
4   Outline the history and controversy surrounding the Whaler's Shrine.
5   Explain why the Makah tribe believed whaling was such an important part of their culture.

6   Compare and contrast Justice McEachern's ruling and the decision of the
     Supreme Court of Canada in the Skeena River Valley land claim.
7   What makes the culture of activism different from other social categories such
     as ethnicity, gender, and age?
8   How did both the environmentalists and the loggers studied by Satterfield
     associate their position with that of Aboriginal peoples? What was wrong with
     this appropriation of Aboriginal culture?

Discussion Questions

1   What is "cultural property," and what rules should apply to its ownership and
     control? Where do the museums stand in all this?
2   Justice McEachern dismissed the evidence put forth by the three anthropolo-
     gists who testified as expert witnesses. What do you think about his decision?
     Should their testimonies have been allowed to stand? Why or why not?
3   Consider an activist group you are familiar with. What types of discourse do
     they utilize to get their message across? Is it effective? Why or why not?
4   How far are you willing to go in your toleration of foreign ways: does it extend
     to whaling, to female circumcision, to arranged marriages, to the wearing of
     prominent religious symbols, to the eating of dogs, dolphins, or chimpanzees,
     etc.? If there are limits, what are they and why?

CHAPTER 7

//

Understanding Gender

LEARNING OBJECTIVES

After reading this chapter, students should be able to

- identify the differences between gender, sex, and sexuality;
- understand gender as a social construct in contrast to the concept of biological determinism, and the social systems that contribute to that construct;
- discuss the importance of a "holistic" approach to the study of gender;
- outline and discuss the work of Thorne and Pascoe among American youth and explain the use of *feminist* and *queer theoretical approaches*;
- summarize Fong's methods and findings surrounding China's one-child policy and the effect on singleton daughters in urban areas; and
- outline Nanda's study of the *hijras* in India and discuss the value of a cross-cultural approach to studying gender.

KEY TERMS

biological determinism	gender	patriarchy
caste	gender role	queer theory
feminist theoretical	hetero-masculinity	transgender
perspective	interpretive perspective	transsexual

Introduction

In this chapter we will explore how **gender** is realized in relation to the social organization of society. What do we mean by gender? The usual answer is to say that sex is a matter of biology and that gender is socially constructed—a set of local ideas related in some way to the biological "fact" of sex. Ideas about gender distinction, however, are not everywhere the same as they are in "mainstream" Euro-North American society, which itself is diverse in attitudes and practices. Some cultural traditions, such as those found in regions of India, have a place for a gender that is neither male nor female. This role is not defined in terms of a contrast between "female" and "male," but is rather a matter of degree, of "more" or "less." In North American society, we often remark that some men are more masculine than others and some women more feminine. What does it mean to say so, and what does it tell us about our own cultural values?

Masculinity and femininity are *social* constructions that must be considered alongside other social categories such as childhood, adolescence, adulthood, and old age. Gender identity varies across an individual's life course—babies, children, and the elderly tend to be regarded differently than when they are in the prime of their reproductive years. Anthropologists consider such issues on the basis of their ethnographic experiences, and their observations have had a great impact on North American public consciousness.

Biologically speaking, we have two primary sexes and several possibilities that stand outside of these two options (inter-sexed individuals with characteristics of both sexes; people with a surplus of X or Y chromosomes). Until quite recently, the nature of sexual identity and reproduction was pretty much a mystery to everyone, and in certain ways it still is. The way the collective imagination tries to explain the mysteries of sexuality relates to the broader structure of society, including the distribution of power within it. In studying gender, we are on the track of deeper issues involving the social definition of personhood, which in turn relates to worldview, religion, economics, and law. These are not just academic concerns: they are as important on a personal level as anything could possibly be, and they are fought over every day in legal courts around the world.

In this chapter we will explore gender and sexuality by considering how these social categories are realized within a particular cultural context. This chapter is heavy on ethnographic case studies, for we feel that gaining a better understanding of a somewhat abstract category such as gender (as well as kinship, race, and religion) is best accomplished through the exploration of how these categories are actually embodied and experienced in the daily lives of individuals around the world. Through case studies, we will see how anthropologists have applied theory to their observations and data, what methods they have used to collect data and arrive at their conclusions, and the significance of this knowledge to how we think about society.

We will begin by considering how gender is learned in a North American context through two ethnographic examples that explore gender from within the American educational system. Barrie Thorne's *Gender Play* considers how elementary school children learn gender behaviors, while C.J. Pascoe investigates masculinity and sexuality in an American high school in her provocatively titled ethnography, *Dude, you're a fag*. Both authors employ a feminist theoretical perspective to make sense of their observations and data. We will consider how this theoretical perspective shapes the perceptions of each author. We will continue our discussion by looking at how China's one-child policy has impacted urban "singleton" daughters born after the policy was implemented. While Vanessa Fong's research demonstrates how gender norms and behaviors have been transformed as a result of the rapid industrialization of the Chinese economy, she also illustrates that cultural understandings of gender are closely related to kinship relations and obligations. Finally, we will conclude our discussion of gender and sexuality by exploring Serena Nanda's ethnography *Neither Man nor Woman*. Nanda's cross-cultural analysis of gender roles employs a comparative approach to "explain alternative gender roles by correlating their presence with other cultural characteristics" (Nanda 1999: 145). A comparative approach operates on the assumption that understanding gender roles in a particular society requires the consideration of other social factors, such as social hierarchy and religion. A cross-cultural analysis that is informed by an interpretive perspective allows for an investigation that does not simplify social systems or discount the people within them, but gives space for the complexity of each situation to be fully considered.

We "Do" Gender

In many Western societies, the term **gender role** is used to describe the seemingly different sets of actions and behaviors associated with girls and boys, men and women. Gender is most often conceived as dichotomous and simply an extension of biological sex. Despite the frequency with which we hear that women are "naturally" (i.e., biologically) more nurturing and better at raising children, while men are "naturally" more ambitious and better at occupying the most powerful positions in the workforce, these roles are cultural constructs. These roles are not universal because they are not biological. Notions of **biological determinism**, in which there is a direct correlation between cultural characteristics regarding gender (or race, or class) with biological traits, has been largely disproved. This way of thinking is continually reinforced and perpetuated by everyday conversations and actions that, however subconsciously, serve to reinforce the idea that girls and boys behave in specific ways that are pre-determined at birth. One need only look cross-culturally to find examples of gender roles that do not fit what many in the West take for granted as "natural." For example, in much of rural Thailand, the difference in physical size between men and women is minimal, the clothing they wear is very similar, and both perform agricultural tasks that are often interchangeable (Miller, Van Esterik, & Van Esterik 2001). While gender roles exist, they are not the same as those found in Euro-Western cultures, which one would assume they would be if gender were in fact biological.

Gender is socially constructed. We "learn" how to be male and female through the social acts that make up the everyday, such as interacting with our family, meeting people and developing friendships, attending school, being employed, watching TV and movies, etc. Within minutes of being born, we are wrapped in pink or blue blankets and our education begins. As sociologist Barrie Thorne states, "gender is not something one passively 'is' or 'has' ... we 'do' gender" (1994: 5). Of course, people are not mindless drones who go about their lives accepting everything they are taught—far from it. The idea that we are socialized into behaving a certain way can become very problematic if we do not consider the agency of the individual. Otherwise, people would be nothing more than inactive bodies with little or no control over their own behavior and beliefs. Culturally defined behaviors and beliefs are very powerful; however, we must be cognizant of the fact that there are many exceptions to these rules.

So how do we go about understanding gender? We continually return to the statement that theory steers perception. Understanding the social organization and relationships of a community or society, whether one is focusing on gender, economics, politics or religion, requires that anthropologists have some way of organizing their thoughts and observations theoretically, so that they don't emerge from the field with a mass of notes that in the end remains, well, a mass of notes! How they make sense of these ideas and observations is dependent on their theoretical perspective.

Anthropology conducted from a **feminist theoretical perspective** operates on the assumption that all social relations and the knowledge of these relations are gendered. Gender, therefore, must be considered alongside class, race, and age as a fundamental social category. Feminists argue that knowledge of the social world has traditionally been taught and learned from a male-centered perspective, and women's experiences, positions, and beliefs have been marginalized and ignored. Women's experiences are extremely diverse, and issues such as class position and ethnicity affect a woman's experience of the world around her. It is therefore not enough to simply consider all women as victims of oppression simply because they are women; rather, the specific circumstances and social position of the woman herself must always be considered. An Australian corporate executive will have a very different experience of employment than that of a Peruvian rural farmer. Simply being a woman does not unite them in a shared oppression, and ignoring individual circumstances overlooks the class and race oppression that many women experience. Feminist anthropologists desire to reshape how knowledge is gathered and interpreted; simply including women in the scope of study does not qualify as a feminist approach.

Feminist research is characterized by a desire to empower women and eliminate oppression, and such research is conducted for the purpose of enacting social change. Moreover, the relationship between the researcher and researched is open and subjective, and the quest for objectivity is considered to be impossible. Feminism is characterized by a multiplicity of sub-fields, including liberal, radical, and Marxist feminism, to name just a few. We will consider two ethnographic examples of research conducted through a feminist lens on the topic of gender.

Gender on the Playground

Barrie Thorne explored gender norms and behaviors by employing a feminist perspective during her ethnographic fieldwork in an elementary school in California in the late 1970s and early 1980s. While this research was conducted over 30 years ago, Thorne provides valuable insight into the various ways in which children "learn" to be boys and girls in the public education system. Thorne's approach to studying children was distinctive, for rather than *observing* kids and *talking* to the teachers and other adults in the school, Thorne both observed and talked to the children themselves. As a result, her findings highlight a number of misleading assumptions about gender behavior in kids that we will explore below. Her approach also exemplifies the importance of two central anthropological tenets—an individual's experience, and context.

Researchers continually look at children as a group in order to understand gender construction, perhaps as an attempt to see the person "in the raw" before the social world fully shapes them into behaving one way or another. In much of this social-scientific and developmental psychology research, children are regarded as adults in the making (James and Prout 1997; Caputo 1995). Their behavior and attitudes are examined with an eye to the future—how will this behavior affect their development in later years? Discussions in the media illustrate that this is a topic that continues to ignite passionate debate. For example, retail giant J.Crew was the focus of such debate when in April 2011, company president Jenna Lyons posed for a photo with her five-year-old son while painting his toenails fluorescent pink. Conservative pundits raged with claims that Lyons was participating in "blatant propaganda celebrating transgendered children," while others rushed to her defense, proclaiming that painting toenails had nothing to do with sexuality. *Forbes* online magazine covered the story, and it sparked debates in print and television media for days (Phillips 2011). Clearly, gender identity and behavior in children is a hot topic in the Western world.

Thorne positions her young research participants as a group who "act, resist, rework and create; they influence adults as well as being influenced by them" (1994: 3). She challenges adults (i.e., teachers and parents, etc.) to consider children's actions as important in the present, and to recognize that they are not simply passive recipients of socialization. To do this requires an awareness of how one's assumptions and stereotypes inform understandings of gendered behavior in children. Parents and other adults tend to exhibit a phenomenon labeled by sociologist Michael Messner as "believing is seeing"—individuals choose what they would like to believe is true rather than allowing what they see to inform their beliefs.

To many teachers and parents that Thorne spoke with, instances that did not fit within a stereotype were regarded as exceptions to the "rule" of gendered behavior rather than evidence of there being many ways to behave as a girl or boy. An often-cited example of the fundamental differences between girls and boys is how they seem to play with those of the same sex. This research, primarily from the field of developmental psychology, has been explained both by evolutionary arguments

(Pellegrini 2009) and through socialization (Fabes, Martin, & Hanish 2003; Hoffmann & Powlishta 2001; Maccoby 1998; Maccoby and Jacklin 1987). Thorne observed this in many instances on the playground and in the classroom, such as kids scrambling over one another to be in line with other girls and boys: "Once when the recess bell had rung and they began to line up for the return to class, a boy came over and stood at the end of a row of girls. This evoked widespread teasing—'John's in the girls' line'; 'Look at that girl over there'—that quickly sent him to the row of boys" (Thorne 1994: 40).

Thorne considers the research on sex segregation and play against her own observations and interpretations of the data. She finds existing explanations found in the literature to be problematic as they rarely account for exceptions, something that she was continually struck with during her time in the schools—the existing theories simply fell short in explaining the behavior that she witnessed before her. One such example became evident to her as she was *talking* with kids about friendships. Thorne learned that *who* kids play with and identify as friends changes depending on the context and situation—who they hang out with in school and why is not always the same as who they hang out with on the weekends, at church, at baseball, etc. She writes: "When I stood on the Ashton playground talking with Melanie, a sixth-grader, I learned of a boy–girl friendship that went underground in school. After Jack walked by without even glancing at her, Melanie whispered to me, 'He's one of my best friends.' 'But you didn't even nod or say hello to each other,' I said. 'Oh,' she replied, 'we're friends in our neighbourhood and at church, but at school we pretend not to know each other so we won't get teased'" (1994: 50).

Girls socializing with other girls on the playground is but one example of friendship; rather than describing this behavior as gendered (i.e., all girls act this way, all boys act that way), Thorne illustrates instead that this is but one example in a specific context. As the dynamic of school is different from the dynamic of the neighborhood, the way kids identify with one another also changes. Researchers tend to conduct their observational studies in schools because working within the realm of an institution is inherently easier than approaching individual families and asking if they can be observed in their home or their neighborhood. When findings from one context are generalized to all contexts, however, the complexity of the situation is lost and grand generalizations emerge, such as the belief that girls and boys play differently and therefore prefer to exclusively socialize with those of the same sex. What are also lost are the voices of the kids themselves, that is, if they were even asked in the first place.

Thorne conveys an understanding of gender that is not fixed and static, but rather fluid and situational. Gender behavior does not follow a set of strict rules informed by what is appropriate for a boy or a girl and what is not; rather, this behavior is flexible and changes depending on the situation, context, and company. Thorne observed many instances of girls and boys enacting and challenging typical gender roles. For example, she writes that "day after day on the Ashton playground I noticed that Evan, a first-grade boy, sat on the stairs and avidly watched girls play jump rope, his head

PLATE 7.1 Children in Gender-Specific Hallowe'en Costumes

and eyes turning around in synchrony with the rope. Once when a group of girls were deciding who would jump and who would twirl (the less desirable position), Evan recognized a means of access to the game and offered, 'I'll swing it.' Julia responded, 'No way, you don't know how to do it, to swing it. You gotta be a girl.' He left without protest" (1994: 45). Sometimes these instances were a result of the rules of the classroom, such as when one teacher assigned seating in her classroom and mixed boys and girls at each table. Here, the girls and boys worked together on class projects and were much more cooperative than the girls and boys in another class that were allowed to pick their own seats. In the latter class, the girls ended up on one side and the boys on the other to create an atmosphere of girls versus boys. No comments were made about the ability of the girls and boys to work together as peers, but for the class segregated by gender, the teacher frequently used the threat of "not having a boys' side and a girls' side" in order to gain quiet and control in the classroom (1994: 37).

To conceive of gender roles as binary and oppositional fails to acknowledge the diversity that exists within these categories, and the desire of many to live outside of them. For the physical and boisterous girl and the boy who sits quietly to be regarded as peculiar simply because they do not "fit" with gender stereotypes places limitations on kids, something we will explore in more detail when we consider Pascoe's work in the next example.

As a feminist scholar, Thorne desires to effect social change related to the hierarchical and unequal relationships between men and women that are inscribed by constructions of gender. Thorne did not simply observe children for the sake of research, but did so with the hope that educators would read her work and think critically about how they organize their classrooms and talk to girls and boys, much on the model of Margaret Mead and her research with adolescent girls in Samoa. Her recommendations focus on how educators can rethink their teaching approaches to challenge assumptions that girls are better students than boys, and that boys have more energy than girls. For example, she notes the importance of challenging the notion that play that perpetuates aggressive masculine behavior is innate and simply a case of "boys being boys."

Creating an environment where children are free to try on and experiment with a diversity of roles is central to challenging the assumption that girls and boys must behave in certain ways. Thorne argues for the importance of continuing to resist and question stereotypical ideas of femininity, masculinity, and social arrangements that are rooted in patriarchal beliefs concerning the "natural" order of things: "A more complex understanding of the dynamics of gender, of tensions and contradictions, and of the hopeful moments that lie within present arrangements, can help broaden our sense of the possible" (1994: 173).

Gender Grows Up

If we fast forward over 20 years, we are presented with another ethnographic exploration of gender, this time one that takes place in an American high school in 2003. C.J. Pascoe conducted fieldwork in a racially diverse California high school with the intent of exploring two socially constructed categories, sexuality and masculinity, which Pascoe asserts are fundamentally linked. Over 18 months, Pascoe conducted ethnographic fieldwork among students in their classrooms, common spaces, and at school events. She conducted over 50 formal interviews with students, faculty, and administrators, and countless other "informal" interviews that took the form of conversation. Like Thorne, Pascoe employs a feminist approach to understanding gender. She also investigates sexuality, in which she employs **queer theory**. How do these theories differ, and what can they tell us about how teenagers identify and live their lives?

Like feminism, queer theory challenges the "assumed naturalness of the social order"—that is, that heterosexuality is a concrete and static category that is natural, and that all other sexual identities, desires, and discourses are not. Queer theory "moves beyond traditional categories such as male/female, masculine/feminine, and straight/gay to focus instead on the instability of these categories. That is, we might think of 'heterosexual' and 'homosexual' as stable, opposing, and discrete identities, but really they are fraught with internal contradictions. To this end, queer theory emphasizes multiple identities ..." (Pascoe 2011: 11).

Pascoe regards sexuality as she does gender—as an "organizing principle of social life," and not simply in reference to an individual's sexual identity. Traditionally, sexuality has been thought of in terms of private, individual acts; however, social science research has illustrated that the meanings we associate with terms and categories such as "gay," "straight" or "bisexual" have implications that reach far beyond what goes on behind closed doors. Take the controversial issue of gay marriage in Canada and the United States. This issue illustrates the significance the public assigns to how individuals define their sexual identity. In Canada, up until 1999 heterosexual couples were awarded rights and benefits from the state that same-sex couples were not. This was officially changed when marital benefits were extended to all co-habiting couples that met the definition of a common-law partnership, whether the relationship was same-sex or not. In the United States, each of the 50 states is responsible for its own marriage laws—at the time of this writing in 2014, 18 states and the District of Columbia allow same-sex marriage. As you will see in the next chapter, debates in the United States about legalizing gay marriage revisit past arguments about interracial marriage, given that some states then allowed it and some did not. The debate around marriage exemplifies how sexuality is a central organizing structure in society, and that institutions, such as the government and the courts, play a role in how we organize sexual life and produce sexual knowledge.

Pascoe considers how the high school, as a social institution much like the government, contributes to our understanding and realization of sexuality and masculinity. By putting sexuality front and center, Pascoe examines how students, faculty, and administrators at this high school created, challenged, and supported expectations around the presumed naturalness of heterosexuality. Some of these activities were seemingly mundane and harmless, such as a feature in the school yearbook that highlighted "best of" categories for girls and boys in each grade. Pictures of boy–girl pairings were placed in categories such as "best dressed," "biggest flake," "best smile," "best looking," and "best couple." There were no pairings of two girls or two boys in this section, a fact that points to the presumed "naturalness" of heterosexual pairings.

Popular school events such as school dances, where public displays of sexuality were much more explicit, showed a contrast between a desire to control student sexuality on the one hand, and a desire to encourage it on the other. Pascoe describes how there were very clear rules around "dancing inappropriately" at these events, and one teacher told her how they were instructed to "'keep our eyes on the chairs.' Surprised, I asked her, 'why the chairs?' She explained, 'Boys like to sit on the chairs and then the girls stand up and dance for them'" (2007: 42). At the same dance, however, scantily clad girls and fully covered boys screamed the lyrics to rapper Nelly singing "It's getting' hot in here / So take off all your clothes" and chanted in unison the word "ho" when the DJ turned down the volume on the chorus of a Tupac Shakur song. Pascoe observed two vice-principals joking with a male and female student as they left early, "You two going to a hotel or what?" (2007: 43). All of these instances served as venues for performing and proving heterosexual identities—"while the staff were concerned with students' sexuality, they also, to some extent, encouraged it through sponsoring these types of rituals and joking around with students" (2007: 43). The staff were less concerned with policing the "gender inequality fostered by such heterosexuality," such as the fact that the teachers appeared to have no problem allowing students to chant the word "ho" at the tops of their lungs (2007: 43).

What Pascoe finds problematic is not that students were exploring their sexuality within the walls of an institution; rather, it is that heterosexuality and a very specific type of masculinity were the *only* options supported by the high school. Holding a girlfriend's hand in public, caring about the appearance of one's clothing, or dating someone of the same sex did not align with the ideals of "**hetero-masculinity**." The consequence of exhibiting these behaviors was at best to be ignored and, at worst, to experience intense harassment and violence. Pascoe tells the story of Ricky, "a lithe, white junior with a shy smile and downcast eyes, [who] frequently sported multicolored hair extensions, mascara, and sometimes a skirt. An extremely talented dancer, he often starred in the school's dance shows and choreographed assemblies" (2007: 65). Ricky was often the subject of abuse and ridicule, at the hands of both other male students and teachers. While the insults and threats he heard from students were overt, many of the teachers did little to protect him or to punish the perpetrators. Ricky used an example of being beaten up in middle school to illustrate the attitudes of many of his teachers: "They gave them a two-day suspension and they kind of kept an eye on me. That's all they could do. The PE coach was very racist and very homophobic. He was just like 'faggot this' and 'faggot that.' I did not feel comfortable in the locker room and I asked him if I could go somewhere else to change, and he said, 'No, you can change here'" (Pascoe 2007: 67). As a non-heterosexual youth who did not conform to a masculine gender role, Ricky was unable to ever break free of the "fag" label. As a result of this relentless and intense bullying, Ricky dropped out of high school.

Dude, you're a fag is a title clearly meant to elicit a reaction in readers. The frequent use of the word "fag" by her research participants led Pascoe to theorize that "becoming a fag has as much to do with failing at the masculine tasks of competence, heterosexual prowess and strength, or in any way revealing weakness or femininity as it does with a [homo]sexual identity" (2011: 54). Pascoe illustrates through a number of ethnographic examples that it was not only those males who identified as gay or bisexual, such as Ricky, that were subject to bullying—it was any male whose behavior was perceived to be outside of the established masculine gender role. The difference was the manner in which these boys were able to shrug off the fag label, and how this was dependent on their ability to perform the masculine gender role. When she asked a student named Ben what kinds of things boys are called fags for, Ben answered, "Anything … literally anything. Like you were trying to turn a wrench the wrong way, 'Dude, you're a fag.' If a piece of meat drops out of your sandwich, 'You fag!'" (2007: 57). Ben's comments illustrate that the term has just as much to do with being incompetent and therefore unmasculine as it does with anything sexual. For this reason, focusing *only* on concepts of sexuality to understand homophobia neglects how the construction of masculinity contributes to the belief that heterosexuality is the norm.

Whether or not you find this type of research interesting, you may be asking yourself "what does it matter?" With so many other social issues in contemporary society, does it really matter how boys and girls in an American high school under-stand masculinity and sexuality? Pascoe provides a compelling argument that attention to the construction of these social categories certainly does matter. Pascoe positions her work in relation to the tragic instances of cyber and face-to-face bul-lying that led to a number of male adolescents taking their own lives in the United States. These cases have been largely classified as instances of homophobia, where boys and young men were teased and taunted because of their presumed or actual sexual preference. Pascoe believes, however, that these cases are as much about step-ping outside the traditional definitions of masculinity, however slight, as they are about homophobia:

> Evidence in several of the cases indicates that their [the victims'] (mildly) non-normative gendered behavior (such as enjoying schoolwork or drama class) was just as likely to turn them into targets as were their sexual identities.... That these cases exist, however few, illustrates how serious the problems are around the contemporary making of masculine identities—and that we need to start thinking about the ways in which young males come to think of themselves and others as masculine. (2011: xi)

So what does Pascoe suggest society do to counteract this activity? As her work is informed by both feminist and queer theory approaches, her ultimate goal is to challenge the status quo. She asserts that students who are subject to harassment, such as gay, lesbian, bisexual, and **transgendered** students, need legal protection. Teachers and administrators must be educated as to what constitutes harassment, and must in turn educate those students who are observed exhibiting this type of behavior. In order to change the way we think, disciplinary action is not enough—education is key, as is critically examining curriculum and student events that do not allow for the expression of sexuality and gender roles that are not "hetero-normative." At the center of both Pascoe's and Thorne's work is the assertion that talking to individuals about their experiences will lead to a better understanding of how kids and teens realize their gender and sexual identities. While talking to adults and situating research within an institution allows for access and an important environment through which kids can be approached, it is always important to remember that labels and identities are often context- and situation-dependent.

We have spent a fair amount of time discussing gender and sexuality as it relates to North American culture, primarily because this is where most of our readers hail from. To learn to think critically about one's own culture is one of the greatest contributions of cultural anthropology—deconstructing what we have learned to think of as normal and natural illustrates that these behaviors are learned and culturally dependent. Next we will consider how policy related to a nation's birth rate has significant consequences on how gender roles are perceived and experienced in the family specifically, and in society as a whole.

Gender and Social Organization:
The Family and the Economy

The construction of gender roles and behaviors has a significant impact on how the social world is organized. While Thorne and Pascoe have offered ethnographic portraits of how kids experience gender in the school system, another realm where gender norms are extremely important is within the family. In what ways are the expectations placed on children by their family related to gender norms, and how do these expectations shift when significant social changes impact the role of women in society? Understanding social organization requires a holistic approach: our lives are not organized by categories titled "gender," "economy" or "religion," but instead are a product of these interrelated roles, beliefs, and behaviors. The ways in which people think about gender roles are influenced by the political, social, and economic climate of the time and directly impact family relationships and social institutions such as schools and the workplace.

Anthropologist Vanessa Fong considers how China's one-child policy has had an impact upon urban-born daughters. China's first official population-control campaign was implemented in 1970, when families were encouraged to have no more than two children. It was not until 1978, when the government set a population target of 1.2 billion people or under by the year 2000, that the one-child policy was officially enforced. The approach was successful in curbing the birth rate: "in 1970, when population control policies began, China's total fertility rate was six births per woman; in 1980, two years after the start of the one-child policy, China's total fertility rate was down to two births per woman" (Fong 2002: 1099). The policy led to enormous international backlash, particularly from the United States. Fong notes that much of the literature exploring the effects of the policy highlights the negative impact on women, detailing instances of forced sterilizations and abortions, and of the blame placed upon women who had daughters instead of sons in a culture where male children were traditionally more valued than females. The preference for male children has had a very real impact on the make-up of urban Chinese society. Demographically speaking, China has a skewed gender ratio with more males than females, the cause of which may have been female infanticide, abandonment, and selective abortion.

Fong takes a slightly different approach to understanding the effects of the one-child policy without diminishing the suffering experienced by many women. She notes that in urban areas where the cost of living is high and space restrictions are significant, resistance to the policy was relatively low. Fong's central thesis is that "urban daughters born under China's one child policy have benefited from the demographic pattern produced by that policy" (2002: 1099). Fong's data suggest that these daughters have an unprecedented power to challenge traditional gender roles in a way that will benefit them. An unintended consequence of the one-child policy has been to force parents to invest, both socially and economically, in their daughters when traditionally they would have invested in their sons.

Fong interviewed grandmothers, mothers, and singleton daughters to gain cross-generational perspectives on the position of women in society. Grandmothers told her that when they were young, they were unable to live with or provide financial and social support to their parents. Even if wage-paying jobs had been a possibility, as a result of having numerous children and a household to manage they would not have had the time to work outside the home. One grandmother explained how having to continually take time away from her factory job to have children hindered her ability to excel: "I got to work upstairs in the factory office because I had gone to school, but I couldn't take a position of responsibility because I always had to take time off when I got pregnant…. After my fourth child, my health was bad all the time, and I had to quit my job" (2002: 1101). The daughters of these women who gave birth to their own children in the one-child–policy era were able to work outside the home because of fewer child-rearing responsibilities. Because they were able to bring home a monthly wage, they were also able to provide financial support to their elderly parents, illustrating that they too could be as filial as sons: "As a junior high school student's mother told her husband when he complained that she was giving too much money to her parents, 'Why shouldn't I give them the money I've earned? You should be grateful that I don't give all my wages to them!'" (2002: 1102).

As a result of the changes in social status of their mothers and grandmothers, singleton daughters are better positioned to take advantage of opportunities that might not have been open to them if they had had to compete with brothers. Despite increased opportunities in school and the workplace, however, their lives continue to be subjected to the societal gender norms and roles that position them as secondary to men. Fong describes the experience of a student she had been tutoring who was waiting to hear her test results. On the one hand, this student was receiving the investment of time and money from her parents to excel at school. On the other, however, she must continually prove her worth to her father:

> Although studious and well behaved, Ding Na was often criticized by her father, who liked to remind her that he had always wanted a son. He worried that she might not score high enough to get into a good four-year college, even though she usually ranked in the top 20 percent of her high school class on practice exams. "What will you do if you don't get into a good college?" he lamented. "If you were a boy, you could study abroad while supporting yourself as a laborer, but what can a girl do abroad besides sit around waiting for remittances I can't afford?" Although her mother praised her for being more willing to help with chores than most other teenagers, whenever Ding Na had trouble helping her father carry groceries or move furniture, he snapped, "Girls are so useless. A boy would have no trouble with this." On July 26, 1999, when Ding Na's college entrance exam scores were released, I began to see the relationship between Ding Na and her father in a different light…. She had scored higher than she had ever scored on a practice exam in high school, and well above the likely cutoff

for her top-choice four-year college. She shouted with joy as we congratulated her. Her father beamed at her with tears in his eyes and said, "I was wrong to have wanted a son. A daughter like you is worth ten sons." (Fong 2002: 1098)

China remains a **patriarchal** society, with a socio-economic system structured by class and gender roles. Singleton daughters must negotiate gender roles in the family, as shown above, to prove they are as filial as sons, as well as in the workplace, where they are pressured to portray desired behaviors such as being more patient and meticulous than men. The ability of singleton daughters to "parody" the typical feminine gender role allows for social mobility and access while subsequently rejecting traditional roles, such as staying home to have numerous children and do all of the housework. Fong states that in some ways middle-class urban men have less social security than their female counterparts. While women face a "glass ceiling" that prohibits them from reaching the elite positions inhabited by men, they also have the protection of "marrying up," an option rarely available to men of the same social status. Urban middle-class males are experiencing a change in their position in society as a result of women's increased social mobility. Aside from having more competition in the workforce, they also explained that it was more difficult to find a wife. Now that singleton daughters are able to contribute to the purchase of an apartment, they have a greater choice of partners. Fong writes that

> a male vocational high school student told me that he could have gone to a college-prep high school if his parents, who ran a small shop, had spent all their savings on extra fees and bribes that would have gotten him in despite his low exam score. He said, "They gave me a choice. Either they could use their savings to send me to the college prep high school, or they could use it to buy an apartment for me so that I'll be able to get a wife when the time comes. I don't like to study, and I didn't think I could make it to college even if I went to a college prep school, so I chose the apartment. (2002: 1105)

The effects of a policy to curb national birth rate has had a substantial impact on all generations of a society that positions family as a central unit of support. Fong's analysis is a snapshot of the effects of the policy in a specific location, among a specific group of people. Her research cannot be generalized to all women in China, as it is specific only to urban women whose families had a very different experience with the one-child policy than those in rural areas. Her work illustrates the way in which politics and kinship intersect with gender roles, and how this has ignited a change in the urban-middle-class perception of the place of singleton daughters specifically, and women more generally, in society.

By looking cross-culturally at how gender is realized, we see that a holistic approach that considers kinship, the economy, and the political system brings to light many key components that factor into how society perceives gender. Thorne and Pascoe situate their ethnographic studies within the education system, and focus specifically on the interactions of the students and teachers themselves. Fong, on the other hand, situates her study more generally in Chinese urban society. Both approaches illustrate the significance of gender to organizing the social world. We will now move on to our final ethnographic example, Serena Nanda's *Neither Man nor Woman*. By stepping far away from traditional binary gender roles, this research illustrates just how socially constructed the concept of gender is.

Rejecting the Gender/Sex Dichotomy: Third Genders and Cross-Cultural Analysis

Our final ethnographic example of the chapter explores gender from a cross-cultural, **interpretive perspective** that considers how symbolism and religion create space in Indian society for an institutionalized third gender. Do people who identify outside of the mainstream gender categories have to contend with social rules and norms in the same way that men and women do? In what ways are their lives different from those who identify with the dichotomous gender systems of mainstream Western society? There are many societies in which a third gender exists, and by applying a cross-cultural approach it becomes clear that gender is simply another social category that serves to organize rules, behaviors, and meanings for the people who exist within it. In this section, we move beyond the dichotomous gender roles of boys and girls, men and women, and consider the existence of a third gender role through a cross-cultural examination of the hijras of India.

Who are the hijras? This is a complicated question that many anthropologists have attempted to answer. Anthropologist Gayatri Reddy provides this definition: "For the most part, hijras are phenotypic men who wear female clothing and, ideally, renounce sexual desire and practice by undergoing a sacrificial emasculation—that is, an excision of the penis and testicles—dedicated to the goddess Bedhraj Mata" (2005: 2). The number of hijras in India varies drastically, depending on the source, with estimates ranging from 10,000 to two million (Reddy 2005). Hijra communities can be found throughout India, although they seem to be concentrated in the northern cities of Delhi and Lucknow, as well as in Hyderabad to the south.

Hijras are socially organized according to lineages and households, and from there they are further organized into a social hierarchy, with one senior hijra occupying a role of respect and dominance. The hijra community itself has further ways of distinguishing who is a hijra, including those who were "born" a hijra by virtue of having ambiguous genitals, those who are "made" a hijra through castration (Nanda 1999), and those who engage in activities deemed unauthentic, such as sex work or displaying sexual desire (Reddy 2005). While there have been a number of studies conducted with the hijra community over the last few decades, they are a highly secretive group, and gaining access to their communities is difficult. As a result, there remains much

PLATE 7.2 Hijra

uncertainty around what the existence of the hijra community can tell us about Indian society and, on a grander scale, the story of human sexuality itself (Lai 1999).

The place of hijras in Indian society cannot be fully understood unless it is contextualized within historical and religious realms. While we do not have the space required to give a comprehensive explanation of this history here, ethnographies by both Serena Nanda (1999) and Gayatri Reddy (2005) provide excellent overviews. Hijras have existed in Indian society for centuries and are described in scholarly and popular literature using an array of terms, including eunuchs, transgendered, homosexual, bisexual, inter-sexed, and hermaphrodites (Lai 1999).

While their historical role can be traced to the presence of eunuchs in the Muslim courts, their religious and spiritual role can be traced to the Hindu religion. The existence and legitimization of this third gender role is attributed to the presence of an array of alternative genders in Indian mythology and culture. Like other Indian **castes**, the origin of the hijras is told through a myth linking them to Hindu deities. This origin myth provides a link with Hinduism, thus not only validating a ritual place for hijras in society, but also linking their gender role with the deities and mythic figures of the religion (Nanda 1999: 13). Within Hindu and Indian mythology, there exist a number of examples of the combined power of men and women, among both deities and humans. These mythical figures are very well known among Indian society, allowing for the hijras not only to exist, but also to occupy a place of ritual significance (Nanda 1999: 20). For example, one of the most significant figures to the hijra community is that of Shiva. Shiva is "a deity who incorporates both male and female characteristics. Shiva is an ascetic—one who renounces sex—and yet appears in many erotic and provocative roles.... One of the most powerful forms of Shiva is that of *Ardhanarisvara*, or half man/half-woman, which represents Shiva united with his shakti (female creative power). Hijras say that worshipers of Shiva give them special respects because of this close identification, and hijras often worship at Shiva temples" (1999: 20).

While situating the hijras within a historical and religious context is important, we must also ask how the hijras see themselves. This answer is extremely varied depending on to whom one speaks, where they live, their age, their social status, etc. It is important to remember that just as in any other community, its members each have their own story and identity. Nanda relays the story of four hijras in her ethnography, and their life stories include tales of how they came to join the hijra community, why they dress and perform the way they do, their working and religious life, and how their relationships, past and present, have informed who they are today. Reddy weaves the views of different hijras throughout her analysis and uses categories such as gender, religion, kinship, and class to structure her ethnography. Regardless of how their stories are represented, however, Reddy notes that it is important to remember that hijras do not see themselves solely as sexual beings. Rather, "they argue explicitly for the roles of kinship, religion, and class, among others, in their constructions of self-identity ... they provide a lens through which to examine the embeddedness of sexuality within other arenas of everyday life" (2005: 33). While it can be tempting to isolate aspects of personhood into categories as a vehicle through which to better understand culture and society, one must stop and ask oneself a question: "Is this how I view my own life? Do I see myself solely through one lens, whether it is ethnicity, age, sexuality or gender?" The likely answer is a resounding "no," as all of our lives are a mélange of experiences, categories, and relationships. This is what makes the individual so fascinating!

The role of hijras in Indian society is both multidimensional and ambiguous. Their formal role, and the way in which they earn social respect, is that of a ritual performer who bestows fertility blessings on newborn babies and new marriages. After the birth of a son, families will often throw a celebratory party where a group of hijras will be invited to perform their ritual dances. If compensated appropriately, the hijras will then bless the baby boy with the power of fertility. Weddings provide a similar scene, with hijras dancing and performing and expecting to be compensated for their time. Families willingly oblige, afraid that to disrespect the hijras will bring about infertility in their loved ones. It may appear somewhat of an odd choice to have impotent and emasculated men confer blessings on babies and newlyweds; these are not simply impotent men, however. Nanda explains that, "As ritual performers, they are viewed as vehicles of the divine power of the Mother Goddess, which transforms their impotence into the power of generativity.... The faith in the power of the hijras rests on the Hindu belief in shakti—the potency of the dynamic female forces of creation that the hijras, as vehicles of the Mother Goddess, represent" (Nanda 1999: 5).

The income garnered from their formal role, however, is rarely enough for a hijra to live on, and many must make ends meet through other means, such as begging or homosexual prostitution. These practices are less socially desirable, and as a result their "true" role as a performer has been undermined. Many hijras themselves condemn prostitution, for it goes against the claims that hijras are ascetics, that is, that they have renounced sexual activity. At the same time, however, hijras must survive, and the wage they earn from prostitution supplements the small wage they earn as performers. As well, discussions with hijras illustrate that many freely admit to having sexual desire. Once again, we see a chasm between the official role and definition on the one hand, and the reality as it is lived in contemporary society on the other. The complex place that hijras occupy in Indian society and the contradictions that characterize their position require a holistic approach in order to gain a better understanding of their social role.

For our purposes here, we are interested in looking at how the existence of the hijras signifies a challenge to the dichotomous gender identities found in the West. Of course, not all Westerners ascribe to this dichotomy, and the prominence of **transsexual** people and their supporters has become increasingly strong over the last 20 years. From a Western perspective, it may be tempting to think of the hijras in terms of Western definitions of transsexuality or homosexuality. These identities, however, do not share the religious and ritual components that the hijra role in Indian society does. One of the central differences between transsexuals and the alternative gender roles found in other cultures is that "trans-sexualism has been defined in such a way as to reinforce our cultural construction of both sex and genders as invariably dichotomous" (Nanda 1999: 137). Transsexuals assert that while they are born with the genitalia of one sex, their gender identity, or "inner psychological conviction," is that of the other sex (1999: 137). The transitional status associated with a man becoming a woman, or a woman becoming a man, negates the possibility of a third gender and serves to reinforce the dichotomy of *either* man *or* woman that is so prominent in the Western world. While hijras are referred to as neither men nor women, the experienced gender identity of many hijras is, on first glance, as women. Can they really be a third gender if their gender identity is as women?

By discussing the deep-rooted place of hijras in Indian society, Nanda illustrates that there exists an institutionalized, or long-established, place in society for a third gender role. A gender role or identity does not mean the same thing for everyone—of the four hijras whose stories she tells, all have different conceptions of their own gender identity that is related to their personal experiences as a child, an adult, a woman, or a man. What they share, however, is a declaration that they are *not* men in either the physical sense, i.e., insofar as they are impotent and have undergone the religious obligation of emasculation, or in the behavioral sense, i.e., insofar as they do not have the sexual feelings and preferences of other men. As one hijra named Krishna states, "We are not men with the ordinary desires of men to get married and have families. Otherwise, why would we choose to live this life?" (Nanda 1999: 16). Hijras wear their hair long, and most dress in women's clothing and take female names when they join the hijra community. They declare, however, that they are not women. Nanda describes how "their female dress and mannerisms are often exaggerations, almost to the point of caricature, and they act in sexually suggestive ways that would be considered inappropriate, and even outrageous, for ordinary women in their significant and traditional female roles as daughters, wives and mothers" (1999: 18). The most important detail that sets them apart from women is their inability to menstruate and have children. Thus, the lived gender identity that hijras experience as a group exists outside of the dichotomous gender system that structures mainstream society in Western countries.

Other anthropological research conducted with communities who do not ascribe to a dichotomous gender system illustrates the socially constructed reality of gender identity and behavior. Research among the kathoey of Thailand, the xanith of Oman, the berdache of Aboriginal North America, and the f'afafine of Polynesia illustrates that a third gender is not a phenomenon limited to India and signifies the diversity of gender construction (Reddy 2005: 31). The work of Nanda, Reddy, and other anthropologists shows us that by looking cross-culturally at how gender roles are conceptualized and realized, the Western dichotomous approach to understanding gender (boy/girl, man/woman) is also a cultural construct, and only one way in a myriad of perspectives.

Theory Steering Perception

Thorne, Pascoe, and Fong approached the study of gender from a feminist perspective; however, their methodologies were very different and, as a result, they asked and answered very different research questions. While Thorne and Pascoe conducted participant observation and held interviews in two schools, Fong conducted participant observation, interviews, and surveys in a variety of locales (e.g., schools, homes). While Fong's approach allowed her to reach many more people than both Thorne and Pascoe, the issues that they were investigating would not have benefited from a survey approach, since the type of data yielded by that kind of approach would not have enriched their understanding of gender and sexuality. Survey data, as used by Fong, were employed to recount *how* things happened—in this case, she wanted the perspectives of mothers and grandmothers concerning their past experiences as daughters, while observation is an interpretation of the immediate present. As well, Fong's scope of analysis included a discussion of the economic and political climate of the time, a necessary component to her understanding of how gender roles have transformed over time. Nanda employed an interpretive, cross-cultural approach that allowed her to consider the existence of third genders in societies across the world, and how these gender roles differed from or were similar to that of the hijras in India. Central to her analysis was a consideration of the symbolism, myth, and history of Indian culture, for an understanding of these components of society allowed her to conclude that the hijras did indeed occupy an "institutionalized" position within society. While all four researchers investigated gender, their approaches, methods, and theoretical perspectives led them to pose and answer very different questions.

Conclusion

Perhaps one of anthropology's greatest contributions is showing how difficult it is to arrive at conclusions about human nature without taking into account the full variety of human experience. Anthropologists do not deny that there is such a thing as human nature. Indeed, some anthropologists have been seriously engaged with finding out the common denominators that underlie the bewildering variety of cultural practices around the world. Seeking to find such a common denominator (if one exists) in constructions of sexuality or gender is but one example of this quest. In this chapter we have considered how constructions of gender contribute to the social organization of society by examining how it is experienced by children and teens in the American public education system, by singleton daughters in urban China, and by individuals who identify as belonging to a third gender in India. Anthropology, like the individuals who practice it, is situated in a specific time and place. It reflects the concerns of the society around it. In the same way that Franz Boas and Margaret Mead were interested in refuting racist ideology and discriminatory policies against immigrants, contemporary anthropologists concern themselves with social issues such as homophobia, the education of children, and women's rights. The aim of research is to bring about a better understanding of issues or questions that the public has deemed significant. Gender and sexuality are social constructs that are very much part of our daily lives, even if we do not think about them as distinct categories. The holistic approach taken up by anthropologists illustrates just how far-reaching into other aspects of society these categories are, and also demonstrates the importance of gaining an understanding of how such categories are constructed, and why.

Study Questions

1   Explain what is meant by the phrase "we 'do' gender."
2   Summarize Thorne's research. How did her methods differ from a typical study of children? What did she discover about how roles are assigned and reinforced in the school environment?

3   Summarize what Pascoe discovered about "hetero-masculinity" and why she argues that homophobia is not just a matter of sexuality.

4   From a feminist theoretical perspective, why is it important to consider gender alongside other categories such as class, ethnicity, and age?

5   Explain how kinship and family relationships relate to social constructions of gender.

6   Compare and contrast the effect of China's one-child policy on urban and rural families. Outline the policy's generational influence on the economic situation of singleton daughters in urban communities.

7   Why is situating the hijras within a historical and religious context important to understanding their role in Indian society?

8   What does it mean to say that theory steers perceptions? Use examples from the chapter.

Discussion Questions

1   Consider the assertion that gender roles and behaviours are situational and fluid, meaning that they are likely to change depending on the company, the context, and one's age. Do you agree with this? Why or why not? Give an example from your own life experience to support your answer.

2   What value does a cross-cultural approach to studying gender and sexuality provide?

3   Consider your own experience growing up. What social cues, activities, policies, influences, rituals, rules, expectations etc. played a role in how you came to understand gender roles and sexuality?

4   Explain what is meant by the phrase "believing is seeing" in relation to gender behavior. In your experience, does this ring true?

CHAPTER 8

//

Race, Science, and Human Diversity

LEARNING OBJECTIVES

After reading this chapter, students should be able to

- understand the historical notion of race as both a biological and political concept;
- explain Darwin's theory of natural selection and his conclusions about the diversity of the human race;
- define *typological thinking* and *anthropometry* and discuss their historical significance;
- outline the history of the eugenics movement and historical attitudes toward "race mixing" and segregation;
- outline the Boasian argument against the connections of race, heredity, culture, and nation by racial nationalists;
- explain the historical circumstances that led to the genocide in Rwanda; and
- summarize the influence of genetics on anthropology's study of human diversity.

KEY TERMS

eugenics movement	natural selection	typological thinking
genome		

Introduction

The problem of human diversity has always been central to anthropology, but physical differences bring that issue to focus in a particularly vivid way. Anyone can see that humanity comes in different flavors; but since all human populations are highly variable, the closer you look the more varieties you see. What are we to make of this? Are these superficial differences, or do they go deeper? What does their presence suggest about the history and future of our species? In this chapter we ask: What kind of a concept is "race"? Just what is it supposed to explain? Does it necessarily lead to "racism"? What is the relation between race, heredity, and culture? Why has it seemed so important to decouple them? In the spirit of the Boasian four-fields ideal, we also ask about the relation between cultural and physical anthropology, and of both to the biological sciences. How are developments in genetics and genomics leading to new forms of social identity and the revision of old ones?

We begin with a historical sketch of the problem and then turn to two historically important examples involving the concept of race. Thomas Jefferson (1743–1826) was the author of the American Declaration of Independence and President of the United States from 1800 to 1808; as we've seen, he also launched the Lewis and Clark expedition to the Pacific coast. In 1772, Jefferson married a local Virginia woman, and together they had a number of children, of whom two—both girls—survived to adulthood. But did he also father a *second* family through his relationship with an African-American domestic slave whose descendants are with us today? This question opens up the broader issue of how race was thought about in what was once a rigidly segregated society—of the social factors that influence how we think about human difference, and of how the lines are drawn between racial categories.

Our second example comes from Africa itself. Rwanda and Burundi are small land-locked countries in eastern Africa. In pre-colonial times, each was ruled by a king who came from an aristocratic cattle-keeping group of clans known as the Tutsi. Those they ruled over were farmers known as Hutu. Following the great land-grab by European powers, they came to be governed by Belgium. After independence in the early 1960s, internal conflict between segments of the population led to increasing violence, culminating in Rwanda in an attempt to wipe the Tutsi from the face of the earth. What was the role of the concept of "race" in the unfolding of this tragic event?

Finally, we'll consider how modern genetic technology is reshaping our concepts of race and social identity. This technology was influential in determining whether Thomas Jefferson did indeed father an African-American family. As always, first some background.

Understanding Diversity

By the early nineteenth century there had already been much speculation about the classification, nature, and origin of human races, accompanied by increasing knowledge about the actual range of human variability. But how did these differences arise? A number of schemes of racial classification were developed, along with theories to explain them. Perhaps physical differences—skin color for instance, or bodily stature—were influenced by the climate, or some other environmental factor. Perhaps the races were created separately in different parts of the world.

Charles Darwin (1809–82) didn't know what to make of human racial difference. And he thought about the question deeply, since variation within a species was key to his theory of evolution through **natural selection**. Natural selection works on variation, choosing variants with adaptive value and rejecting or ignoring those without it. In the long term those individuals with useful variations leave more offspring, and evolution moves on in the direction indicated by the selective process. Darwin thought of a race as an "incipient species." Species give rise to races—relatively minor variants—then to sub-species, and finally to true species that have lost the ability to interbreed with their cousins. As time goes by, the differences between the offspring of a common ancestor grow increasingly pronounced—and so we arrive at the classic image of evolution as a branching tree growing upward from its roots, but with some branches dropping off through extinction. What then of ourselves?

Darwin considered the various ways in which human races differ from one another and concluded that they are relatively superficial in comparison to what we have in common: "numerous points of resemblance are of much more importance than the amount of similarity or dissimilarity in a few points" (1998: 154). Thus, all humanity clearly belongs to one species. Put clothes on Fuegians and they're remarkably like Englishmen.[1] But racial difference still needed to be accounted for. Darwin's own theory—sexual selection—didn't attract many fans. He couldn't see that the distinctive racial traits have any selective value, and therefore turned to the notion that in the distant past they might have arisen out of local standards of beauty.

There were more plausible lines of argument. Maybe racial differences did (or once did) confer some hidden selective advantage. Perhaps natural selection isn't the only evolutionary mechanism. Perhaps the different human races separated from the common ancestral population at different times, or evolved on their own at different rates due to geographical separation after migration from wherever humanity originated.

With factors like these thrown in, it was still possible to talk about more or less "advanced" races while retaining the notion of common descent. On the other hand, if it could be shown that we all branched off from one another quite recently in evolutionary time and differ only in very minor ways, this would reinforce the argument for biological racial equality, and hence for social equality. Once again, scientific debates have moral and political implications. We've seen this already in the contrasting views of human nature held by Rousseau and Hobbes (see Chapter 3). Such debates persist, and general texts on paleoanthropology and human evolution contain the details.

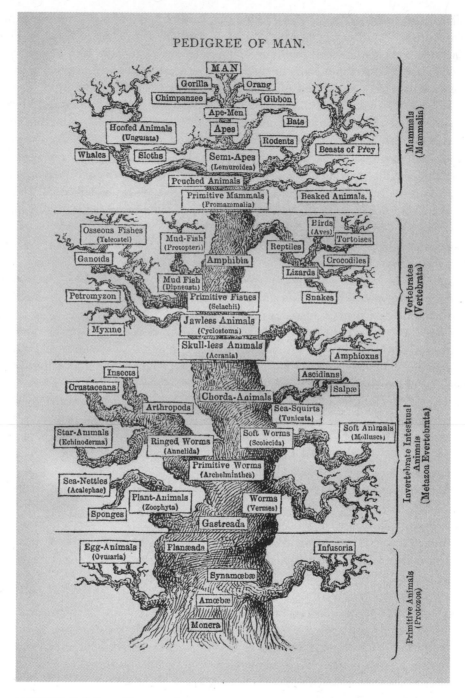

FIGURE 8.1 Evolutionary Tree

The Urge to Classify

Here we want to highlight two related points. The first has to do with the way in which biological classification is carried out—slotting organisms into a common category on the basis of physical or genetic similarities and designating it as a species, sub-species, or merely a race. The criteria for doing so can be quite elaborate. The first modern system was devised in the eighteenth century by a Swede, Carl von Linné (or Linnaeus; 1707–78), in order to classify plants. He assigned them Latin names on the basis of similarities between their flowers. Thus we have *Primula vulgaris*, the common primrose, and so on. Linnaeus established the basis for the classification system still in use for all organisms, such as the two sub-species of the genus *Homo*: *Homo sapiens* ("Wise Man"), as distinguished from *Homo neanderthalensis* (extinct, and presumably less wise). Paleoanthropologists argue about whether their latest fossil discovery is sufficiently distinctive to be assigned to a species of its own or is merely a variant of one that's already been unearthed. There's always glory in a new discovery.

This is **typological thinking**, and racial thinking *is* typological thinking. The physical anthropologists of not so long ago classified humanity into a large number of types and sub-types, using criteria such as skull shape, skin color, hair texture, and eye configuration. Thus we get the big three: Caucasoid, Negroid, and Mongoloid, and sub-classes within each type. Each could be defined by a "pure" or ideal example, and actual people regarded as variations more or less close to it. Older textbooks in physical anthropology often feature photographs of individuals representing these idealized types. The skull was exceptionally important because of its accessibility and what it contains, i.e., the brain.

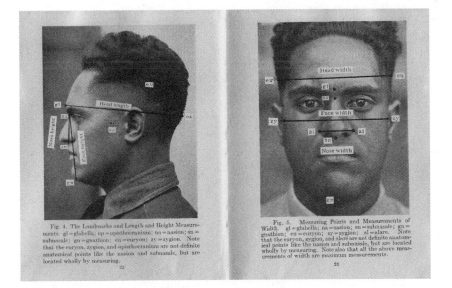

Fig. 4. The Landmarks and Length and Height Measurements. gl = glabella; op = opisthocranium; na = nasion; sn = subnasale; gn = gnathion; eu = euryon; zy = zygion. Note that the euryon, zygion, and opisthocranium are not definite anatomical points like the nasion and subnasale, but are located wholly by measuring.
22

Fig. 5. Measuring Points and Measurements of Width. gl = glabella; na = nasion; sn = subnasale; gn = gnathion; eu = euryon; zy = zygion; al = alare. Note that the euryon, zygion, and alare are not definite anatomical points like the nasion and subnasale, but are located wholly by measuring. Note also that all the above measurements of width are maximum measurements.
23

PLATE 8.1 Anthropometry

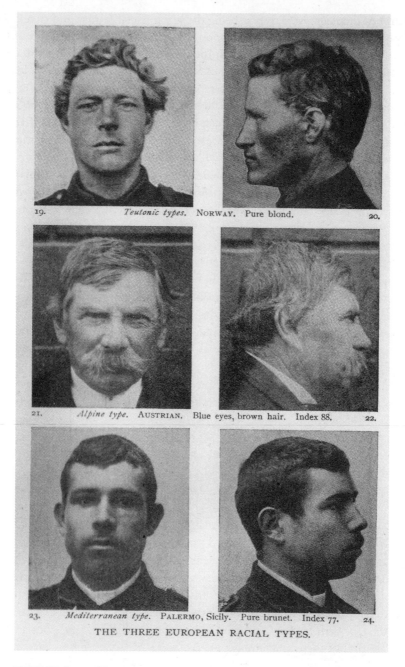

19. *Teutonic types.* NORWAY. Pure blond. 20.

21. *Alpine type.* AUSTRIAN. Blue eyes, brown hair. Index 88. 22.

23. *Mediterranean type.* PALERMO, Sicily. Pure brunet. Index 77. 24.

THE THREE EUROPEAN RACIAL TYPES.

PLATE 8.2 Races of Europe

For example, through skull shape the European peoples were sorted into several major branches: the Mediterranean, the Alpine, and the Nordic (or Teutonic).

Such measurements were seen as being the key to racial history and to unpacking the composition of present-day populations—say the relative proportions of Celtic and Anglo-Saxon ancestry in the British Isles, or of Nordic and Alpine in Germany. Skull-measurement techniques were once standard items in the anthropology curriculum. But, given the internal variability of all populations, the findings arrived at in this manner were difficult to interpret, so some important statistical methods were invented to deal with such problems. Franz Boas, for example, took a keen interest in anthropometry (the science of human body measurement) and published extensively on his own anthropometric research.

The second point we want to emphasize is central to our story. "Race" as it's actually used in common speech is a fuzzy notion, and was even more so in the nineteenth and early twentieth centuries. It falls somewhere between "race" in a biological sense, and "people" or "nation" in a political sense. For example, it was possible to speak about belonging to "the British race" as something to be distinctly proud of, some essential quality of one's own being. This is the rhetoric of nineteenth-century nationalism. If race and nation are essentially the same, then national character is a reflection of the nation's racial makeup. Whereas we now tend to assume that national traits are a product of culture and history, racial nationalists claimed that race and culture are inextricably linked. Nazi racial ideology was an extreme version of that idea, as we see in the words of Adolf Hitler:

> All the human culture, all the results of art, science, and technology that we see before us today, are almost exclusively the creative product of the Aryan. If we were to divide mankind into three groups, the founders of culture, the bearers of culture, the destroyers of culture, only the Aryan could be considered as the representative of the first group. [The state] must set race in the center of all life. It must take care to keep it pure. (Hitler 1998: 292, 403)

The nature of heredity was poorly understood. There was a common and usually unspoken assumption that the historical experience of a nation, a people, or a race somehow gets imprinted on its hereditary material and is expressed over the generations in the behavior and capacities of individuals. Ethnic stereotypes reflect these assumptions: Italians are passionate, Irish are alcoholics, Jews are acquisitive, the French undependable, Germans solid, Negroes lecherous, Chinese crafty, and so on. Early in the twentieth century, a prominent writer on heredity and eugenics speculated what the impact of these new immigrants might be on the American character: "… It appears certain that … the population of the United States will, on account of the great influx of blood from South-eastern Europe, rapidly become darker in pigmentation, smaller in stature, more mercurial, more attached to music and art, more given to crimes of larceny, kidnapping, assault, murder, rape and sex-immorality …" (Davenport 1911: 219).

The Boasians took aim at this kind of thing. The concept of culture in its modern form was one response to the conscious and unconscious racism of the day. The context was an early-twentieth-century North America in the throes of radical social change brought about by a huge upsurge of internal and external migration. African-Americans were moving in large numbers from rural areas to the cities. Foreign immigration increasingly stemmed from sources outside northern Europe and the British Isles: Italy, Greece, the Balkans, Poland, and Russia, for example. Many Eastern European Jews came to North America as part of this wave. In the US, Canada, and Australia, Chinese immigration was discouraged by racial exclusion laws. Economic anxieties were one factor behind this; trade unionists believed that cheap Chinese labor would undercut their bargaining position. But there was also a general sense of racial incompatibility. Here's a Canadian example from 1902: "They come … with customs, habits and modes of life fixed and unalterable…. They form, on their arrival, a community within a community, separate and apart, a foreign substance within but not of our body politic, with no love for our laws or institutions; a people that cannot assimilate and become an integral part of our race and nation" (quoted in Anderson 1991: 73).

The problem of immigration was very much on the public mind when Boas began talking about race. Another factor was the rise of the **"eugenics" movement**. The term is derived from Greek and means "well born." It was coined by Charles Darwin's cousin, Francis Galton (1822–1911), who had become interested in the issue of heredity and racial "quality" with regard to the future of Great Britain. He believed that it should be possible to improve the British race, or at least to prevent it from degenerating due to the different birthrates between the upper and lower classes, between law-abiding citizens and the social problem groups: criminals, the insane, drug addicts, drunkards, prostitutes, the feeble-minded, and the welfare dependent. He therefore advocated social policies aimed at encouraging the upper classes to reproduce more enthusiastically and to discourage the lower orders from doing so.

The concept of "feeble-mindedness" turns out to be exceptionally significant, since it is related to the broader factor of innate intelligence. And that is related in turn to the rise of intelligence testing, a seemingly scientific way of judging the quality of individuals and groups. The IQ (intelligence quotient) test was originally devised by Alfred Binet (1857–1911) in France as a way of measuring the accomplishments of students in relation to the abilities of other children in their age group. An IQ of 100 was defined as the average; if students came in well under or well over that average, they might be recommended for remedial education or moved into a more advanced class.

But as time went on many, particularly in the United States, came to see IQ as reflecting an innate and possibly hereditary factor influencing intelligence and hence social capacity. If some group—a racial minority, say, or the poor—scored lower than the average, this could be seen as an expression of group heredity. In the early twentieth century the "feeble-minded" were seen as a social menace; if allowed to breed freely, it was thought, they would ultimately lead to the degeneration of the nation as a whole. If entire racial or national groups were judged of lesser or greater intelligence, this could be used to explain their level of relative cultural advancement (see Gould 1996).

The underlying assumption was that social class and national quality are largely facts of nature. We also owe the opposition between "nature" and "nurture" to Galton, who believed that the former is paramount in determining racial quality. What Galton said about eugenics in 1904 reflects the influence of his famous cousin:

> Eugenics co-operates with the workings of Nature by securing that humanity shall be represented by the fittest races. What Nature does blindly, slowly, and ruthlessly, man may do providently, quickly, and kindly. The improvement of our stock seems to me one of the highest objects that we can reasonably attempt. I see no impossibility in Eugenics becoming a religious dogma among mankind.... (Galton 1909: 42–43)

Some early feminists were interested in eugenics in addition to women's rights, and the planned-parenthood movement was one outcome—making contraception easily available to working-class women.[2]

Eugenics migrated to North America and became another element in the debate about the genetic future of the American and Canadian peoples. Unlike in Britain, this led to concrete social-policy initiatives, and a number of states and two Canadian provinces (Alberta and British Columbia) passed "eugenic sterilization" legislation aimed at the genetically "unfit"—usually people in state institutions or caught up in the welfare bureaucracy.[3] The National Socialist government in Germany took this further still, but eugenic legislation was also enacted in Scandinavia.[4] Many thousands were sterilized as a result, and in North America the fallout from these policies is still with us in the form of official apologies and financial compensation for the victims. Boas had himself warned against the excesses of the eugenics movement: "Eugenics should not be allowed to deceive us into the belief that we should try to raise a race of supermen, nor that it should be our aim to eliminate all suffering and pain. Eugenics is not a panacea that will cure human ills; it is rather a dangerous sword that may turn its edge against those who rely on its strength" (1916: 478).

We've noted that it was commonly thought that the character of a nation is determined by its racial composition. Anxiety about "race mixing" was therefore very much in the air as well, given the fact that North America seemed to be going through the greatest experiment of this kind that the world had ever seen. There were concerns about what would happen as the old social order lost its northern-European character and became increasingly "mongrelized." A number of influential studies investigated people of mixed-race background, for example in Canada, the Caribbean, and the German African colonies. It was thought that the greater the distance between two races, the more likely that crosses between them would

175

be unstable in some way—less fertile perhaps, or morally unbalanced, a collection of discordant ethnic traits warring with one another. In South Africa and in the American South the fear of race mixing was addressed through "anti-miscegenation" legislation, to which we'll return shortly.

Franz Boas discussed all this in a lecture series that was published in 1911 as *The Mind of Primitive Man*, which we introduced in Chapter 3. It amounts to a Boasian manifesto—a statement of general principles that can be seen in his own writings and in those of his students for many years to come. In it Boas systematically tries to decouple race from culture, and presents the problem clearly in his introductory lecture:

> It appears that neither cultural achievement nor outer appearance is a safe basis on which to judge the mental aptitude of races. Added to this is the one-sided evaluation of our own racial type and of our modern civilization without any close inquiry into the mental processes of primitive races and cultures....
>
> The object of our inquiry is therefore an attempt to clear up the racial and cultural problems involved in these questions. Our globe is inhabited by many races, and a great diversity of cultural forms exists. The term "primitive" should not be applied indiscriminately to bodily build and the culture as though both belong together by necessity. It is rather one of the fundamental questions to be investigated whether the cultural character of a race is determined by its physical characteristics. The term race itself should be clearly understood before this question can be answered. If a close relation between race and culture should be shown to exist it would be necessary to study for each racial group separately the interaction between bodily build and mental and social life. If it should be proved not to exist, it will be permissible to treat mankind as a whole and to study cultural types regardless of race. (Boas 1963: 30–31; see also Boas 1969)

Boas set out to prove that there is in fact *no* close relation between race and culture, that "race" itself is an incoherent concept, and therefore that humankind can be studied as a whole "regardless of race" (see Stocking 1968). He set out to show that even skull shape is an unstable form and that it varies with changing environmental conditions. The task then becomes that of trying to understand individual cultural forms in all their complexity.

His students took on this challenge with enthusiasm, and some of them also wrote on the race issue. In 1942 Ruth Benedict and her colleague at Columbia University, Gene Weltfish (1902–80), drafted a pamphlet on *The Races of Mankind* that was intended for distribution to US troops. The military was still segregated; even the military blood supply was segregated (see Kenny 2006). Nazi propaganda didn't fail to point out the hypocritical element in a war that was supposedly being fought to defend democracy! Benedict and Weltfish stressed "the unity of the human race" and suggested organizing a racially integrated army division as a social experiment: "With America's great tradition of democracy, the United States should clean its own house and get ready for a better twenty-first century. Then it could stand unashamed before the Nazis and condemn, without confusion, their doctrines of a Master Race … sure that victory in this war will be in the name, not of one race or of another, but of the universal Human Race" (Benedict 1943: 192). The pamphlet was never distributed to the troops; Conservative congressmen thought it was subversive (Marks 2008: 245).[5] Nevertheless, segregation in the US armed forces was ended by presidential order in 1948.

But the most significant work coming from the Boasian group on the problem of race was *Man's Most Dangerous Myth: The Fallacy of Race* (1942). The author was Ashley Montagu (1905–99), an Englishman who had first studied anthropology in Britain and then immigrated to the United States where he did his Ph.D. under Ruth Benedict at Columbia. Montagu outlined the history of the traditional race concept, pointing out how superficial and dangerous it is given the true nature of human diversity being revealed by the geneticists. He concluded that "the so-called 'races' represent different kinds of temporary mixtures of genetic materials common to all mankind." For him the human varieties usually called "races" can be accurately described only in terms of gene frequency (Montagu 1942: 41). The problem then becomes determining what causes this variability.

Like the other Boasians, Montagu found no relationship whatsoever between "race" and "culture" or the capacity for culture. His stance was thoroughly relativistic, "by which I mean that all cultures must be judged in relation to their own history, and all individuals and groups in relation to their cultural history, and definitely not by the arbitrary standard of any single culture such … as our own" (1942: 147):

> What seemed to me wrong with the concept of "race" was that no one appears ever to have examined the presuppositions upon which it was based. Those preconceptions, which were taken for granted, even as axiomatic, were that an individual's race was determined by three conditions: (1) his physical characteristics, (2) his inherited mental capacities, and (3) the character of his group's cultural development. These three conditions were indissolubly linked with each other…. No one seemed to understand that there was really no biological connection between physical and mental characteristics or the ability to achieve a state of high civilization either for the individual or for the group. (quoted in Lieberman, Lyons, & Lyons 1995: 840)

Man's Most Dangerous Myth has never gone out of print, and it is currently in its sixth and much expanded edition. Montagu was also an instrumental figure in producing the influential UNESCO (United Nations Educational, Scientific, and Cultural Organization) *Statement on Race* (see Montagu 1972).[6]

The Rise of Genetics

The year 1900 was a big one for the understanding of human diversity: Gregor Mendel's (1822–84) breeding experiments with garden peas came to light again, and Karl Landsteiner (1868–1943) showed that hereditary factors in human blood are the source of harmful and sometimes fatal immune reactions during transfusion.

As mentioned, the nature of heredity was very poorly understood. This troubled Darwin, among others, because he knew that there had to be a mechanism for the preservation and transmission of useful variations; his theory wouldn't work otherwise. Mendel's experiments seemed to show that there are indeed hereditary unit traits that retain their identity and that are expressed in subsequent generations according to precise laws. Though the nature of this process wasn't known, it stood to reason that there had to be some biological factor with the capacity to preserve and transmit information of this kind. It was proposed to call it a "gene."

Landsteiner demonstrated that blood falls into groups—now called A, B, AB, and O—which, like the traits of pea plants, are passed on according to definite statistical rules. This discovery marked the beginning of human genetics as a science. It then turned out that these blood types are not evenly distributed across the globe, but have concentrations in certain regions. Type B, for example, has a peak in south-central Asia and India, while type O is virtually universal among the native peoples of the Americas but is also common in northern Europe and Japan. Such findings gave rise to human population genetics, and to quite different questions than could be answered by skull measuring (Mourant 1983). It was now possible to talk about "gene frequencies" and to diagram them on charts that look a lot like old-fashioned weather maps—derived by connecting the dots for equal frequencies of the genetic trait of interest. The concept of "race" now seems very static; anthropologists and medical researchers turn instead to population genetics in order to explore evolutionary processes and historical connections between populations. We'll have more to say about this in the conclusion, but for now we turn to our case studies.

Red, White, and Black

Sex is one of the factors that serve to define community boundaries. Who is a legitimate mate? Who is in, and who is out? The traditional caste system of India provides a striking illustration: castes are theoretically endogamous; they only marry internally. Marriage and sex outside very narrow boundaries is considered polluting. "Honor killing" might well be the fate of someone—a woman particularly—who steps outside and brings shame upon her family.

But sex is hard to regulate. When Captain Cook reached Hawai'i he tried and failed to prevent his crews from associating with Hawaiian women and spreading venereal disease. When the English settled in Virginia in the early seventeenth century, there were soon liaisons between European men and Native American women. The mixed-race Métis population of Canada, and the Mestizos of Mexico, are results of this process. The most famous example is the "princess" Pocahontas (Smith 1966: 49). What happened between English naval captain John Smith (c. 1580–1631) and Pocahontas (c. 1595–1617) has become the stuff of myth. All we really know is what Smith himself tells us in his *History of Virginia*. Whether it's also a *true* story need not concern us. Smith says he was captured by the Tsenacommacah chief Powhatan's warriors and brought before the king, where there was a debate about what to do with him:

> The conclusion was, two great stones were brought before Powhatan; then as many could laid hands on [Smith], dragged him to them, and thereon laid his head, and being ready with their clubs, to beat out his braines, *Pocahontas* the Kings dearest daughter, when no intreaty could prevaile, got his head in her armes, and laid her owne upon his to save him from death: whereat the Emperor was contented he should live. (Smith 1966: 49)

It's all very romantic, and the names of John Smith and Pocahontas have been joined together ever since. But when it came to marriage she was not joined to Smith but to an English widower named John Rolfe (1585–1622)—"an honest Gentleman, and of good behavior" (Smith 1966: 113). There had been trouble between Powhatan's people and the English, and the marriage helped to smooth things over for the time being. Rolfe already had children by his first marriage, and with Pocahontas he had a son named Thomas (1615–80). He and Pocahontas, now named Rebecca, went to England and were introduced to King James; but she died as they were about to set sail back to America. John Rolfe's descendants by his first marriage came to be known as the "White Rolfes" and those through Pocahontas as the "Red Rolfes." Today some 100,000 people proudly claim "Red" descent.

That was a special case. As the English became more established in their new colony, a more familiar pattern set in. Conflict with Native Americans led to open war, and war coupled with disease led to the destruction of the Native chiefdoms. As Jefferson said in his 1785 *Notes on the State of Virginia*, "spirituous liquors, the smallpox, war, and an abridgment of territory ... had committed terrible havoc among them" (1964: 91).[7] With the realization that tobacco could be a valuable export, there was an increasing demand for labor; Africans were imported as early as 1620, and this in time led to the slave-based plantation system. But Native people hadn't vanished, and poor rural communities of mixed white, black, and Indian ancestry took form that still retained a sense of their Aboriginal identity.

Jefferson was interested in the Indians, and he engaged in a bit of local archaeology himself. Lewis and Clark were instructed to take detailed note of the native people they encountered along the way, and they did so—in part to explore the potential for trade (Wallace 1999: 101). Jefferson speculated about the Indians' ultimate origins:

> Great question has arisen from whence came those aboriginals of America? ... The late discoveries of Captain Cook, coasting from Kamschatka to California, have proved that if the two continents of Asia and America are separated at all, it is only by a narrow strait.... The resemblance between the Indians of America and the eastern inhabitants of Asia, would induce us to conjecture, that the former are the descendants of the latter, or the latter of the former.... (1964: 96)

He was also concerned with the problem of slavery and the characteristics of blacks as a people. By his count there were in 1785 close to 300,000 free inhabitants in Virginia and about 270,000 slaves. In the American Declaration of Independence (1776) he had written, "We hold these truths to be self-evident, that all men are created equal, that they are endowed by their Creator with certain unalienable Rights." This document was hugely significant for the development of the concept of human rights. It was followed in the same century by the revolutionary French *Declaration of the Rights of Man* (1789) and the American *Bill of Rights* (1791), and more recently by the United Nations *Universal Declaration of Human Rights* (1948) and the Canadian *Charter of Rights and Freedoms* (1982). The UN declaration virtually quotes Jefferson in recognizing the "inherent dignity and the equal and inalienable rights of all members of the human family [as] the foundation of freedom, justice and peace in the world."

Yet Jefferson himself remained a slaveholder and was keenly aware of the inconsistency between his great words and the actual American situation—which he called a "blot" and a "great political and moral evil" that he hoped would one day lead to "a complete emancipation of human nature" once the public was ready for it (1964: 86). But he wondered whether black and white Americans could ever live together in peace or would somehow have to be separated (1964: 138–39).

Jefferson's personal circumstances remain obscure. Even while he was alive, rumors circulated about a relationship with a slave woman named Sarah (Sally) Hemings (1773–1835). As it happens, Sally was the half-sister of Jefferson's wife, Martha. Martha Wayles Skelton (1748–82) was a young widow when she married Jefferson in 1772. Her father, John Wayles, in addition to his white family had another family through Elizabeth Hemings, a slave and Sally's mother. Martha died in 1782 shortly after the birth of the last of their six children. Jefferson never married again, nor did he have a male legal heir. Only two daughters with Martha survived until adulthood. As can be seen, this all gets a little complicated.

Sally Hemings was a household servant. In 1785 she accompanied Jefferson and his daughters to Paris, where he served as American ambassador. She lived much of her life at Monticello, Jefferson's home and now a famous tourist attraction.[8] The historian of the Hemings family believes that Jefferson was the father of Sally's seven children—three boys and four girls—two of whom died in infancy (Gordon-Reed

2008). However, neither Jefferson nor Hemings left any account of the nature of their relationship; the evidence for it is mainly circumstantial. Jefferson granted freedom to all three of Sally's sons; other slaves were sold when he died to help pay off his debts. The genetics of the male line turned out to be an important factor in deciding "scientifically" whether Jefferson was indeed their ancestor (see below).

Jefferson died in 1826, and Sally Hemings in 1835. In the years that followed, the slavery issue finally led to the American Civil War. After the defeat of the South, slavery was abolished and constitutional amendments enacted that were aimed at protecting the civil rights of all citizens. Many of these gains were later reversed in the South by legislation restricting the rights of blacks. In Virginia the influence of the eugenics movement resulted in the 1924 *Act to Preserve Racial Integrity*, which declared that "it shall hereafter be unlawful for any white person in this State to marry any save a white person, or a person with no other admixture of blood than white and American Indian" (Kenny 2002: 272). Sixteen states—not all of them Southern—had similar laws.

Ashley Montagu ran through the list in his 1942 book on race. In California, marriage was prohibited with "Negroes, Mongolians, Mulattoes, or members of the Malay Race." In Florida, marriage was prohibited with "Any Negro" (person having one-eighth or more of negro blood)." Montana excluded "Negros or a person of negro blood or in part negro. Chinese person. Japanese person." The list goes on (Montagu 1942: 189–93). In Virginia, a "white person" was defined as having no known trace of non-white blood (including Asian)—*except* those who were 1/16 native Indian or less. This logic was based on a perception of who most people claiming Indian ancestry actually were. Given a long history of intermixture ("miscegenation") between white, Native American, and black communities, it was assumed that virtually all "Indians" were legally black. The exceptions applied mainly to those with no record of black ancestry, who were clearly white in cultural terms, and who could demonstrate a line of descent leading back to Pocahontas.

What finally ended this form of discrimination was a case brought before the US Supreme Court in 1967. It was called *Loving versus Virginia*, and was on behalf of Richard and Mildred Loving. Richard (1933–75) was white and Mildred (1939–2008) was of mixed African-American and Rappahannock Indian ancestry. The couple had married in Washington, DC, where interracial marriage was legal, but had taken up residence back in Virginia where they ran afoul of the Racial Integrity Act. The authorities learned of their status and had them arrested; the Lovings were convicted and sentenced to jail in 1959, but they were allowed to leave the state on the condition that they not return. The Virginia trial judge had said that "Almighty God created the races white, black, yellow, malay and red, and he placed them on separate continents.… The fact that he separated the races shows that he did not intend for the races to mix." Some applied the same logic in defense of segregated schools: if schools were to be integrated, that would naturally lead to miscegenation, and finally to racial degeneration.

The Loving decision was appealed through the state system, but got nowhere. It was then brought before the US Supreme Court as a clear violation of the Lovings' civil rights, The Justices voted unanimously to overturn the Virginia decisions: "under our Constitution, the freedom to marry, or not marry, a person of another race resides with the individual and cannot be infringed by the State. These convictions must be reversed. It is so ordered."[9] And, legally speaking, that was the end of it.[10]

African Racism

When European explorers first reached the interior of East Africa in the 1860s, they were surprised to find centrally organized kingdoms. The largest of these was Buganda, first visited in 1864 by two British officers—John Hanning Speke (1827–64) and James Grant (1827–92). What motivated their trip was an attempt to find the source of the Nile, the Holy Grail of Victorian geography. Speke described his first sight of the royal court, near the present city of Kampala, the capital of Uganda:

> The palace or entrance quite surprised me by its extraordinary dimensions, and the neatness with which it was kept. The whole brow and sides of the hill on which we stood were covered with gigantic grass huts, thatched as neatly as so many heads dressed by a London barber, and fenced all round with the tall yellow reeds of the common Uganda tiger-grass; while within the enclosure, the lines of huts were joined together, or partitioned off into courts, with walls of the same grass. (Speke 1863: 287)

Speke and Grant were followed by the famous journalist and explorer Henry Stanley (1841–1904), who was impressed by the seemingly advanced nature of the Ganda kingdom. Royalty was something the Europeans understood and, as the British had done in India, local African rulers were incorporated into the structure of the colonial state by a kind of treaty arrangement: "A sharp line of separation was drawn between the royal family and commoners, and the blood royal was held to be most sacred" (Roscoe 1911: 187).

Speke records his reaction upon first meeting Kabaka Mtesa, the King: "A more theatrical sight I never saw. The king, a good-looking, well-figured, tall young man of 25, was sitting on a red blanket spread upon a square platform of royal grass, encased in tiger-grass reeds, scrupulously well dressed in a [bark-cloth toga]. A white dog, spear, shield, and woman [the symbols of Uganda] were by his side, as also a knot of staff officers, with whom he kept up a brisk conversation" (1863: 291). The King represented the nation; when a new king was installed he went through a ceremony in which he symbolically "ate Uganda." A rich oral tradition pointed back some 30 generations to the foundation of the kingdom. Though the royal clan was unique, it wasn't clear whether its power had arisen through conquest or had grown up

PLATE 8.3 Mutesa

organically from within (Kenny 1988). The economy was based on banana cultivation and fishing in Lake Victoria, with a lesser role for herding.

The situation was quite different in the neighboring kingdoms to the southwest. Here society was divided up into caste-like groups, with a strongly defined contrast between cattle-keeping clans and the agriculturalists whom they were said to have conquered sometime in the distant past. The cattle-keepers dominated the farmers and extracted tribute from them in the form of grain, beer, and labor; but bonds of reciprocity were established by lending cattle to commoners—a form of feudalism. The entire system was held together through the person of the king, who was the symbolic and economic focus of the social order.

That is the situation that the Europeans found in Rwanda and Burundi. Cattle-keeping aristocrats, the Tutsi, dominated the agriculturalists, the Hutu, who were seen as their serfs. Relations between them were based on what Belgian anthropologist Jacques Maquet called "the premise of inequality"—the notion that categories of people are superior or inferior by nature, "the fundamental ... cultural premise underlying the social roles of the ruler and the subject" (Maquet 1961: 163–64). The Europeans saw Tutsi dominance as being based on their racial superiority, and this perception had a role in the Rwandan genocide.

As discussed above, all human populations are variable, and that's no less true in Rwanda and Burundi. Their populations had three components: Tutsi, Hutu, and a small minority of Twa—short-statured hunter-gatherers who had once made a living in the tropical forest. Maquet, who worked in Rwanda in the 1950s, outlined the local stereotypes of what these three groups are supposed to be like:

> The Twa are hunters, potters and iron-workers. Twa hunters are not numerous, as game is rare in most parts of Rwanda owing to the scarcity of forest. Some of them make a living as singers, dancers, and buffoons. The Hutu are agriculturalists and the Tutsi pastoralists. The statuses of the three groups are hierarchically ranked. The Tutsi group constitutes an aristocracy, the Hutu are commoners, and the Twa are said, half jokingly ... to be more akin to monkeys than human beings. A definite physical appearance is considered typical of each group. According to the socially accepted descriptions of the three stereotypes the typical Twa is short ... with a head low in the crown, face and nose flat, cheek-bones prominent, forehead bulging, eyes narrow and slightly oblique. Hutu characteristics are wooly hair, flat broad nose, thick lips ... and middle stature. Tutsi are very slender and tall. They often have a straight nose and a light brown skin color. (1961: 10)

From a European point of view, the physical and moral characteristics that seemed to separate Tutsi from Hutu were perfectly natural. They were the same qualities that separated aristocratic Europeans from their own working classes and peasantry. The Tutsi—tall, proud, and light of skin—were born to rule; they were thus people the colonial rulers could deal with. The theory was that their ancestors came from the Ethiopian highlands and were culturally and racially superior to those they came to rule over. The following appears in a 1925 Belgian colonial document:

> The Mututsi of good race has nothing of the negro, apart from his colour. He is usually very tall. He is very thin. His features are very fine: a high brow, thick nose and fine lips framing beautiful shining teeth. Batutsi women are usually lighter-skinned than their husbands, very slender and pretty in their youth.... Gifted with a vivacious intelligence, the Tutsi displays a refinement of feelings which is rare among primitive people. He is a natural-born leader, capable of extreme self-control and of calculated goodwill. (quoted in Prunier 1995: 6)

In practice it wasn't all that easy to tell Hutu and Tutsi apart: there has been a history of intermarriage; they fade into one another as physical types and speak the same

PLATE 8.4 King of Rwanda

Bantu language; they are not separate "tribes" but live in the same communities. Not all Tutsi kept cattle; not all Hutu were poor. So what happened?

Rigid distinctions between Hutu and Tutsi were a creation of the colonial order itself. They were not so strongly defined before the coming of the Europeans, who imported their racial preconceptions along with them. There was certainly the "premise of inequality" that Maquet described, but it became increasingly rigid because the Belgian administration favored the Tutsi. People claiming Tutsi identity became a ruling class and virtually monopolized the positions of power that could be occupied by Africans within the framework of a white-ruled colonial state.[11]

> When the Belgians chased the Germans out of the territory in 1916, they discovered that two groups of people shared the land. The Tutsis, who were tall and quite light-skinned, herded cattle; the shorter, darker Hutus tended vegetable plots. The Belgians viewed the minority Tutsis as closer in kind to Europeans and elevated them to positions of power over the majority Hutu, which exacerbated the feudal state of peasant Hutus and overlord Tutsis. Enlisting the Tutsis allowed the Belgians to develop and exploit a vast network of coffee and tea plantations without the inconvenience of war or the expense of deploying a large colonial service. (Dallaire 2003: 47)

These developments set up the preconditions for the Rwandan genocide and similar conflicts in Burundi. Hutu politicians read Marx and Lenin and took aim at Tutsi class oppression. Class war became race war. A historian of the conflict in Burundi describes how such a thing could have happened in a part of Africa that originally seemed so promising: "From a society characterized by complex sociopolitical hierarchies, Burundi has now become greatly simplified, consisting of separate and mutually antagonistic ethnic aggregates. In time of crisis, Hutu and Tutsi emerge as the only relevant defining characteristic of group identities, reducing all other social roles to ... marginal social significance" (Lemarchand 1996: 15).

Since Belgium left Rwanda and Burundi in the early 1960s, Tutsi have killed Hutu, and Hutu have killed Tutsi in both countries. In Rwanda the kingship was overthrown and many Tutsis became refugees in Uganda. Moderates on both sides were murdered or forced to flee. In short, the warring factions became racists. In the United States, a complex history of intermixture was boiled down to the opposition between "black" and "white"; in Rwanda and Burundi, an equally complex history was reduced to the distinction between "Tutsi" and "Hutu." But in Rwanda the outcome was attempted genocide, and 800,000 people died because of it—the result of a carefully orchestrated and politically motivated campaign of systematic murder, an African Holocaust. Canadian general Roméo Dallaire, who headed the UN Peacekeeping mission in Rwanda, found himself unable to stop the genocide; instead, he was forced to witness it from the sidelines because of what he saw as the indifference and double-dealing of the outside world. But, he concluded: "Let there be no doubt: the Rwandan genocide was the ultimate responsibility of those Rwandans who planned, ordered, supervised and eventually conducted it. Their extremism was the seemingly indestructible and ugly harvest of years of power struggles and insecurity that had been deftly played upon by their former colonial rulers" (2003: 515). The failure of the UN mission broke General Dallaire's heart.

Genetic Identities

So far we've been dealing mainly with how "racial" identities are socially constructed—how they are products of history and politics, not biology. Critics of the race concept such as Boas, Benedict, and Montagu sought to demonstrate that there is no biologically rooted connection between race and culture. Their target was the racism of the day, and the notion that entire groups of people are superior or inferior because of their racial inheritance. The culture concept was a weapon in that struggle. But does this mean that biology is irrelevant to the study of human differences? No: human population genetics is a thriving field with many applications. It's clear that certain medical conditions are genetically caused and the statistical prevalence of many others influenced by genetic factors. If you look at contemporary medical journals you will see that research in these areas is a major growth industry.

Like blood groups, genetically related disorders have an uneven global distribution. Many examples could be cited: the frequency of sickle cell anemia found among African Americans, but also in the Mediterranean region and India; a number of inheritable disorders among Jews of Eastern European descent; genetic disorders among Arab groups with a long history of cousin-marriage; the unusual frequency of an iron-overload blood disorder and of cystic fibrosis in western Europe; diabetes among Native North Americans; and so on. Such tendencies can become the focus for political action, such as seeking targeted research funding (see Wailoo & Pemberton 2006).

By the 1990s it had become possible to speak of "molecular anthropology" based on "genomic" analysis. The term "**genome**" applies to the entirety of one's genetic heritage, that is, all the hereditary information one carries. It has a structure that reflects the deep history of one's family line. Technologies and analytical techniques have been developed that make it possible to assess the structure of particular genetic samples quickly and at increasingly low cost.[12] They make it possible to reconstruct one's past in genetic terms, and that of the groups with which one shares a common history.

These two applications of population genetics—medical and anthropological—came together in a controversial case involving the Nuu-chah-nulth of Vancouver Island. They became involved with medical genetics due to a high incidence of rheumatoid arthritis among them. Blood samples were gathered in the hope of getting at the root of this problem. No definite conclusions emerged, however, and it was later learned that these blood samples were used by the geneticist, who was then at the University of British Columbia, to aid another project for which consent had never been granted—genetically based research into the history of human settlement in the Americas:

> Leaders of the Nuu-chah-nulth ... describe the research as another example of exploitation of indigenous peoples. Some have demanded the return of the samples. The Nuu-chah-nulth problem came to the attention of UBC authorities after an indigenous peoples' newspaper reported tribal unrest over the use of their samples for non-arthritis research. [Policies have been introduced] that require researchers to obtain consent each time they wish to conduct new research on stored samples. (Dalton 2002: 111)

The timing and nature of human settlement in the Americas have been issues since Columbus's time. Columbus himself thought about it, as did Thomas Jefferson, Robert Fitzroy, and Charles Darwin. Boas and his group devoted much attention to the problem of cultural affiliations between the tribal peoples of the Northwest Coast and northeastern Russia.[13] The UBC researcher in this case used his samples to show "that the Nuu-chah-nulth contains lineage clusters that predate the colonization of the Americas"—in other words that they originated in Asia (Ward et al. 1991: 8723). Though he thanked them for their collaboration, evidently the Nuu-chah-nulth weren't informed that these samples might be used for a purpose other than the one that was originally intended.

Did this constitute a violation of professional ethics? No, probably not by the standards of the day. But standards change in response to cases like this. How you think about your "origin" is a matter of perspective: "To a Native American, origin might also signify the landscape feature or event where his or her people emerged or acquired their identity" (Lee et al. 2009: 39). The Nuu-chah-nulth sought the return of the blood samples in order to bury them with the bones of their ancestors.[14]

Family Histories

And so we come up against identity issues again. Some native North Americans reject the "scientific" account of their origins and turn to their own stories instead. Others might well find genomics a useful tool in reconstructing the drama of how their ancestors settled the Americas. But probably all of us are interested in our family histories, in one way or another. There have been professional genealogists around for some time, and many families have members who make a hobby of it. Their activities are based on documentary evidence, birth and death records, immigration certificates, and so on. But new possibilities have appeared, enhanced by the power of the Internet.

One of the first practical uses of blood-typing was paternity testing. If paternity was in dispute, then a blood test could at least determine that Mr. X *wasn't* the culprit. Now the new genomic technologies make it possible to situate oneself relative to what has been called "deep time"—evolutionary time. Population genetics and genomics have led to a new form of identity-creation via the founding of genetic ancestry search services (Kenny 2009). This may prove especially appealing if there is really no other way to get a handle on one's past, say if one is African American and the African side of one's ancestry has been lost. The human genome research center at Howard University, a historically African-American school, has spun off a commercial enterprise called AfricanAncestry that aims at helping people recover that lost past:

> Do you know where you are from? Where you are really from? Not the town you were born in or the city you call home. Before the Middle Passage and the time of slavery in the Americas. The place where your bloodline originated and the roots of your family tree truly began. Many of us know we come from Africa but could not claim a specific ancestral homeland. That is, until now! With African Ancestry you can … connect your ancestry to a specific country in Africa and often to a specific African ethnic group. Now you can know "where you are from" and redefine "who you are."[15]

This is also typological thinking, in that the focus is on essential identities, the core of selfhood. AfricanAncestry is now one of a number of services that use increasingly high-powered analysis to tell you about yourself, your near past, and your deep past all the way back to the origins of the human species in Africa. These services identify what ethnic groups you may be genetically affiliated with, about the movements of your ancestors long ago, and—by the way—give an estimate of your disease risks. Whatever you make of them, these services give us new ways of talking about ourselves and conceiving of our relations with others.

The simpler genetic tests they use focus on analysis of the Y-chromosome, and/or on mitochondrial DNA (mtDNA). You probably know that the Y-chromosome determines male sex (XY = male; XX = female). It can be transmitted only down the male line. Mitochondrial DNA is found in small structures in every cell and is essential for cellular energy production, but it is transmitted only down the female line. Both pass from generation to generation largely unchanged, and therefore the analysis of their structure points to processes and events that took place a very long time ago.

AfricanAncestry tells its potential subscribers that "there is no test for racial identification. Race is a social construct, not genetically determined. Similarly, ethnicity is more cultural than biological." This is certainly true, and yet some findings may have a considerable impact on the understanding of both your family's past and your own present circumstances. AfricanAncestry warns men interested in their service that it might turn out that their male line is derived from a European, not someone of African descent. As you've seen above, this would not be surprising given the history and nature of slavery. Conversely, in Brazil, which also has a multiracial history— white, black, and Aboriginal—it's been found that many who think of themselves as of European descent actually carry mtDNA derived from Africa or Native America. The maternal ancestors of their lines were slaves or Indians, or both. The researchers who described these findings hoped that Brazilians, once aware of this complex biological history, "would tend to value the genetic diversity of their own country more and would build a more just and harmonious society" (Santos & Maio 2004: 371; see also Alves-Silva et al. 2000).

The controversy surrounding Thomas Jefferson's bi-racial family was given a new twist in 1998, when a team of geneticists announced in the journal *Nature* that "Jefferson fathered slave's last child" (Foster et al. 1998: 27–38). The child in question was Thomas Eston Hemings (1808–56), who is remembered as resembling Jefferson and having quite light skin (Gordon-Reed 2008: 271, 602). Jefferson's will stated that, upon his death, Eston should be given his freedom, which he was. He subsequently left Virginia, moved to the Midwest where he made his living as a musician, changed his name to Eston Hemings Jefferson, and in effect became "white."

How were the geneticists to get at the truth of this? Jefferson left no sons. However, he had an uncle—Field Jefferson—whose male line, like Eston's, has continued on into our own day. Both were therefore available for Y-chromosome analysis. To make a long story short, there was a match between the two; other families suspected of having Jeffersonian ancestry showed no match and were thus excluded. Even that didn't *quite* settle the issue, but it was pretty close:

> We cannot completely rule out other explanations of our findings based on illegitimacy in various lines of descent. For example, a male-line descendant

of Field Jefferson could possibly have illegitimately fathered an ancestor of the presumed male-line descendant of Eston. But in the absence of historical evidence to support such possibilities, we consider them to be unlikely. (Foster et al. 1998: 27–28)

The Thomas Jefferson Association, consisting of Jefferson's Euro-American descendants through his daughters, has invited the Hemings descendants to their meetings, and some from both sides appeared on the *Oprah Winfrey Show*. There have been joint gatherings at Jefferson's home, Monticello.

Conclusion

The concept of "race" has had a troubled career. From the beginning it was linked to the basic question of human origins and destiny, but also to the problem of how to interpret physical diversity. In the nineteenth century "race" became a key element in colonial discourse, and thus a projection of European political dominance. Caucasians were born to rule the colored races, if only to bring them up to the level where they could rule themselves. Colonized peoples have been paying the price for this assumption ever since. The ethical issues that have arisen within anthropology in recent years are one expression of that fact.

But "race" was an element in scientific discourse as well. The concept of evolution has, since Darwin's time, been a central factor in how human diversity is understood. This didn't necessarily work to the advantage of colonized peoples, since it was always possible to think of them as less "evolved." But race was a powerful factor within the European world as well, in that it was one expression of ethnic nationalism. Nevertheless, the evolutionary approach led to some challenging questions, and some very provocative answers, right down to our own time and the rise of "molecular anthropology." That story continues, and so we wonder if the career of race as an intellectually viable concept is coming to an end, or merely is in the process of changing into a new form driven by the circumstances of our time.

Notes

1 See Stepan (1982) and Stocking (1982) for background; see also Chapter 3.
2 For a general overview of the eugenics movement see Kevles (1995); for how it unfolded in the United States see Paul (1995), and in Canada, McLaren (1990).
3 See Carlson (2001).
4 We are speaking here only of what was done under the laws of these various states. In Nazi Germany much more was done "unofficially"—beginning with the mass killing of patients in mental institutions.

5   In the early 1950s, Gene Weltfish was investigated for suspected communist sympathies, and she lost her university job because of it.

6   The American Anthropological Association and the American Association of Physical Anthropologists have their own statements on race: http://www .aaanet.org/stmts/racepp.htm; http://www.physanth.org/association/position -statements/biological-aspects-of-race/.

7   See Wallace (1999: 74–101) for details of Jefferson's views and the fate of the Virginia Indians.

8   See http://www.monticello.org/.

9   See http://caselaw.lp.findlaw.com/scripts/getcase.pl?court=us&vol=388&invol=1.

10   Advocates for the legalization of same-sex marriage cite the Loving case as a precedent. At the time of writing in 2014, 18 US states and the District of Columbia allow it; the rest, including Virginia, do not. What happens to people who are legally married in one jurisdiction and move to another where such marriages are not recognized? It's clearly an unstable situation. Canada has allowed same-sex marriage since 2006.

11   The American Anthropological Association Statement on Race points out that "ultimately 'race' became a strategy for dividing, ranking, and controlling colonized people used by colonial powers everywhere."

12   If you're interested in the details of how this is done, see Jobling, Hurles, & Tyler-Smith (2004).

13   To investigate this issue, Boas organized what was known as the Jesup North Pacific Expedition, which is remembered as "a research project of such scientific importance and geographical scope that it still ranks as the foremost expedition in the history of American anthropology" (Freed, Freed, & Williamson 1988: 7).

14   There are other cases of this sort. One involves the Yanomamo, who live in the borderlands between Venezuela and Brazil, from whom blood was taken in aid of a project on the population genetics of small tribal groups (see Couzin-Frankel 2010). Another relates to the Havasupai, a small tribe that lives in and around the Grand Canyon in Arizona, from whom blood samples were taken in the course of research undertaken to understand an unusual incidence of diabetes (Dalton 2004).

15   See http://www.africanancestry.com/home/.

Study Questions

1   Explain how the stories of Pocahontas and Thomas Jefferson illustrate our historical understanding of race as a biological and social concept.

2   What is eugenics? What did Galton mean when he said that "eugenics co-operates with the workings of Nature by securing that humanity shall be represented by the fittest races"?

3 Outline the Boasian stance on the relationship between culture and race using examples from the various scholars mentioned in the chapter.

4 Explain Benedict and Weltfish's argument against racial segregation in World War II.

5 How does the history of Thomas Jefferson and his descendants mirror how our understanding of race and identity has evolved over time?

6 Explain how Europeans perceived the relationship between the Hutu and the Tutsi in Rwanda and Burundi. How was this perception informed by the way in which their own social classes were organized at home? What were the implications of their perceptions?

7 Explain the controversial case of the Nuu-chah-nulth of Vancouver Island and the geneticist from the University of British Columbia who took the blood samples. What does this case suggest about the ethics of genomic research?

Discussion Questions

1 How can cultural anthropology contribute to a better understanding of the way in which race is conceptualized? What questions can an anthropologist interested in studying race as a cultural construct pose?

2 Most anthropologists and other social scientists recognize that race is a socially constructed category, yet the concept of race persists in our culture. Why is this?

3 The rise of genetic ancestry search services such as AfricanAncestry reflects a desire among the public to learn about their genetic past. Why do you think this desire exists? In what ways does society contribute to the importance placed on genetic ancestry?

CHAPTER 9

//

Anthropology, Cultural Change, and Globalization

LEARNING OBJECTIVES

After reading this chapter, students should be able to

- understand why studying globalization is important and why anthropology is well suited to understanding the processes of globalization;
- define the terms *change*, *progress*, and *modernization* using examples from the chapter;
- understand how globalization has created a shift in the relationship between culture and place;
- discuss how the movement of people and goods around the world has changed cultures and how we understand the concept of culture; and
- discuss how mass communication, technology, and global markets have changed both how and what anthropologists study.

KEY TERMS

change
cultural imperialism
de-territorialization
economic migrant

globalization
isolationism
macro vs. micro levels
migration

modernization
multi-site ethnography
progress

Introduction

In this final chapter we will consider the issues of cultural change and globalization, and the place of anthropology, a discipline traditionally associated with the past, in our rapidly changing social world. We will consider two case studies that illustrate ways in which anthropological methods and research may lead to a better understanding of the complex processes of globalization on a local level. First, however, it is important that we define the terms used to describe these processes. In so doing, we will also examine some of the assumptions that are embedded in these seemingly neutral terms.

The Language We Use: Important Terms and Concepts

We continually hear of how the world is shrinking, how before long there will exist only one (Americanized?) culture, and that in a relatively short time the global political climate will look vastly different than the way it does today. The term **globalization** is used by politicians, activists, journalists, and everyday citizens. If asked to define globalization, what would you say? Would you focus on the economic processes? The negative effects of industrialization on the environment? The mass migration of people in search of wage labor and a better life? Or the increased ability to share information, art, ideas, and beliefs with people across the globe? These are all components of globalization and illustrate the all-encompassing manner in which the process of change affects aspects of life for people in very different ways. By this point in the book, we hope you have come to understand the importance of considering the impact of complex economic, political, and social processes on the individual person living in a specific community. Understanding the processes of globalization is no different; however, as the processes of globalization are not limited to activities occurring in specific communities and nation-states, it is imperative that the scope of analysis also be broadened.

In Kearney's words, globalization refers to "social, economic, cultural, and demographic processes that take place within nations but also transcend them, such that attention limited to local processes, identities, and units of analysis yields incomplete understanding of the local" (Kearney 1995: 548). This definition illustrates the complexity of globalization: while these processes and changes occur within the nation-state and are therefore experienced within specific communities by individual people, these also travel beyond the seemingly well-defined borders of individual countries. While anthropologists specialize in focusing their lens on "the local," to limit their analysis to one geographic area would neglect the fact that these processes may very well have originated in a nation far removed from the one under study.

Culture and Place: A New Relationship

Cultural change is occurring at breakneck speed all over the world. The ability to communicate across vast geographical spaces in a manner that makes time nearly irrelevant has greatly changed the way in which many people live their lives. The Internet and other technological developments have introduced a new dimension to the concept of diffusion. While the diffusion of goods and ideas is nothing new—for example, tobacco first spread from the tropics of the Western hemisphere to North and South America, and then on to the rest of the world after 1492—the ways in which these ideas are moving, and the implications of such movement, are having profound effects on how we live our lives.

With the advent of mass communication systems, information is passed without the necessity of personal travel. And because not everyone has equal access (or any access at all) to these communication systems, information continues to circulate via word of mouth. Teenagers in China are infatuated with pop stars from Taiwan and Hong Kong, the elderly in Canada practice tai chi in community centers, and kids in the Philippines watch Disney cartoons in their living rooms. As anthropologists Jonathan Inda and Renato Rosaldo state, "culture is highly mobile" (2008: 11). Traditionally, we have thought of cultural practices and customs as tied to geographic locations. This is no longer the case: globalization has "weakened" the relationship between culture and place (Inda & Rosaldo 2008).

Despite the weakening of cultural ties to place, or the "**de-territorialization**" of culture, there will always exist an element of place, or "territoriality," within culture because people live and operate in local environments, and it is in these locations that culture moves, changes, and is experienced (Inda & Rosaldo 2008). The relationship between culture and place has changed with the increased movement of people across national boundaries and borders. We are familiar with the ease with which those with the financial means can travel across the world or speak with others in places far removed from oneself. But what about the "flow" of cultural ideas and goods—is this movement unidirectional? In other words, is one culture stronger and more pervasive than others?

The notion that the world is becoming smaller and more homogeneous (or the same) due to the processes of globalization is an often-repeated sentiment. Notions of the "one-world culture," "**cultural imperialism**" or "the West and the rest" imply that the cultural diversity of the world is in danger of extinction, and that as communication systems, travel, and modernization initiatives continue to flourish, it won't be long before everyone is wearing the same clothes, eating the same food, and living in the same style of houses. Western, or more specifically American, culture (both material goods and ideologies) appears to be absorbing the cultural diversity of the world. From an anthropological perspective, do you think that this is true, or even possible? When cultural traits are borrowed, they often undergo a major change in order to "fit" with local circumstances. People will always have their own cultural lens through which they see the world—this will not change just because they have access to Hollywood films or Nike shoes.

The notion that culture flows from the West to the rest of the world is simplistic. Consider the restaurants in your neighborhood or community—what cuisines are represented? Or the medical treatments that are available to you here in North America—perhaps you have consulted a naturopath or an acupuncturist. The music that you listen to? The centers for worship in your city or town? While it may be true that Western cultural ideas and goods are well known in all corners of the globe, to say that the West is not a cultural *consumer* of other cultures is to imply that non-Westerners are only passive recipients of cultural knowledge and are not engaged in the sharing of information and ideas. Furthermore, the culture and population of the West are themselves extremely heterogeneous—consider Canada. How would you describe the culture of Canada without discussing the tremendous multiculturalism that the nation is so well known for? The line that differentiates "the West from the rest" is no longer as clear as we once believed it to be, and as the movement of ideas and people continues to develop in new and exciting ways, it will become more blurred as technology surges forward.

The Meaning of Change

What examples come to mind when you hear the word **progress**? What images come to mind? Do you think of technology? Industry? A way of thinking? Definitions of progress suggest a positive development, usually of a gradual move toward achieving a goal or reaching a higher standard. Definitions that consider progress in relation to people suggest the advancement of society toward "an improved or more advanced condition" (OED). This forward movement implies a positive change from one state to another, a leaving behind of something outdated to embracing something new. Now consider the term **change**. Change is a much broader concept that, on its own, has no direction or value—change is the result of action or thought, whether it is intentional, accidental, beneficial or harmful. Cultural change most often occurs in politically and economically stable societies in a gradual manner—cultural systems are, for the most part, stable systems. When change occurs in a rapid and abrupt manner, it often results in extreme modification to social relationships, particularly when beliefs and understandings of cultural values and institutions have been challenged.

Despite their difference in meaning, the words *progress* and *change* are often used interchangeably. To use the term progress to describe cultural change implies that this cultural change is for the better. Progress, however, is not a *cause* of cultural change but rather a particular way of describing such change. Change is an altering of the social and/or material world that may or may not be beneficial or welcome. This is an important distinction to keep in mind when discussing cultural change, particularly in the context of globalization. How can we judge whether or not a change has been positive? Must it be positive for all members of a society in order for it to be considered progress? Social change affects individuals in very different ways—what may be a positive change for some may result in a negative transformation for others. The experiences of cultural change are intricately entangled with social, political, and economic factors that bring about very different circumstances depending on where one is located in the social order of things.

The term **modernization** is often used to describe political, economic, and social changes. Like the notion of progress, modernization implies a value-laden transformation from antiquated to current, and usually includes material and technological progress and individual betterment. Modernization can be defined as the process of cultural and socio-economic change, and is often linked to urbanization, industrialization and the spread of education. The effects of modernization reach far beyond the economic systems of society—these changes creep into the social and political realms of everyday life. From a Western perspective, modernization brings with it many of the elements of social life that we hold dear, such as increased access to formal education, democratic political processes, and secularization; however, the effects of these changes often materialize in unexpected and unwelcome ways. Supporters of modernization assert that the benefits gleaned from the process make any inconveniences (whether they are social or environmental) worth the cost, while critics (including many anthropologists), state that the rapid cultural change brought about by modernization often leads to increased social inequality and environmental degradation.

An example of the unexpected consequences of modernization is evident in the case of the Skolt Lapps, a group who live in northern Finland and who have traditionally supported themselves through fishing and herding reindeer. Reindeer were an integral part of the Skolt Lapp way of life—they provided meat and hides, were given as gifts, were a good to be traded or sold, and also provided a means for transportation, pulling sleds in the winter and packing in the summer. In the 1960s, the reindeer herders adopted the snowmobile, a move that was believed to make herding easier and more efficient. The unexpected consequences of this change, however, were enormous and far reaching. The cost of purchasing the snowmobiles and maintaining them is large, and this created a dependency on outside economic transactions, a dependency that had not existed to this extent before. As a result of the need for cash, the men were required to leave the village for wage work or depend on government assistance. Ironically, the adoption of the snowmobile contributed to a decline in reindeer herding—the number of deer in a herd fell drastically, from around 50 to 12. Not only is this number too small to maintain and receive any benefit from, but the deer are also constantly attempting to flee and join a larger herd. The relationship between the men and the deer has drastically changed, for the deer are fearful and suspicious of the noisy and aggressive machines that the men ride (Pelto 1973).

The consequences of mechanized herding has been experienced in the economic sphere, where men have been required to leave the village and enter into the cash-credit economy, as well as culturally, as herding and conceptions of manhood are deeply linked. While it would be correct to say that the Skolt Lapp economy has been modernized, it would be difficult to say that this change signified *progress* if we associate the word with a positive transformation.

The Flow of Goods

Another product of modernization is the increased flow of capital and goods across the world. Multinational corporations are companies that operate worldwide but are centrally controlled from one location. Motivated by profit, multinational corporations make decisions that will bring the highest return in the economic sector. At times, these decisions are made with little understanding of or regard for the impact on the interests and well-being of those who live where the product is sourced, manufactured, and distributed. While the presence of a manufacturing plant may bring numerous jobs to the area and circulate capital into the local communities for other services, such as restaurants, grocery stores, taxis, etc., the payment that workers receive is necessarily low in order for the corporation to benefit from setting up shop there. To keep costs low, the working conditions of many manufacturing plants are dismal, putting the lives of thousands at risk for the sake of profit. While some point fingers at the individuals who own these plants to ensure that their workers have safe conditions, others redirect this responsibility to the corporation, stating that plant owners have little choice but to pay their workers next to nothing in order to meet the demand for extremely cheap goods.

In April 2013, the Rana Plaza, a building housing over 1,000 garment workers in Savar, Bangladesh, went up in flames. Bars on the windows prevented people from escaping, and over 1,100 people perished when the eight-story building collapsed following a fire. The building was owned by a local businessman, who rented the space to two international clothing manufacturers. Bangladesh is a very poor country—43 per cent of residents live below the poverty line, and it ranks 146th out of 186 on the United Nations Development Index.[1] The garment industry is an extremely important source of income for the four million Bangladeshi textile workers, 40 per cent of whom are women. In response to this tragedy, clothing manufacturers have called upon the governments of their own nations and those of the host nation to enact stricter control on workplace conditions. It is yet to be seen whether any significant changes will occur, and what impact this will have upon the people who spend their days in the factories. This example illustrates the complexity of conducting business in a global economy, and how one decision made in a boardroom in the United States (or Canada, Spain, France, etc.) can have extreme consequences for thousands of people living in very precarious situations.

Anthropology is well suited, both theoretically and methodologically, to consider the impact that these macro (or worldwide) processes have upon individuals in communities all over the world, and how these individuals respond in culturally informed ways. There are a number of anthropological studies that have considered the relationship between multinational corporations and the local communities where their goods are produced, such as Laetitia Cairoli's *Girls of the Factory: A Year with the Garment Workers of Morocco* (2012), an ethnography that considers the lives of the female garment workers in Fez, Morocco.

Understanding Processes of Change: An Anthropological Perspective

The value in anthropological research of understanding the processes of globalization lies in its ability to consider how global processes that are concerned with economics, politics, and the social world are experienced on a local and individual level: "[Anthropology] is preoccupied not just with mapping the shape taken by the particular flows of capital, people, goods, images and ideologies that crisscross the globe, but also with the experiences of people living in specific localities when more and more of their everyday lives are contingent on globally extensive social processes" (Inda & Rosaldo 2008: 5).

The methods that characterize anthropology as a social science position the voices and experiences of the individual as central to analysis. A researcher engages in participant observation, speaks with local citizens, and conducts interviews with those living in a specific place and time so as to understand how their daily lives are affected by the opening of a new manufacturing plant, the spread of cell phones, or access to the Internet. Anthropologists consider how individuals make sense of these processes through their own cultural lens. Globalization touches all aspects of life, and, as such, anthropologists have investigated how these processes have materialized in a diversity of social realms. Below, we take a brief look at how anthropologists have approached the study of globalization in terms of migration, international adoption, protest, activism, and the development of local economies.

Migration of People, Migration of Culture

The movement of people takes many forms and is motivated by a diversity of factors. There are those who move from rural environments to urban ones in search of wage labor and the desire for a better standard of living; students who travel across the world to continue their studies in different countries; families who are forced from their home because of the threat, or the actuality, of political, ethnic or religious violence; and men and women who cross national borders in order to earn a living as nannies, engineers, nurses, and maids. The movement of people is nothing new—pastoralists and foragers have always relocated regularly, and European expansion and exploration began hundreds of years ago. What characterizes the current state of migration as distinct, however, is the sheer *volume* of people who are no longer living in the nation in which they were born or raised, and the relative ease with which migrants can keep contact with their home country/community and the friends and family who remain there.

PLATE 9.1 Burmese Refugees Waiting to be Registered by a Thai Policeman

Migration is the movement of a person or people from one place to another. The movement of people has been a popular area of study for anthropologists, particularly in terms of *why* people decide to move, *how* they adapt to their new surroundings, and more recently, how this move affects their cultural and individual identity (which we explored in Chapter 5). Migration takes many forms. Perhaps the most common form is the movement of people within a nation from rural areas to urban centers. According to the "push-pull theory," because of the increase in population, rural environments are less able to support residents economically. As a result, people flock to urban centers with the hope of finding employment. The reality of this situation is often bleak—individuals are separated from their support networks and the fast pace of city life can be difficult to adjust to. Moreover, employment often comes in the form of low-paying and low-skilled work, such as cleaning or factory work, which may have grave psychological effects, as well as making it extremely difficult to make ends meet.

Migration has increased dramatically since the mid 1980s—it is estimated that nearly 2 per cent of the world's population lives abroad.[2] While rates of international migration are on the rise (a 37-per-cent increase from 1990 to 2010), it is still relatively uncommon, with nine out of every ten people in the world living in their country of birth (United Nations Department of Economic and Social Affairs 2010). Women make up approximately half of the population of international migrants, a relatively new trend over the last 50 years.

Immigration patterns have also changed. During the first part of the twentieth century, the majority of immigrants moving to countries such as Canada, the United States, and Australia were European, specifically from countries in western and northern Europe. The fact that these immigrants were coming from predominantly white nations was not coincidental—the receiving countries had strict immigration policies outlining who were and were not "desirable" populations. Australia, for instance, once had an explicitly "White Australia" policy. In Canada, the changing labor needs and a desire to improve the national image ignited a transformation and restructuring of these problematic immigration policies in the 1960s. In the last 20 years, Canada and the United States have experienced an increase in immigrants from Asia, Mexico, Latin America, and the Caribbean, as well as most recently from central and eastern Europe. It would be wrong, however, to say that migration is only happening from developing to developed countries—while 70 per cent of international migrants hail from the "South," roughly half of this population has migrated to other economically developing countries.[3]

Economic migrants, or individuals who relocate for a limited period of time in order to work, have no intention of making their move permanent. Asian women are the fastest-growing group of migrant workers—there are approximately 1.5 million Asian women working abroad. The majority of these women head to Saudi Arabia, Kuwait, Hong Kong, Singapore, and Japan and are employed primarily in the domestic service sector and professions such as nursing and teaching (Miller, Van Esterik, & Van Esterik 2001). Most of these individuals remain connected to their homeland and often send wages home to family. Indeed, remittances from migrants provide a major source of capital for many developing nations.[4] A number of anthropologists have investigated the complex experiences of migrant workers all over the world. In Canada, the Philippines became the nation's largest source of short- and long-term migrants in 2010. The edited collection *Filipinos in Canada: Disturbing Invisibility* (Sintos Coloma et al. 2012) explores how understandings of gender, youth, and identity intersect with migration and labor practices in Canada's Filipino community. In that volume, anthropologist Lisa Davidson investigates the experiences of Filipina women who travel to Canada to work as nannies under the Live-In Caregiver Program, a program designed to address shortages of child and elder care while offering permanent residence status to those workers who have stayed for two years.

Sharon Nagy (2006) explores the employment of transnational household workers in Doha, the capital city of Qatar, a small country on the Arabian Peninsula. The end of the twentieth century was a period of rapid urbanization in the Arabian Gulf. This transformation required an influx of workers in all sectors to meet building and development demands. While these workers were primarily international, village dwellers and Bedouin communities within Qatar also moved into Doha, establishing the city as a true mix of cultures and nationalities. Over six years of fieldwork (1994–2000), Nagy considered the social interactions occurring in Doha along two lines: those between Qatari citizens and foreign nationals, and those between groups who share

Qatari citizenry but who hail from very different cultural backgrounds. Nagy was interested in understanding how these social relationships and cultural understandings manifest in the spatial organization of the city. She describes how the impact of land and building grants, immigration laws, and employment regulations "facilitate residential isolation and limited interaction between groups. In addition, the way space is divided is linked to prevailing attitudes towards social differentiation and the existence of multiple ideologies of difference is reflected in multiple spatial phenomena" (2006: 135). Qataris prefer to live near those who are similar to themselves—this preference excludes non-Qataris, as well as Qataris who hail from different cultural, class, and religious backgrounds.

Nagy's research also explores the manner in which household relationships "reproduce" global hierarchies that are informed by ideas of gender and nationality. Within the relatively confined space of the household, Qatari women and children come into contact with foreigners whom they would not normally meet due to their restricted public movement. The domestic workers themselves, particularly the women, also have limited interactions with people outside of their house of employment. The household setting informs both employers' and employees' knowledge of the wider cultural backgrounds of each group (see Nagy 1998). Nagy's research illustrates that the processes involved in international economic migration are experienced on a multitude of levels—from the political and economic circumstances of sending and receiving countries, to the spatial organization of a city, to the individual households and lives of the employers and employees themselves.

Culture, Identity, and Citizenship: International Adoption

The act of adopting children across national borders has ignited heated debate among all sectors of society, from academics to politicians to families sitting around the dinner table. This practice touches on a number of issues that people tend to have very strong opinions about—the nature of family, the well-being of children born into poverty, the right of wealthy nations to adopt children from poorer ones, and the significance, if any, between biological origins and cultural identity. While there are a number of angles to this debate, we will focus our discussion on how the culture concept has been invoked on a number of levels in critiques of international adoption. Our discussion will consider how changes at the global and national levels altered the way in which American citizens viewed their responsibility as a global super-power. This cultural transformation ignited the interest of American interest groups and citizens to the plight of children in war-torn or poverty-stricken situations, and the drive to offer assistance through adoption was set in motion. Sixty-five years later, adoption has become a legitimate method to create a family by those with the means to do so. Finally, at a more individual level, the practice by adoptive parents of instilling a cultural education for children adopted across national borders is illustrative of an understanding of culture that is tied to biological traits.

Before we begin, however, it is important that we contextualize our discussion of adoption. As we have already seen in Chapter 4, the act of defining the family is a complex and culturally sensitive process. Definitions of who is family and who is not have far-reaching implications that are social, political, economic, and religious in nature. Clearly, this is not a process to be taken lightly. Western constructions of adoption operate on the premise that an orphan child is taken in by a nuclear-style family unit. The child becomes part of this family unit through a legal process rather than a biological one. This is but one understanding of both the orphan and adoption concepts, but it is far from universal. There has been extensive anthropological literature examining the practice of adoption and fostering and how it "fits in" to the larger concept of kinship.[5]

One example of this type of research is by anthropologist Jessica Leinaweaver (2007), who examines the practice of child-circulation in Ayacucho, a poverty-stricken area of Peru that witnessed political violence and upheaval in the 1980s and 1990s. In many cultures, such as Hawaiian and Chinese, the nuclear family unit is not the core unit and the act of caring for one's children often requires the cooperation of extended family and, at times, the larger community. In Ayacucho, Leinaweaver examined the practice of child-circulation, which involves the relocation of a child to a household of a family relative. This relocation is not regarded as permanent, and the child can move back and forth between the homes. Both parties involved stand to gain benefits, such as relief from feeding a child by the sending family and the additional help another set of hands can bring to the receiving household. As well, each party pays a price, such as incurring the cost of a new family member or the hardship of having one's child live somewhere else.

Leinaweaver (2007) describes how child-circulation is a common practice in this region of Peru and serves the purpose of strengthening ties between families, allowing for better opportunities for children and assistance to adults. One Peruvian anthropologist declared that the concept of the orphan simply did not exist in Ayacucho as a relative would always be able to take in a child. This statement, however, refers only to the time before the political upheaval and violence that killed so many mothers and fathers. In 1983, the first orphanage was opened. Twenty years later, this institution has become a home to many children whose parents and relatives are *temporarily* unable to care for them. Most parents who leave their children here have every intention of taking them back once they are able to provide for them again.

Leinaweaver (2007) also tells the stories of two girls. Her first story concerns Luisa, a baby girl whose mother died during childbirth. Her elderly and poor father could not take care of her and so gave her to her mother's brother to be taken care of. Luisa's health took a turn for the worse, and, in panic, her uncle took her to the local orphanage to receive medical treatment and care. Because of Luisa's poor health and the unlikely event that her family would be able to financially care for her, the state intervened and declared that it would be in Luisa's best interest to be put up for permanent adoption. In discussion with Luisa's uncle and father, Leinaweaver learned that it was never their intention that Luisa be taken permanently from their family—they had hoped she would receive the medical care she so desperately needed and would then be returned to them when she was healthy. In essence, this is the practice of child-circulation that also involves a state-run institution rather than just family members.

In the second story, Milagros lived with her mother and two siblings when they fled the rural highlands of Ayacucho after her father had been taken by the rebel forces during the war. After the family stayed with her mother's sister for three years in an urban area, everyone decided that Milagros would continue living with her aunt while her mother and siblings relocated to another area. Her aunt was better off financially, and this meant that Milagros would be able to continue going to school rather than having to get a job to help support her mother and siblings if she lived at home. There was no involvement of the Peruvian legal system. This is an example of child-circulation that did not involve the intervention of the state.

The stories of these two girls illustrate an example of child rearing that is different from what is found in North America. While Milagros's story appears quite positive in that she was able to take advantages of opportunities without losing contact with her biological mother, Luisa's story illustrates the consequences of two clashing systems: on the one hand, a type of child rearing found in the rural region of Ayacucho, where children may circulate between the households of extended families for periods of time, and on the other, Peru's Code of Children and Adolescence, which is informed by a belief that it is in the best interest of the child to be cared for by those who are kin only if they have economic means to do so. In this situation, economic capability took precedence over kinship, and Luisa was put up for adoption.

Child rearing takes many forms, and the systems that govern kinship relations are subject to cultural worldviews and belief systems. Adoption, whether by those related by blood to a child or not, is a meaningful and legitimate act of creating a family. It is a process that challenges the assumption that blood kin are the only legitimate people who can raise a child. As we turn our lens toward international adoption, a process that crosses legal and cultural boundaries, it is important to consider the meanings of terms such as orphan, family, and adoption by all parties involved. Our focus in the next section is on the culture of adoption in North America, primarily from the perspective of the receiving nations and the adoptees.

As World War II came to an end in 1945, America was transformed from an **isolationist** nation to a major player on the international stage. American citizens had been awakened to the horrors of war as media reports circulated the globe, and over the next few decades, America would increasingly become involved in international struggles. As a result of these political, economic, and social forces in the international realm, a cultural shift in the American public occurred. Perhaps most devastating to many Americans in the 1950s were accounts of innocent children who had been victims of war-related violence. While these reports would likely have caused concern at any time, America's new position of power seemed to ignite feelings of responsibility. Reports of children orphaned as a result of the atomic bombing of Hiroshima led to an outcry by Americans who wished to sponsor orphans and bring them to the United States where they could be adopted (Klein 2003). Liberal groups sought adoptive parents for those children fathered and left behind by American and European servicemen in the Philippines, Japan, China, Korea, and later Vietnam (Marre & Briggs 2009). Protestant Evangelical Christians believed it was their duty to spread the word of God and halt "godless communism." This movement inspired the creation of World Vision, a Christian organization still in operation today that facilitates the sponsoring of children in developing nations by those who send a monthly dollar amount. This religious movement inspired a number of Christian American families to make a further commitment by actually adopting children from Korea. It was not

PLATE 9.2 Korean Children with Their American Parents

long before American-financed overseas orphanages and adoption services appeared (Marre & Briggs 2009).

As the culture of the United States was changing to reflect the nation's relatively new status, changes at home were having an impact on women's social position in society. Women were gaining higher social standing—their wages were creeping higher and professional opportunities previously closed to them were slowly opening. By the 1960s, fewer and fewer unwed mothers were putting their children up for adoption: "a combination of state supports for parents and rising wages and employment opportunities for women enabled them to keep their children. As soon as single mothers could afford to keep their children, they did" (Marre & Briggs 2009:10). These social changes, alongside the legalization of birth control and abortion in the 1970s, led to a falling birth rate and far fewer babies being put up for adoption in North America.

These changes to the demography of American society, combined with social and religious movements, led many prospective adoptive parents to look overseas (Yngvesson 2009). The number of transnational adoptions has nearly doubled since the late 1980s, with the United States representing the largest receiving nation at 22,884 adoptions in 2004 (Selman 2009). In this same year, China, Russia, Guatemala, and South Korea were the largest sending nations. The process of adopting a child transnationally is lengthy, arduous, and, in most cases, expensive. Estimates put the cost of arranging a transnational adoption to Canada at approximately $35,000–$45,000,[6] ensuring that only those with economic means are able to engage in this type adoption. While the sending nations as a whole are not necessarily poor, the families who tend to put children up for adoption are. This creates a highly unbalanced relationship, and many critics argue that the right of individuals from wealthy nations to adopt children from poorer nations is morally questionable. Tales of corruption, trafficking in children, and unwed mothers being forced to put their children in orphanages placed transnational adoption under international scrutiny. In 1993, the *Hague Convention on the Protection of Children and Co-operation in Respect of Intercountry Adoption* was signed, stating that countries must do whatever possible to keep the child within their own family, or to find a family for that child in their home country. Transnational adoption was to be the third option: "The convention insisted on a child's right to an identity and to the right to 'grow up in a family environment, in an atmosphere of happiness, love and understanding'" (Volkman 2005: 5).

Herein lies one of the major issues at the heart of international adoption. While considering the practice on a **macro** level, the act of wealthy nations adopting the children of poorer nations appears to be a band-aid solution to the problems of economic inequality in the world. When considered on a **micro** level, however, if an individual child who cannot be cared for by their kin can be spared a life of poverty by being adopted by a family from overseas, it is difficult to say that this process is corrupt. It is for this reason that the topic of international adoption ignites such passionate debate.

A shift in national cultural values, powerful religious movements, an increase in women's social position, and international legislation committed to protecting a child's right to a cultural identity have all contributed to establishing transnational adoption as a relatively accepted practice. The discourses employed to discuss this type of adoption have also changed over the last few decades. Originally, adoptive parents and the agencies that they went through assumed that an international adoption was a "closed" adoption—the child was adopted, brought to their new home, and raised as an American (or Canadian, Spaniard, etc.). Over time, however, the importance of cultural identity became a prominent topic of debate among those involved. Many adoptees began to challenge, question, and speak out about how transnational adoptions were carried out and discussed in mainstream society. It was not long before

> adoptees were expected, or at least invited, to explore their multiple identities: to retain a name, to imagine their birth families, to learn about "birth cultures," perhaps even to visit their birth countries and seek out relatives. Many Korean adoptees had grown up and had shaken off their sense of isolation as they met other adoptees like themselves. They began to speak forcefully, sometimes with anger and pain, about how they were not simply the white Minnesotans (or Swedes, or Californians) whom their parents and the culture as a whole had expected them to be. Some articulated their sense of dislocation, uncertainties about where they fit as they struggled to reconcile their outer appearance and inner sense of self, the ambiguities of simultaneously belonging and not belonging. (Volkman 2005: 5)

Many adoptive parents are now committed to providing a cultural education for their adopted children—language and cultural education classes, introducing children to adult role models of the same ethnicity, living in a diverse area, and traveling to the birth country have all become increasingly common. The Internet has an abundance of chat groups for adoptees and adoptive parents, providing virtual communities for those who have experienced adoption in one way or another. This desire for support and dialogue suggests that the realization of an individual's cultural identity is a complex process that touches on a number of issues, including kinship, geography, and appearance. Conceptualized in this way, identity is "associated with a root or ground of belonging that is inside the child (as 'blood,' 'primal connectedness,' and 'identity hunger') and is unchanging. But it is also outside the child in the sense that it is assumed to tie him or her to others whom he or she is like (as defined by skin color, hair texture, facial features, and so forth). Alienation from this source of likeness produces 'genealogical bewilderment' and a psychological need for the adopted child to return to where he or she 'really' belongs" (Yngvesson 2009: 26). If culture is indeed learned, does this move to associate the birth culture with transnationally adopted individuals raised in very different surroundings seem unusual, or do you believe that the notion of cultural origins is important for all individuals, whether they remember them or not?

Understanding culture is a complex undertaking, and it is not an easy task to create an environment where children are supported to foster aspects of their identity that they deem important. Through anthropological research, the voices of adopted children and their adoptive parents are increasingly being heard, and with them the challenges and successes of this complex approach to family making are better understood. Due to the circumstances of transnational adoption, however, the voices of the birth parents remain largely silent, a situation that reflects the power imbalance between those with the means to adopt children and those in the unfortunate situation of having to give their children up (Marre & Briggs 2009).

Protest

In the last days of 2010, the world watched as protests erupted across many parts of the Arab world, including Tunisia, Egypt, Libya, and Yemen, in a movement that became known as the Arab Spring. Protesters were rallying against repression, censorship, and violence from authorities, including governments and militia. While each protest took on a meaning of its own to reflect the situation in that nation, they shared a common approach of strikes, demonstrations, and marches and used social media such as Facebook to organize and communicate their cause. As a result of the protests, governments in Tunisia, Egypt, Libya, and Yemen fell, and other leaders announced their decision to step down at the end of their current terms.

In January 2011, Cairo, Egypt, took center stage as thousands of Egyptians occupied Tahrir Square to protest 30 years of power by President Hosni Mubarak. For weeks, television coverage documented the protests and protesters, from families spanning multiple generations to individual youth, united in their determination to bring about change. Anthropologist Lila Abu-Lughod watched the protests unfold from the living rooms of friends in a small Egyptian town south of Cairo where years earlier she had conducted ethnographic research. She was struck by the absence of footage or reporting from outside of Tahrir Square—what was happening in the countryside? How were the majority of Egyptians who lived *outside* of Cairo reacting to the revolution?

As an anthropologist, Abu-Lughod was interested in how the fight for democracy and freedom that was occurring on the streets of Cairo was experienced by the rural Egyptians living a life far removed from the busy metropolis. How were these momentous events affecting the daily lives of rural Egyptians? According to Abu-Lughod, "Affected by the same national policies and state institutions, each region and location experienced them through the specific problems they created for people locally. And each group that felt itself to be part of what these young men described as this 'glorious revolution' has taken up a different set of projects" (2012: 25). Abu-Lughod had already established a trusting relationship with many individuals in the village, and because of this was able to observe and speak with people about their experiences of abuse and oppression at the hands of government authorities (police, councils, politicians). This small town was an important heritage site that attracted both local and international tourists, and because of this had ignited political and commercial interest. This interest was accompanied by corruption, and locals had been plagued with issues such as shortage of food and a lack of public services. Just as in Cairo, local youths used social media such as Facebook to come together to discuss local issues, as well as strategies to initiate improvements that would affect daily life, such as the distribution of bread and bottled cooking gas.

While differences in motivations existed in the country and the city, Abu-Lughod asserts that the acts of resistance she witnessed and that were described to her must be considered in the same vein of protest as those occurring in Cairo, despite the fact that they were geographically removed and out of the spotlight of the international media. She describes how the language used to describe the struggle in the village was somewhat different from that used in Cairo, reflecting the importance of community and social responsibility: "The youth speak the moral language of responsibility, self-lessness and community welfare, the struggle against corruption and self-interest. It is a strong language of social morality, not of rights. They do not speak of democracy, but in tackling problems directly and personally; they are living it" (2012: 25).

Abu-Lughod's work illustrates the value of an anthropological approach to under-standing an event that gains international attention. Through observation and inter-views, the perspectives of those who are not included in the international media are given space to be heard, and through this discussion offer a more complete snapshot of the impact of such a significant event.

Meeting Foreign Demand: Ecotourism and Mining

Anyone who has perused the glossy pages of a *National Geographic* or watched an episode of the reality television show *Survivor* knows the allure of a secluded tropical beach or pristine mountain range. Traveling to distant countries where the types of food eaten, the dress worn, and the language spoken are totally different from one's own is an exciting and at times terrifying experience. Encounters with different people, landscapes, and cultures can be a powerful tool for instilling a sense of social respon-sibility, particularly if the areas traveled to are at risk as a result of overuse, pollution or poor management. It is this sense of social conscience that travel agencies and tour groups hoped to tap into when the concept of ecotourism was developed.

As an industry, ecotourism is relatively new to the tourist trade. Becoming enor-mously popular in the 1990s and reaching its peak when the United Nations declared 2002 the "year of ecotourism," it was an approach that many believed would be beneficial for all involved: "The outcome of ecotourism ought to be win-win-win: ecotoursits ought to win by getting to experience the 'natural areas' that attract them, people living alongside such 'natural areas' ought to win through opportunities for work enabled by the presence of wealthy outsiders in their midst, and those interested in the protection of these natural areas ought to win as everyone else involved becomes invested in the mission of conservation" (Walsh 2012: 51). Of course, not all great ideas translate into great products, and ecotourism has proven not to be the magic bul-let it was thought to be. As we will see in anthropologist Andrew Walsh's ethnographic study of Madagascar, the reality for residents of this hot ecotourist destination was far from pristine.

The Ankarana region of Madagascar is home to an ecosystem unlike any other in the world. Ankarana National Park consists of 150-million-year-old limestone formations, caves, underground rivers, and sunken forests—as one can imagine, an awe-inspiring sight. It is also home to some very valuable natural resources, the most sought-after being sapphires. Walsh's ethnography *Made in Madagascar: Sapphires, Ecotourism and the Global Bazaar* explores the emergence of two seemingly disparate trades in Madagascar: sapphire mining and ecotourism. While mining and

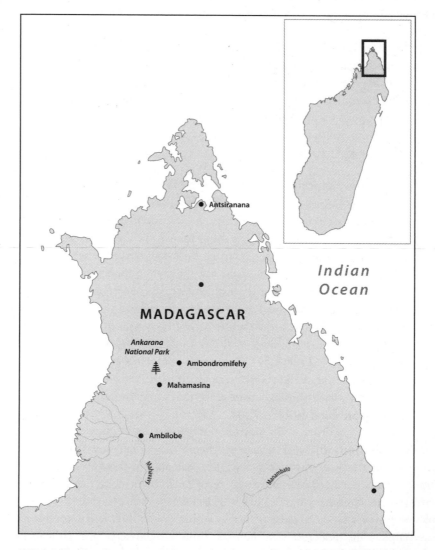

MAP 9.1 Madagascar

environmentalism represent two vastly different approaches to development, Walsh illustrates that to the local people witnessing their region's inundation with outsiders (both foreign and from within the country), these two trades are fundamentally connected, and not simply because they are concerned with the natural resources of the area.

To the Antankarana people who live alongside the park, the Ankarana massif is a sacred site for instilling blessings related to prosperity, fertility, and health. During a ceremony known as "entry into the caves," hundreds of people from around the area gather to spend three days in the caves at the tombs of past rulers. There are stories, dances, and songs; blessings are sought for rain, for more children, for more cattle. Essentially, those seeking blessings are seeking a fertile and prosperous future, just as their ancestors have done for years before them. This site is not simply meaningful to the locals, however. Conservation agencies such as the World Wildlife Federation are also intent on protecting the area's ecosystem. Ecotourists flock here to see one of the world's largest population of lemurs, and over 100 species of bird, 50 reptile species, and 10 frog species, as well as over 350 different species of plant.[7] Unfortunately, the goals of prosperity and fertility are quite different from—even opposed to—those of the conservation societies and ecotourists who have pledged to protect the area. While both groups want the area to thrive, their reasons for doing so are very different. As Walsh writes,

> For those who seek access to blessings inside the massif, success will be measured in new births, expanding herds, and increasing yields of rice and cash crops; the growth they desire will come to the local landscape in the form of new and bigger houses, more grazing cattle, and fields of newly planted sugar cane. As you can imagine, indications of growth such as these would not be signs of success to those whose goal is protecting Ankarana's distinctive biodiversity; in fact, the work of conservation is founded in an ethos that lends itself to quite dissimilar aspirations. As Keller puts it, "the conservation ethos" is one founded on the ideal of maintaining "equilibrium among the different species present on the planet" (2008: 251). And when the protection of biodiversity and the conservation of the present state of things is the goal, the kind of growth ensured by sacred sites like those to be found within the Ankarana massif will always represent a problem. (2012: 13)

Walsh talked to individuals who made their living, in one way or another, through the ecotourism industry by acting as guides, entrepreneurs, drivers, and park guards. One guide in particular, Robert, had years of experience within and outside the Ankarana area working with researchers, individual tourists, and tourist groups. Robert is a sought-after guide because of his agreeable personality, language abilities, and knowledge of the biodiversity in the park. Robert, like many other guides, does not come from the Ankarana area. For local individuals with little experience in guiding or dealing with tourists, the competition from experienced outsiders such as Robert has proven difficult to contend with.

The failure of the ecotourism industry to benefit those who live closest to the areas under protection is an accepted reality for many locals. The local perception in Ankarana is that ecotourism benefits outsiders much more than the local person, whether it is the conservation groups and ecotourists or the guides who move to the area to show these groups around. Alongside this resignation, Walsh began to uncover a great deal of speculation about why foreigners were willing to travel so far at such great expense to visit the park. One park employee told Walsh how an elderly relative could not believe his ears when she explained why foreigners were coming in droves to their home:

> There was an elder relative of mine [who] asked me, "Hey, my child, what is the reason for the visits of these *vazaha* … why is it that they have come? I laughed. "Do you want to know the reason for their visits? They come to see chameleons. They come to see lizards. Half of them come to see ants. Some come to see birds, and then there are some who come to see only trees." "IS that so!?!," he said. "Ya!" I said. "Haaa! Kakakakaka!" He almost fainted he was laughing so hard…. "Really my daughter!?! … [He said,] I was thinking there were sapphires there, I thought there was gold there … but that is all they are here to see?" [I answered] "Ya … they come to see animals, to see snakes." He laughed and laughed. (2012: 66)

This was a common sentiment expressed by locals, Walsh states. Many locals also believe that foreigners are given access to valuable resources within the park that they themselves are restricted from, and that the purpose of the foreign conservation offices set up around the park is to ensure foreigners exclusive access while keeping locals out. The thought that people would travel from all over the world simply to observe animals, caves, and trees simply does not make sense to those who have been living among these objects their whole lives.

The realization that Ankarana's pristine biodiversity is also home to an enormous supply of sapphires has sparked the interest of an entirely different group of foreigners. Unfortunately, the goals of this group diverge from those of the local peoples much more starkly than in the case of the conservationists described above. Walsh notes that when he visited one small town in the area in 1995, there were a mere 400 people residing there. Two years later, this number had grown to an astounding 15,000 after word had circulated that foreigners were willing to pay a tremendous amount for the small blue stones that young children used as ammunition in their slingshots. Sapphires were a hot commodity, and everyone wanted a part.

Once again, speculation as to *why* sapphires were so valuable to foreigners was rampant in the local communities. Again, too, locals debated the real purpose of these stones: Were they used in the production of expensive electronics? Of watch faces?

Of bullets and bombs? Walsh comments, "The idea that these foreigners were, as he [one local] and others in town had been assured by local conservation officials, tourists intent on 'taking nothing but pictures and leaving nothing but footprints' in Ankarana National Park was as hard to believe as the idea that the region's sapphires were being used in the manufacture of jewelry" (2012: 48). What was widely accepted, however, was the understanding that while Madagascar had valuable resources that foreigners were willing to pay enormous amounts of money for, local people were simply not reaping the rewards.

While the mining industry is leaving its ugly mark on the pristine land that so many held so dear, it is also having an impact on traditional male roles in Madagascar culture. For most of these young men, earning a wage in the dangerous and risky mining industry has resulted in a shift in priorities—no longer is buying a house, supporting a family or providing for their parents a main concern. Rather, it is "*la vie!*," or living a lifestyle characterized by drinking, sex, and partying funded by the "hot money" earned in the pits. Not surprisingly, local Ankaranans (particularly the elderly) and conservationist groups alike have deemed the sapphire rush a "total fiasco," both for the damage imposed on the area by the rapid influx of people and for the ecological devastation brought on by mining practices. The environmental impact of this mining has taken a serious toll on the area, and Ankarana National Park saw a 50-percent drop in visitors in one year. Most ecotourists are not interested in traveling to a park defaced with mining pits and shacks. One thing is for certain: "both [industries] stand to fall apart as soon as foreign consumers lose interest in what the region has to offer them" (2012: 72).

Walsh closes his ethnography by asking a question that has likely come into your own head at some point during your time reading this introductory text—*so what?* Why is this important? Why should I care? According to Walsh, these events are relative to all our lives because we are all *active* players in the "global bazaar," that very real marketplace where goods and services are traded from all over the world. If sapphires and ecotourism are not your thing, then perhaps coffee, tea or cell-phone batteries are. It is very difficult, if not impossible, to be a consumer in today's society without participating in this global bazaar. Through research and reporting, the public can become better informed consumers and can ignite change through their purchasing and travel practices.

The Globalization of Anthropology: Multi-Site Ethnographies and Virtual Worlds

We have seen how anthropologists have contributed to a better understanding of the processes of globalization, but we should also pause to consider how anthropology as a discipline has changed as a result of these same processes. One of the most interesting developments is in how the practice of fieldwork has changed over the last few decades.

Anthropologists are increasingly embarking on **multi-site ethnographic studies**, where the focus is not one geographic location but a number of sites that share a common group of people, task or ideology. For example, anthropologist Christina Garsten (1994) explored the organizational culture of Apple Computer in the Silicon Valley, Paris, and Stockholm, while Ulf Hannerz (2003) explored the social world of foreign news correspondents in Jerusalem, Tokyo, and South Africa.

A key component of multi-site ethnography involves identifying and exploring the links or relationships between the various sites—these anthropologists are not simply comparing a handful of locales, but are instead examining a group of sites that are in some way related. In Garsten's ethnography, she explores the ways in which company culture is influenced by national culture, as well as the difference between the center of the company (Silicon Valley) and its peripheral sites. For his part, Hannerz examines the relationship between the correspondent and the news agency for which they work, as well their relationship to other news agencies with correspondents in the field. Interviews or focus groups often play a predominant role in data collection, for there is less time to spend on participant observation when an anthropologist has a number of field sites.

Another change in fieldwork practices can be seen in the case of anthropologists who are focusing their research on the virtual world. Tom Boellstorff explores the culture of Second Life in his ethnography *Coming of Age in Second Life*, "a virtual world owned and managed by a company, Linden Lab, where by the end of my fieldwork tens of thousands of persons who might live on separate continents spent part of their lives online" (2008: 4). Created in 2003, Second Life is one of many online virtual worlds where, as of this writing, millions of people have created communities, bought and sold virtual goods, attended social activities, and discovered friendship and love. News of the thriving actual economy of Second Life attracted world media coverage when it was reported that US$1 million of economic activity occurred daily.

Boellstorff is a professor of anthropology at the University of California, Irvine, and an ethnographer who has published extensively on his research studying gay cultures in Indonesia. In *Coming of Age in Second Life*, Boellstorff was interested in exploring what anthropology could contribute to understanding culture in a virtual world. He wanted to investigate the notion of a "virtual worldview": "What might the set of assumptions and practices that make up Second Life culture teach us about such a virtual worldview?" (2008: 24). Boellstorff conducted fieldwork within Second Life between June 2004 and January 2007 as Tom Bukowski, an avatar or character that exists within the environment of Second Life. Unlike Cathy Small's research at AnyU, Boellstorff fully disclosed his anthropologist status in his profile and openly discussed his research with other residents of Second Life.

You may recognize the similarity in title with another ethnography that we discussed in this book—that of Margaret Mead's *Coming of Age in Samoa*. The similarity in title is indeed intentional—like Margaret Mead 70 years before him, Boellstorff uses traditional anthropological methods such as participant observation and interviewing to explore a cultural world that seems strange and foreign to many who do not live there. He notes the importance of participant observation in particular, explaining that by engaging with one's surroundings, the anthropologist does not rely on individuals to explain their culture, but instead watches and participates in how a culture unfolds. Participant observation considers how all aspects of a culture relate to one another: it is "useful for gaining a conceptual handle on cultural assumptions that may not be overtly discussed…. Participant observation can illuminate debates and issues of which the researcher was unaware prior to the research, and so could not have thought to include on a list of interview questions or survey form" (2008: 76). Boellstorff also notes the importance of recognizing that his fieldwork and the resulting ethnography constitute a specific snapshot of a 2.5-year time period in this world. While this is an important reminder for readers of all ethnographies, the point is particularly pertinent in this case due to the rapid and constant technological updates in the environment under study.

While Boellstorff employed traditional anthropological methods to embark on an untraditional approach to fieldwork, he did have some unique methodological decisions to make. Boellstorff was faced with deciding whether or not to engage with participants in the *actual* world. While many researchers studying virtual worlds have done so, Boellstorff decided to restrict his research to events and individuals who existed within the virtual world, as this was the culture that he was interested in investigating: "I made no attempt to meet Second Life residents in the actual world or learn their actual-world identities, though both happened on occasion. I took their activities and words as legitimate data about culture in a virtual world. For instance, if during my research I was talking to a woman, I was not concerned to determine if she was 'really' a man in the actual world, or even if two different people were taking turns controlling her" (2008: 61).

Boellstorff's ethnography offers a detailed analysis of this virtual world, exploring place and time as they exist in Second Life, as well as concepts of personhood, relationships, and community. Also included are the topics of economy, politics, governance, and issues of inequality, much as one would see in ethnographies where the fieldwork took place in the actual world. Rather than focusing on a specific aspect of Second Life culture, Boellstorff instead chose to present the culture as an interrelated whole, examining how aspects of this culture relate to one another. Because of this holistic approach, Boellstorff was required to be somewhat brief in his discussion of the social world. This book is therefore as much an ethnography of Second Life as it is a discussion of anthropology's role in understanding virtual worlds more broadly.

Boellstorff concludes that "virtual worlds are distinct domains of human being, deserving of study in their own right" and not simply as a product of technology produced in the actual world (2008: 238). While traditional anthropological methods are effective for gathering data in order to understand the virtual world, this is a culture that is distinct and separate from the actual world. Boellstorff argues that while virtual worlds are relatively new, "being virtual" in the way that humans have always been able to imagine themselves in different settings and locales, including those they have never been to or may not even exist, is part of human culture: "online worlds draw upon a capacity for the virtual that is as old as humanity itself" (2008: 238). We will no doubt see more ethnographies exploring the virtual world in the years to come, and they will likely take very different forms than what Boellstorff has offered, due in large part to the rapidly changing context in which they are set.

Conclusion

Our discussion of globalization tells us that we must consider the economic, political, and social processes on both a macro and micro, or national/international and local, level in order to fully understand the all-encompassing nature of global change. Anthropology is well suited to investigating how individuals negotiate these changes, changes that very well may have been initiated thousands of miles away but that are experienced in the day-to-day activities of local citizens. As we have seen, cultural change does not necessarily imply progress, nor does modernization necessarily imply an improvement in the quality of life. The use of these value-laden terms without consideration for what they imply perpetuates the notion that the "West" is what all other nations should strive to imitate.

We have considered a number of prominent issues connected with global change: political and social protest, the transnational flow of people, and development and ecotourism. The anthropologists who spent time dealing with these issues illustrate that while the processes of globalization have far-reaching implications, the manner in which individuals experience these processes in their daily lives requires important consideration. As a discipline, anthropology has also been changed, most notably in its methodology, as we see with the increase in multi-site ethnography and research conducted in the virtual world. While the discipline will continue to change and adapt its methods and approaches to better understand the ways in which we live, the focus on the individual experience will always remain.

Notes

1   See   http://www.cbc.ca/news/business/story/2013/06/17/f-vp-evans-bangladesh -women.html.

2   See http://www.un.org/esa/population/migration/Akhtar_Sweden_Feb_2013_FIN .pdf.

3   See http://www.un.org/esa/population/migration/Akhtar_Sweden_Feb_2013_FIN .pdf.

4   See http://www.unfpa.org/pds/migration.html.

5   See Weismantel (1995) on Zumbagua, Ecuador; Howell (2003) on Norway; and Aptekar (1988) on Colombia.

6   See http://www.theglobeandmail.com/life/parenting/the-painful-new-realities-of
     -international-adoption/article547159/?page=all.

7   See http://www.travelmadagascar.org/PARKS/Ankarana-National-Park.html.

Study Questions

1   Drawing on the tragedy in Bangladesh, explain how the increased flow of capital
     and goods has local and international implications.

2   Compare and contrast the concepts of *change* and *progress* using examples from
     the chapter.

3   Identify the benefits and challenges associated with modernization, using the
     Skolt Lapps as an example.

4   Explain the processes of migration and outline the effects of economic migration
     across the world in general, and specifically in Qatar.

5   Outline the history of international adoption in the West and explain why the
     practice has a profound effect on cultures at both the macro and micro levels.

6   Outline Walsh's work in Madagascar and explain why the goals of local residents
     are inconsistent with the foreign demands of mining and tourism. Why is it
     important for those living outside of Madagascar to understand how the pro-
     cesses of globalization have an impact upon those living there?

7   Explain the difference between traditional ethnography and multi-site ethnog-
     raphy, using examples from the chapter.

8   Outline Boellstorff's ethnographic study *Coming of Age in Second Life*, including
     his methodological choices, his findings, and what his work suggests about the
     future of cultural anthropology.

Discussion Questions

1   Discuss the practical value anthropology can offer us in understanding our
     globalized world. How are the processes of globalization influencing fieldwork?

2   Consider the ethnographic examples put forth in this chapter. Identify how the
     processes of globalization have influenced citizens of these locales. Are these
     consequences positive or negative? Are the ramifications cultural, political,
     economic?

3   Why is the notion of cultural imperialism too simplistic to explain the processes
     of globalization? Use examples from the text and from your own experience in
     your discussion.

4   Do the benefits of globalization outweigh the harms? Should modernization be
     abandoned to protect cultures (e.g., should the Lapps eschew snowmobiles)?
     How can anthropology help places and cultures find a middle ground?

Conclusion

As we mentioned in the Introduction, anthropologists are storytellers too. In this book we have looked at many stories that reflect the circumstances of their time and place. We hope you can see how anthropology arose as a discipline and the topics that have engaged our attention at various points in the history of the subject. As we've noted a number of times, the world changes, and anthropology changes along with it. Nevertheless, we think it's possible to identify persistent themes and questions that transcend particular historical circumstances. The emergence of a distinctive anthropological method—ethnography—is another unifying factor. As for persistent themes, we might consider the following:

Nature and Culture: the light that comparative anthropological research can shed on the problem of what basic human nature is, as opposed to what culture and circumstances lead us to be.

The Dynamics and Direction of History: the central problem of social evolutionary thought, and one of the reasons why so-called primitive peoples have proved so fascinating as a "natural laboratory" of human possibility.

The Bonds of Community: how we come together in groups, whether they be families, tribes, nations, or the transnational communities made possible by social media and the Internet. This includes the symbolism and rituals of group identity.

Collective Visions: The process of imposing meaning on experience; how culture and social life steer our understandings of how the world works—our cosmologies, our religions, our interpretations of why things happen the way they do, our very selves.

Anthropologists engage in "fieldwork" to get at a problem that is seen as significant given the current state of the discipline. In earlier times much research was exploratory—aimed at documenting the range of human diversity. But usually there is some theoretical motivation as well, for example looking at how global processes affect local activities and perceptions. The usual output is an academic paper, addressed to other scholars as part of the normal give-and-take of any discipline. Sometimes the product is more substantial: a book on some specific theme, perhaps, or a full-scale ethnography. Such work falls somewhere between science and literature, and in recent times anthropologists have devoted considerable attention to the nature of the creative process itself—ethnographic writing as an art.

Occasionally such work attracts a wider audience because it addresses something of public concern, such as hunger, human rights, sexuality or the environment. Of course, prominent figures such as Margaret Mead are rare; nevertheless, you've seen that anthropologists are out there in the "real world" as advocates, working in applied settings, and commenting on social issues. You've also seen that small-scale societies often far removed from the Western world were once the focus of most anthropologists' attention. But today anthropologists are just as likely to be engaged in researching a public school, a scientific laboratory, an IVF clinic, a video gaming parlor, sporting events, a religious community, a business organization, or a political movement. A common denominator is actually *being there*—participant observation. Though disciplinary boundaries are seldom clear-cut, this approach distinguishes anthropology from the other social sciences.

And here we must stop. We encourage you to reflect on how what you've read in this book can be applied to your own experience and understanding of local and global events. Remember that anthropology is a way of seeing.

Glossary

Introduction

Globalization: the process of international integration arising from the interchange of worldviews, products, ideas, and other aspects of culture

Interpretation: the process of creating meaning out of experience

Meaning: a complex concept, difficult to define. A "culture" can be thought of as a system of symbolic communication in which "meaning" emerges out of the manner in which cultural elements are related to one another—as in a spoken language, or in a ritual or art form. The anthropologist's goal is to "interpret" and understand such things

Social evolution: the transformation of one social form into another, as for example the "evolution" of organized states out of previously tribal societies. In nineteenth-century thought, this was seen as the emergence of complexity out of simpler modes of organization

Social memory: how social life affects the processes of memory and forgetting, whether on an individual psychological level or in terms of how groups think of their collective history

Chapter 1

Archaeology: the study of the material remains of past and present cultures

Comparative method: how a particular theory fares when applied cross-culturally

Cultural relativism: the idea that one should suspend moral judgment and assumption in order to appreciate and understand a culture on its own terms, rather than in comparison to one's own

Culture: the complex whole that includes knowledge, belief, art, morals, law, custom, and any other capabilities and habits acquired by humans as a member of society

Culture shock: refers to the feelings of confusion and insecurity that arise from living in a new culture or surroundings

Ethnocentrism: the act of judging other cultures by the standards and values of one's own

Ethnography: a theoretically informed description and explanation of a way of life

Holistic approach: involves looking at the complete picture rather than individual parts

Inductive approach: starting from specific ideas or observations and moving into broader theories of thought

Linguistic anthropology: the study of the relationship between culture and language

Participant observation: joining and engaging in the culture and customs of the people who are the focus of one's study over an extended period of time

Physical anthropology: the study of human variation, adaptation, and change

Reflexive thinking: how our personal opinions and beliefs influence the ways in which we see the people and activities around us

Socio-cultural anthropology: the study of human culture, social organization, and behavior

Chapter 2

Applied anthropology: the application of anthropological theory, methodology, and knowledge to solving practical problems, usually at the commission of a specific organization or client

Diffusion: the spread of tools, practices or other features from one culture to another

Historical particularism: an approach to understanding society whereby the unique history of each culture is considered influential and central to understanding the present

Medical anthropology: a "sub-field" of anthropology that employs anthropological theory and method in exploring understandings of health and health care from a cross-cultural perspective

Purposeful sampling: a method whereby research participants are selected based on having certain characteristics that the researcher deems necessary for inclusion

Qualitative research: aims to understand the why and how of human behavior through methods such as participant observation and interviews

Structural functionalism: an approach to understanding society whereby the major structures of society are comparable to the organs of a biological organism

Chapter 3

Paradigm: a model or framework about how a group of ideas relate to one another

State of nature: a term used by early social and political theorists for the imagined condition of humankind before the rise of civilization

Totemism: the belief that humans are thought to have a spiritual connection or a kinship with another physical being, such as an animal or plant

Chapter 4

Bride-service: the situation where a man works for his in-laws in return for their daughter

Bridewealth: valuable property transferred from the family of the man to that of his prospective bride

Descent: the connection an individual has to their ancestors

Dowry: property that accompanies a woman into the marriage relationship— a kind of pre-inheritance that in an ideal world would be passed on to her offspring

Endogamy: marriage within a group, as opposed to exogamy, marriage outside

Kinship: relationship by blood or marriage

Kinship systems: how kinship relations are organized into structured wholes

Marriage: a legally recognized relationship between people who intend to live together as sexual and domestic partners

Matrilineage: the transmission of all titles, rights and property in the female line

Patrilineage: kin who define their relationship through male descent—father to son, etc.

Polygyny: the custom of being married to more than wife at a time

Rite of passage: a ritual marking and celebrating of a change in social status, such as a birth, marriage, graduation, or funeral

Chapter 5

Culture: the complex whole that includes knowledge, belief, art, morals, law, custom, and any other capabilities and habits acquired by humans as a member of society

Epistemology: the theory of the scope and nature of knowledge

Ethnology: a branch of anthropology that compares and analyzes the characteristics of different peoples and the relationship between them

Habitus: the meaningful yet unconscious activity that pervades our daily lives

Mana: the distinguishing characteristic of any sacred being

Paradigm: an accepted model of how ideas relate to one another, forming a conceptual framework within which research is carried out

Sociocentric theory: an approach to understanding society that looks internally for causes, rather than to impersonal notions such as fate or physical causality

Chapter 6

Activism: action in pursuit of a political or social goal

Essentialism: the belief that a group of people possess a set of inherent characteristics often used in discussions related to race, gender, class, and sexuality

Noble savage: refers to the notion that "there are simple people, living in an Edenic landscape and gentle climate, whose powers of reason and ability to live in harmony with nature ensure relief from the evils of civilization" (Satterfield 2002: 100)

Oral traditions: "the means by which knowledge is reproduced, preserved and conveyed from generation to generation. Oral traditions form the foundation of Aboriginal societies, connecting speaker and listener in communal experience and uniting past and present in memory" (Hulan & Eigenbrod 2008: 7)

Potlatch: a form of ceremonial gift-giving marking notable occasions such as a marriage, inheriting an important title, or erecting a totem pole

Revitalization movement: an organized effort by members of a society or group to construct a more satisfying culture (Wallace 1956: 265)

Savage beast: a construct that portrays Aboriginal peoples as living in a constant state of violence, disorganization, and chaos

Treaty: an agreement made under law; in the context of Aboriginal land, it is a contract between an Aboriginal people and another governing body

Chapter 7

Biological determinism: the notion that there is a direct correlation between cultural characteristics regarding categories such as gender, race, or class with biological traits

Caste: an explicitly hierarchical social system based on hereditary, endogamous groups, in which each is characterized by a specific status, occupation, mode of life, and pattern of customary interactions with other such groups" (Winthrop 1991:27)

Feminist theoretical perspective: an approach whose central tenet is that all social relations and the knowledge of these relations are gendered; this approach highlights the role of patriarchy in maintaining the oppression of women in society

Gender: the socially constructed roles, behaviors, activities, and attributes that a given society considers appropriate for men and women (World Health Organization)

Gender roles: the seemingly different sets of actions and behaviors associated with girls and boys, men and women, that a society deems appropriate

Hetero-masculinity: the cultural pressure exerted on males to be masculine in traits and heterosexual in orientation or else be viewed as feminine and socially unacceptable (Theodore & Basow 2000)

Interpretive perspective: an approach that considers the meaning that social actors give to what they and others do

Patriarchy: a system of power in society whereby relationships are organized to maintain male supremacy

Queer theory: a paradigm that does not lend itself easily to a simple definition or explanation, as it has been conceptualized by those who engage with it in a diversity of ways. While there is no one definition of queer theory, in the broadest sense queer theory is a "theoretical perspective from which to challenge the normative" (Goldman 1996: 170), or a "radical questioning of social and cultural norms, notions of gender, reproductive sexuality, and the family" (Smith 1996: 280)

Transgender: when one's gender identity does not match one's biological sex

Transsexuals: individuals who assert that their gender identity is that of the other sex

Chapter 8

Eugenics movement: social policies aimed at encouraging the upper classes to reproduce more enthusiastically and to discourage the lower orders from doing so

Genome: the entirety of one's genetic heritage

Natural selection: the selection by natural processes of genetic variants with adaptive vaule and the rejection of those without it; in the long term those individuals with useful variations leave more offspring, and evolution moves on in the direction indicated by the selective process

Typological thinking: The concept that organisms of a species conform to a specific norm; in this view variation is considered abnormal (Genscript)

Chapter 9

Change: the result of action or thought, whether it is intentional, accidental, beneficial or harmful, with no particular direction or value

Cultural imperialism: the imposition of a powerful country's culture on another country or group of people

De-territorialization: moving away from social, political or cultural ties to native geographic entities or populations

Economic migrant: an individual who relocates for a limited period of time in order to work, and who has no intention of making their move permanent

Globalization: "social, economic, cultural, and demographic processes that take place within nations but also transcend them, such that attention limited to local processes, identities, and units of analysis yields incomplete understanding of the local" (Kearney 1995: 548)

Isolationism: a foreign-policy approach advocating non-involvement in other nations' affairs on the premise that this will best serve one's own national interests

Macro vs. micro levels: the macro level of analysis considers social structures and institutions, while the micro level occurs at the individual, face-to-face level

Migration: the movement of a person or people from one place to another

Modernization: the process of cultural and socio-economic change, often linked to urbanization, industrialization, and the spread of education

Multi-site ethnography: identifying and exploring the links, or relationships, of various study sites that are in some way related

Progress: a gradual move toward achieving a goal or reaching a higher standard; definitions that consider progress in relation to people suggest the advancement of society toward a state of greater civilization; this forward movement implies a positive change from one state to another, a leaving behind of something outdated in order to embrace something new

References

Introduction

Beaglehole, J.C. 1974. *The Life of Captain James Cook*. Stanford: Stanford University Press.

Columbus, Christopher. 1989. *The Diario of Christopher Columbus's First Voyage to America 1492–1493*. Trans. Oliver Dunn and James E. Kelley. Norman: University of Oklahoma Press.

Columbus, Christopher. 1991. *The Libro de las profecias of Christopher Columbus*. Trans. Delno C. West and August Kling. Gainesville: University of Florida Press.

Connerton, Paul. 1989. *How Societies Remember*. Cambridge: Cambridge University Press. http://dx.doi.org/10.1017/CBO9780511628061.

Cook, James. 1967. The Journals of Captain James Cook on his Voyages of Discovery Vol. III: *The Voyage of the* Resolution *and* Discovery *1776–1780*, part one (edited by J.C. Beaglehole). Cambridge: Cambridge University Press.

de Las Casas, Bartolomé. 1992. *In Defense of the Indians*. Trans. Stafford Poole. DeKalb: Northern Illinois University Press.

Diaz del Castillo, Bernal. 1928. *The Discovery and Conquest of Mexico*. Trans. A.P. Maudsley. London: George Routledge & Sons.

Fentress, James, and Chris Wickham. 1992. *Social Memory*. Oxford: Basil Blackwell.

Fraser, Simon. 1960. *The Letters and Journals of Simon Fraser*. Toronto: Macmillan.

Friedman, John Block. 2000. *The Monstrous Races in Medieval Art and Thought*. Syracuse, NY: Syracuse University Press.

Gomez, Nicolas Wey. 2008. *The Tropics of Empire: Why Columbus sailed south to the Indies*. Cambridge: MIT Press.

Pagden, Anthony. 1982. *The Fall of Natural Man: The American Indian and the origins of comparative ethnology*. Cambridge: Cambridge University Press.

Todorov, Tzvetan. 1984. *The Conquest of America*. New York: Harper Perennial.

Wickwire, Wendy. 1994. "To See Ourselves as the Other's Other: Mlaka'pamux contact narratives." *Canadian Historical Review* 75 (1): 1–20. http://dx.doi.org/10.3138/CHR-075-01-01.

Williams, Glyn. 2008. *The Death of Captain Cook: A hero made and unmade*. Cambridge, MA: Harvard University Press.

Chapter 1

Amit, Vered. 2000. "Introduction: Constructing the Field." In *Constructing the Field: Ethnographic fieldwork in the contemporary world*, 1–18. New York: Routledge.

REFERENCES

Barrett, Stanley R. 2000. *Anthropology: A student's guide to theory and method.* Toronto: University of Toronto Press.

Caputo, Virginia. 1995. "Anthropology's Silent 'Others': A consideration of some conceptual and methodological issues for the study of youth and children's cultures." In *Youth Cultures: A cross-cultural perspective*, ed. Vered Amit-Talai and Helena Wulff, 19–42. London, New York: Routledge.

Dyck, Noel. 2000. "Introduction." In *Games, Sport and Cultures*, 1–9. Oxford, New York: Berg.

Fernea, Robert. 1970. *Shaykh and Effendi: Changing patterns of authority among the El Shabana of Southern Iraq.* Cambridge, MA: Harvard University Press.

Fernea, Elizabeth Warnock. 1969. *Guests of the Sheik: An ethnography of an Iraqi village.* Garden City, NY: Anchor Books Doubleday & Company.

Geertz, Clifford. 1973. *The Interpretation of Cultures.* New York: Basic Books.

Gluckman, Max. 1958. *Analysis of a Social Situation in Modern Zululand.* Manchester: Manchester University Press.

Hassan, Fayza. 2001. "Elizabeth Warnock Fernea: Part of it all." *Al Ahram Weekly Online* 527 (19 March–4 April). http://weekly.ahram.org.eg/2001/527/profile.htm.

Malinowski, Bronislaw. 1922. *Argonauts of the Western Pacific.* London: Routledge & Kegan Paul.

Malinowski, Bronislaw. 1966. *Coral Gardens and Their Magic.* London: Allen & Unwin.

Malinowski, Bronislaw. 1967. *A Diary in the Strict Sense of the Term.* Trans. Norbert Guterman. New York: Harcourt Brace & World.

McGee, R.J., and R.L. Warms. 1996. *Anthropological Theory: An introductory history.* London: Mayfield Publishing Company.

Narayan, Kirin. 1993. "How Native is a 'Native' Anthropologist?" *American Anthropologist* 95 (3): 19–32.

Nathan, Rebekah. 2005. *My Freshman Year: What a professor learned by becoming a student.* Ithaca, NY and London: Cornell University Press.

Rhode, David. 2007. "Army Enlists Anthropology in War Zones." *New York Times*, Oct. 5. http://www.nytimes.com/2007/10/05/world/asia/05afghan.html?pagewanted=all&_r=0.

Stocking, George. 1995. *After Tylor: British social anthropology 1885–1951.* Madison: University of Wisconsin Press.

Young, Michael W. 2004. *Malinowski: Odyssey of an anthropologist 1884–1920.* New Haven, CT: Yale University Press.

Chapter 2

Attaran, A., Donald R. Roberts, Chris F. Curtis, and Wenceslaus L. Kilama. 2000. "Balancing Risks on the Backs of the Poor." *Nature Medicine* 6 (7): 729–31. http://dx.doi.org/10.1038/77438.

Barrett, Stanley R. 2000. *Anthropology: A student's guide to theory and method.* Toronto: University of Toronto Press.

Behague, D., C. Tawiah, M. Rosato, S. Telesphore, and J. Morrison. 2009. "Evidence-Based Policy-Making: The implications of globally-applicable research for context specific problem-solving in developing countries." *Social Science & Medicine* 69 (10): 1539–46. http://dx.doi.org/10.1016/j.socscimed.2009.08.006.

Boas, Franz. 1911. *The Mind of Primitive Man*. New York: The Macmillan Company.

CDC (Centers for Disease Control). 2012. Malaria: FAQs. http://www.cdc.gov/malaria/about/faqs.html.

Erikson Paul, A., and D. Murphy Liam. 2013. *A History of Anthropological Theory*. 4th ed. Toronto: University of Toronto Press.

Feinberg, R. 1988. "Margaret Mead and Samoa: *Coming of age* in fact and fiction." *American Anthropologist* 90 (3): 656–63. http://dx.doi.org/10.1525/aa.1988.90.3.02a00080.

Firth, Raymond. 1985. "Audrey Richards 1899–1984." *Man* 20 (2): 341–44.

Freeman, D. 1983. *Margaret Mead and Samoa: The making and unmaking of an anthropological myth*. Cambridge, MA and London: Harvard University Press.

Gilliam, A. 1993. "Symbolic Subordination and the Representation of Power in *Margaret Mead and Samoa*." *Visual Anthropology Review* 9 (1): 105–15. http://dx.doi.org/10.1525/var.1993.9.1.105.

Hahn, R.A., and M. Inhorn. 2009. "Introduction". *Anthropology and Public Health: Bridging Differences in Culture and Society*, 1–31. Oxford, New York: Oxford University Press. http://dx.doi.org/10.1093/acprof:oso/9780195374643.003.0001.

Hausmann-Muela, S., and J. Muela-Ribera. 2003. "Recipe Knowledge: A tool for understanding some apparently irrational behavior." *Anthropology & Medicine* 10 (1): 87–103. http://dx.doi.org/10.1080/13648470301265.

Hausmann-Muela, S., J. Muela-Ribera, and M. Tanner. 1998. "Fake Malaria and Hidden Parasites—The ambiguity of malaria." *Anthropology & Medicine* 5 (1): 43–61.

Herzfeld, M. 2001. *Anthropology: Theoretical practice in culture and society*. Oxford and Malden, MA: Blackwell Publishers.

Janes, C., and K. Corbett. 2009. "Anthropology and Global Health." *Annual Review of Anthropology* 38 (1): 167–83. http://dx.doi.org/10.1146/annurev-anthro-091908-164314.

Kamat, Vinay. 2009. *The Anthropology of Childhood Malaria in Tanzania. Anthropology and Public Health: Bridging differences in culture and society*. Oxford, New York: Oxford University Press.

Knauft, B. 2006. "Anthropology in the Middle." *Anthropological Theory* 6 (4): 407–30. http://dx.doi.org/10.1177/1463499606071594.

Lewis, H.S. 2001. "The Passion of Franz Boas." *American Anthropologist* 103 (2): 447–67. http://dx.doi.org/10.1525/aa.2001.103.2.447.

Malinowski B. 1944. *Argonauts of the Western Pacific*. London: G. Routledge & Sons.

Maslove, D., A. Mnyusiwalla, E. Mills, J. McGowan, A. Attaran, and K. Wilson. 2009. "Barriers to the Effective Treatment and Prevention of Malaria in Africa: A systematic review of qualitative studies." *BMC International Health and Human Rights* 9 (26): n.p. http://dx.doi.org/10.1186/1472-698X-9-26.

McCoy, D., J. Kembhavi, J. Patel, and A. Luintel. 2009. "The Bill & Melinda Gates Foundation's Grant-Making Programme for Global Health." *Lancet* 373 (9675): 1645–53. http://dx.doi.org/10.1016/S0140-6736(09)60571-7.

Mead, Margaret. 1973. *Coming of Age in Samoa*. New York: Morrow Quill.

Miller, Barbara D., Penny Van Esterik, and John Van Esterik. 2001. *Cultural Anthropology*. Canadian Edition. Toronto: Pearson Education Canada.

Mosse, David. 2005. *Cultivating Development: An ethnography of aid policy and practice*. London and Ann Arbor, MI: Pluto Press.

Mosse, David, ed. 2011. *Adventures in Aidland: The anthropology of professionals in international development.* Studies in Applied and Public Anthropology, vol. 6. New York and Oxford: Berghahn Press.

Mukhopadhyah, C.C., and Y.T. Moses. 1997. "Reestablishing 'Race' in Anthropological Discourse." *American Anthropologist* 99 (3): 517–33. http://dx.doi.org/10.1525/aa.1997.99.3.517.

Murray, Gerald. 1987. "The Domestication of Wood in Haiti: A case study in applied evolution." In *Anthropological Praxis Translating Knowledge into Action*, ed. Robert M. Wulff and Shirley J. Fiske, 223–42. Boulder, London: Westview Press.

Radcliffe-Brown, A.R. 1922. *The Andaman Islanders: A study in social anthropology.* Cambridge: Cambridge University Press.

Richards, Audrey I. 1939. *Land, Labour and Diet in Northern Rhodesia: An economic study of the Bemba tribe.* London: Oxford University Press.

Richards, Audrey I. 1948. *Hunger and Work in a Savage Tribe: A functional study of nutrition among the Southern Bantu.* Glencoe: The Free Press.

Richards, Audrey I. 1956. *Chisungu: A girl's initiation ceremony among the Bemba of Northern Rhodesia.* London: Faber & Faber.

Society for Medical Anthropology. 2014. http://www.medanthro.net/blog/about-the-blog.

Stocking, George, ed. 1984. *Functionalism Historicized.* Madison: University of Wisconsin Press.

Woelk, G., K. Daniels, J. Cliff, S. Lewin, E. Sevene, B. Fernandes, A. Mariano, S. Matinhure, A. Oxman, J. Lavis, and C. Lundborg. 2009. "Translating Research into Policy: Lessons learned from eclampsia treatment and malaria control in three southern African countries." *Health Research Policy and Systems* 7 (31): n.p. http://dx.doi.org/10.1186/1478-4505-7-31.

The World Health Organization. http://www.who.int/en/.

The World Health Organization. 2008. *Key Facts, Figures and Strategies: The global malaria action plan.* http//rbm.who.int./gmap/GMAP_Advocacy-ENG-web.pdf.

Chapter 3

Burrow, J.W. 1968. *Evolution and Society: A study in Victorian social theory.* Cambridge: Cambridge University Press.

Cook, James. 1968. *The Voyage of the Endeavour 1768–1771.* Ed. J.G. Beaglehole. Cambridge: Cambridge University Press.

Darwin, Charles. 1966. *Narrative of the Surveying Voyages of His Majesty's Ships Adventure and Beagle*, vol. 3. New York: AMS Press.

Darwin, Charles. 1979. *The Origin of Species by Means of Natural Selection.* New York: Avenel Books.

Darwin, Charles. 1989. *The Voyage of the Beagle.* Harmondsworth: Penguin.

Darwin, Charles. 1998. *The Descent of Man.* Amherst, NY: Prometheus Books.

Evans-Pritchard, E.E. 1963. *The Comparative Method in Social Anthropology.* London: Athlone Press.

Fitzroy, Robert. 1966. *Narrative of the Surveying Voyages of His Majesty's Ships Adventure and Beagle*, vol. 1 & 2. New York: AMS Press.

Goodall, Heather. 1996. *Invasion to Embassy: Land in Aboriginal politics in New South Wales, 1770–1972.* Sydney: Allen and Unwin.

Gusinde, Martin. 1971. *The Sek'nam: On the life and thought of a hunting people on the Great Island of Tierra del Fuego*. New Haven, CT: Human Relations Area Files.

Hobbes, Thomas. 1962. *Leviathan*. New York: Collier Books.

Kuper, Adam. 1988. *The Invention of Primitive Society: Transformations of an illusion*. London: Routledge.

Locke, John. 2002. *Second Treatise on Government*. Mineola, NY: Dover Publications.

Lothrop, Samuel K. 1928. *The Indians of Tierra del Fuego*. New York: Museum of the American Indian.

Morgan, Lewis Henry. 1851. *The League of the Ho-de-no-sau-nee, or Iroquois*. Rochester: Sage & Brothers.

Morgan, Lewis Henry. 1877. *Ancient Society*. New York: Henry Holt & Co.

Rousseau, Jean-Jacques. 1992. *Discourse on the Origins of Inequality*. Trans. Judith Bush et al. Hanover: Dartmouth College.

Trautmann, Thomas R. 1987. *Lewis Henry Morgan and the Invention of Kinship*. Berkeley: University of California Press.

CHAPTER 4

Eggan, Fred, ed. 1955. *Social Anthropology of North American Tribes*. Chicago: University of Chicago Press.

Evans-Pritchard, E.E. 1940. *The Nuer*. Oxford: Oxford University Press.

Evans-Pritchard, E.E. 1951. *Kinship and Marriage Among the Nuer*. Oxford: The Clarendon Press.

Fortes, Meyer. 1969. *Kinship and the Social Order*. Chicago: Aldine.

Fox, Robin. 1967. *Kinship and Marriage: An anthropological perspective*. Harmondsworth: Penguin.

Franklin, Sarah, and Susan McKinnon, eds. 2001. *Relative Values: Reconfiguring kinship studies*. Durham, NC: Duke University Press.

Kenny, Michael G. 1999. "A Place for Memory: The interface between individual and collective history." *Comparative Studies in Society and History* 41 (3): 420–37. http://dx.doi.org/10.1017/S0010417599002248.

Lafitau, Joseph François. 1974. *Customs of the American Indians Compared with the Customs of Primitive Times*, trans. William Fenton and Elizabeth Moore, vol. 1. Toronto: The Champlain Society.

Malinowski, Bronislaw. 1954. *Magic, Science and Religion. Garden City*. Doubleday.

Mauss, Marcel. 1990. *The Gift: The form and reason for exchange in archaic societies*. Trans. W.D. Halls. London: Routledge.

Miller, James Rodger. 1996. *Shingwauk's Vision: A history of native residential schools*. Toronto: University of Toronto Press.

Morgan, Lewis Henry. 1851. *The League of the Ho-de-no-sau-nee, or Iroquois*. Rochester, NY: Sage & Brothers.

Morgan, Lewis Henry. 1871. *Systems of Consanguinity and Affinity of the Human Family*. Washington, DC: Smithsonian Institution.

Morgan, Lewis Henry. 1877. *Ancient Society*. New York: Henry Holt & Co.

REFERENCES

Nanda, Serena. 2000. "Arranging a Marriage in India." In *Stumbling Toward Truth: Anthropologists at work*, ed. Philip R. Devita, 196–204. Long Grove, IL: Waveland.

Perdue, Theda, and Michael D. Green. 2005. *The Cherokee Removal: A brief history with documents*. 2nd ed. Boston: Bedford/St. Martin's.

Perdue, Theda, and Michael D. Green. 2007. *The Cherokee Nation and the Trail of Tears*. New York: Viking.

Proctor, Robert N. 1988. *Racial Hygiene: Medicine under the Nazis*. Cambridge, MA: Harvard University Press.

Radcliffe-Brown, A.R. 1950. "Introduction." In *African Systems of Kinship and Marriage*, ed. A.R. Radcliffe-Brown and C. Daryll Forde, 1–85. London: Oxford University Press.

Radcliffe-Brown, A.R. 1952. *Structure and Function in Primitive Society*. London: Routledge and Kegan Paul.

Richards, Audrey. 1950. "Some Types of Family Structure amongst the Central Bantu." In *African Systems of Kinship and Marriage*, ed. A.R. Radcliffe-Brown and C. Daryll Forde, 207–51. London: Oxford University Press.

Sahlins, Marshall. 2013. *What Kinship Is—And Is Not*. Chicago: University of Chicago Press. http://dx.doi.org/10.7208/chicago/9780226925134.001.0001.

Schneider, David M. 1980. *American Kinship: A cultural account*. 2nd ed. Chicago: University of Chicago Press.

Schneider, David M. 1984 *A Critique of the Study of Kinship*. Ann Arbor: University of Michigan Press.

Schneider, David M., and Kathleen Gough, eds. 1962. *Matrilineal Kinship*. Berkeley: University of California Press.

Smith, John. 1624. *The General Historie of Virginia, New-England, and the Summer Isles*. London: Michael Sparkes. [facsimile edition]

Strathern, Marilyn. 1992. *Reproducing the Future: Essays on anthropology, kinship, and the new reproductive technologies*. Manchester: Manchester University Press.

CHAPTER 5

American Psychiatric Association. 2013. *DSM V: Diagnostic and statistical manual of mental disorders*. Washington, DC: American Psychiatric Association.

Benedict, Ruth. 1959. *Patterns of Culture*. Boston: Houghton Mifflin.

Benedict, Ruth. 2005. *The Chrysanthemum and the Sword: Patterns of Japanese culture*. Boston: Houghton Mifflin.

Bourdieu, Pierre. 1977. *Outline of a Theory of Practice*. Trans. Richard Nice. Cambridge: Cambridge University Press. http://dx.doi.org/10.1017/CBO9780511812507.

Darnell, Regna. 2001. *Invisible Genealogies: A history of Americanist anthropology*. Lincoln: University of Nebraska Press.

Daws, Gavan. 1968. *Shoal of Time: A history of the Hawaiian Islands*. Honolulu: University of Hawaii Press.

Durkheim, Émile. 1995. *The Elementary Forms of Religious Life*. Trans. Karen E. Fields. New York: The Free Press.

Durkheim, Émile, and Marcel Mauss. 1965. *Primitive Classification*. Trans. Rodney Needham. Chicago: University of Chicago Press.

Evans-Pritchard, E.E. 1937. *Witchcraft, Oracles and Magic among the Azande*. Oxford: Clarendon Press.

Foucault, Michel. 1988. *The History of Sexuality*. Vol. 3: The Care of the Self. Trans. Robert Hurley. New York: Vintage Books.

Foucault, Michel. 1990. *The History of Sexuality*. Vol. 1: An Introduction. Trans. Robert Hurley. New York: Vintage Books.

Geertz, Clifford. 1973. *The Interpretation of Cultures*. New York: Basic Books.

Hall, Edward. 1959. *The Silent Language*. Garden City: Doubleday.

Hall, Edward. 1966. *The Hidden Dimension*. Garden City: Doubleday.

Kuhn, Thomas. 1970. *The Structure of Scientific Revolutions*. 2nd ed. Chicago: University of Chicago Press.

Lévi-Strauss, C. 1969. *The Elementary Structures of Kinship*. Boston: Beacon Press.

Luhrmann, Tanya. 2012. *When God Talks Back: Understanding the American evangelical relationship with God*. New York: Vintage Books.

Luhrmann, Tanya. 2013. "Belief Is the Least Part of Faith." *New York Times*, May 29. http://www.nytimes.com/2013/05/30/opinion/luhrmann-belief-is-the-least-part-of-faith.html.

Malinowski, Bronislaw. 1947. "The Problem of Meaning in Primitive Languages." In *The Meaning of Meaning*, ed. C.K. Ogden, and I.A. Richards, 296–336. New York: Harcourt, Brace.

Mauss, Marcel. 2006. "Techniques of the Body." In *Techniques, Technology and Civilization*, ed. Nathan Schlanger, 77–95. New York: Berghahn.

Pew Forum on Religion and Public Life. 2008. U.S. Religious Landscape Survey. "Religious Affiliation." http://www.pewforum.org/Topics/Religious-Affiliation/.

Post, Emily. 1922. *Etiquette in Society, in Business, in Politics, and at Home*. New York: Funk & Wagnalls.

Sacks, Oliver. 1995. *An Anthropologist on Mars*. Toronto: Vintage Canada.

Sahlins, Marshall. 1985. *Islands of History*. Chicago: University of Chicago Press.

Sahlins, Marshall. 1995. *How "Natives Think: About Captain Cook for example*. Chicago: University of Chicago Press. http://dx.doi.org/10.7208/chicago/9780226733715.001.0001.

Satterfield, Terre. 2002. *Anatomy of a Conflict: Identity, knowledge, and emotion in old-growth forests*. Vancouver, Toronto: UBC Press.

Stanner, W.E.H. 1979. *White Man Got No Dreaming: Essays 1938–1973*. Canberra: Australian National University Press.

Stocking, George. 1995. *After Tylor: British social anthropology 1888–1951*. Madison: University of Wisconsin Press.

Tylor, E.B. 1903. *Primitive Culture*. London: John Murray.

Wilson, Bryan, ed. 1970. *Rationality*. Oxford: Blackwell.

Wright, Susan. 1998. "The Politicization of 'Culture'." *Anthropology Today* 14 (1): 7–15. http://dx.doi.org/10.2307/2783092.

Yengoyan, Aram. A. 1986. "Theory in Anthropology: On the demise of the concept of culture." *Comparative Studies in Society and History* 28 (2): 368–74.

CHAPTER 6

Adams, John W. 1973. *The Gitksan Potlatch: Population flux, resource ownership and reciprocity*. Toronto: Holt, Rinehart & Winston of Canada.

REFERENCES

Arima, Eugene, and Allan Hoover. 2011. *The Whaling People of the West Coast of Vancouver Island and Cape Flattery*. Victoria: Royal BC Museum.

Benedict, Ruth. 1959. *Patterns of Culture*. Boston: Houghton Mifflin.

Boas, Franz. 1963. *The Mind of Primitive Man*. 4th ed. New York: The Free Press.

Boas, Franz. 1996. "The Study of Geography." In *Volksgeist as Method and Ethic: Essays on Boasian ethnography and the German anthropological tradition*, ed. George W. Stocking, 3–16. Madison: University of Wisconsin Press.

Brody, Hugh. 1981. *Maps and Dreams: Indians and the British Columbia frontier*. Vancouver: Douglas & McIntyre.

Brown, Michael F. 2003. *Who Owns Native Culture?* Cambridge, MA: Harvard University Press.

Clifford, James. 1988. *The Predicament of Culture: Twentieth-century ethnography, literature, and art*. Cambridge, MA: Harvard University Press.

Cole, Douglas. 1985. *Captured Heritage: The scramble for Northwest Coast artifacts*. Vancouver, Toronto: Douglas & McIntyre.

Cole, Douglas. 1999. *Franz Boas: The early years, 1858–1906*. Vancouver, Toronto: Douglas & McIntyre.

Cole, Douglas, and Ira Chaikin. 1990. *An Iron Hand upon the People: The law against the potlatch on the Northwest Coast*. Vancouver, Toronto: Douglas & McIntyre.

Colson, Elizabeth. 1953. *The Makah Indians: A study of an Indian tribe in modern American society*. Minneapolis: University of Minnesota Press.

Cook, James. 1967. *The Voyage of the Resolution and Discovery 1776–1780*. Ed. J.G. Beaglehole. Cambridge: Cambridge University Press.

Coté, Charlotte. 2010. *Spirits of our Whaling Ancestors: Revitalizing Makah & Nuu-chah-nulth traditions*. Seattle: University of Washington Press.

Cove, John J. 1982. "The Gitksan Traditional Concept of Land Ownership." *Anthropologica* 24 (1): 3–17. http://dx.doi.org/10.2307/25605083.

Culhane, Dara. 1998. *The Pleasure of the Crown: Anthropology, law and First Nations*. Burnaby, BC: Talonbooks.

Darwin, Charles. 1998. *The Descent of Man*. Amherst, NY: Prometheus Books.

Erikson, Patricia Pierce. 1999. "A-Whaling We Will Go: Encounters of knowledge and memory at the Makah Cultural and Research Center." *Cultural Anthropology* 14 (4): 556–83. http://dx.doi.org/10.1525/can.1999.14.4.556.

Freed, Stanley, Ruth S. Freed, and Laila Williamson. 1988. "Capitalist Philanthropy and Russian Revolutionaries: The Jesup North Pacific Expedition (1897–1902)." *American Anthropologist* 90 (1): 7–24.

Johnston, Hugh M., ed. 1996. *The Pacific Province: A history of British Columbia*. Vancouver, Toronto: Douglas & McIntyre.

Jonaitis, Aldona. 1999. *The Yuquot Whaler's Shrine*. Seattle: University of Washington Press.

LaViolette, F. 1961. *The Struggle for Survival: Indian cultures and the Protestant ethic in British Columbia*. Toronto: University of Toronto Press.

Lee, Jeff. 2013. Muchalaht Wrestle with Emotions caused by Loss of Shrine. *Vancouver Sun*, April 15: A4.

Loo, Tina. 1992. "Dan Cranmer's Potlatch: Law as coercion, symbol, and rhetoric in British Columbia, 1884–1951." *Canadian Historical Review* 73 (2): 125–65. http://dx.doi.org/10.3138/CHR-073-02-01.

Mauss, Marcel. 1990. *The Gift: The form and reason for exchange in archaic societies* Trans. W.D. Halls. London: Routledge.

McEachern, Allan. 1991. *Reasons for Judgment* [in the Delgamuukw Case]. Vancouver: Criminal Court Registry Office.

Mills, Antonia. 1994a. *Eagle Down is our Law: Witsu'wit'en Law, feasts, and land claims*. Vancouver: University of British Columbia Press.

Mills, Antonia. 1994b. "Rebirth and Identity: Three Gitksan cases of pierced-ear birthmarks." In *Amerindian Rebirth: Reincarnation beliefs among North American Indians and Inuit*, ed. A. Mills and Richard Slobodin, 211–41. Toronto: University of Toronto Press.

Mills, Antonia, ed. 2005. *Hang Onto those Words: Johnny David's evidence*. Toronto: University of Toronto Press.

Parker, Arthur C. 1913. *The Code of Handsome Lake, the Seneca Prophet*. Albany: University of the State of New York.

Persky, Stan. 1998. *Delgamuukw: The Supreme Court of Canada decision on Aboriginal title*. Vancouver: Greystone Books.

Price, Sally. 2001. *Primitive Art in Civilized Places*. 2nd ed. Chicago: University of Chicago Press.

Satterfield, Terre. 2002. *Anatomy of a Conflict: Identity, knowledge, and emotion in old-growth forests*. Vancouver, Toronto: UBC Press.

Sproat, Gilbert Malcolm. 1868. *Scenes and Studies of Savage Life*. London: Smith, Elder & Co.

Tennant, Paul. 1990. *Aboriginal Peoples and Politics: The Indian land question in British Columbia, 1849–1989*. Vancouver: University of British Columbia Press.

United Nations. 2007. United Nations Declaration on the Rights of Indigenous Peoples. Resolution 61/295. New York.

United States Congress. 1990. *An Act to Provide for the Protection of Native American Graves (Public Law 101–601)*. Washington, DC: Government Printing Office.

Vansina, Jan. 1985. *Oral Tradition as History*. Madison: University of Wisconsin Press.

Wa, Gisday, and Delgamuukw. 1992. *The Spirit in the Land: Statements of the Gitksan and Wet'suwet'en hereditary chiefs in the Supreme Court of British Columbia, 1987–1990*. Gabriola Island, BC: Reflections.

Wallace, Anthony F.C. 1956. "Revitalization Movements." *American Anthropologist* 58 (2): 264–81. http://dx.doi.org/10.1525/aa.1956.58.2.02a00040.

Wallace, Anthony F.C. 1972. *The Death and Rebirth of the Seneca*. New York: Vintage.

CHAPTER 7

Caputo, Virginia. 1995. "Anthropology's Silent 'Others': A consideration of some conceptual and methodological issues for the study of youth and children's cultures." In *Youth Cultures: A cross-cultural perspective*, ed. Vered Amit-Talai and Helena Wulff, 19–41. London, New York: Routledge.

Fabes, Richard A., Carol Lynn Martin, and Laura D. Hanish. 2003. "Young Children's Play Qualities in Same-, Other-, and Mixed-Sex Peer Groups." *Child Development* 74 (3): 921–32. http://dx.doi.org/10.1111/1467-8624.00576.

Fong, Vanessa L. 2002. "China's One-child Policy and Empowerment of Urban Daughters." *American Anthropologist* 104 (4): 1098–109. http://dx.doi.org/10.1525/aa.2002.104 .4.1098.

Hoffmann, Melissa L., and Kimberly K. Powlishta. 2001. "Gender Segregation in Childhood: A test of the interaction style theory." *Journal of Genetic Psychology* 162 (3): 298–313. http://dx.doi.org/10.1080/00221320109597485.

James, Allison, and Alan Prout. 1997. *Constructing and Reconstructing Childhood: Contemporary issues in the sociological study of childhood.* 2nd ed. London: Routledge.

Lai, Vinay. 1999. "Not This, Not That: The Hijras of India and the cultural politics of sexuality." *Social Text* 61: 17(4).

Maccoby, Eleanor E. 1998. *The Two Sexes: Growing up apart, coming together.*

Maccoby, Eleanor E., and Carol Nagy Jacklin. 1987. "Gender Segregation in Childhood." In *Advances in Child Development and Behavior* 20: 239–87. http://dx.doi.org/10.1016/S0065-2407(08)60404-8.

Miller, Barbara D., Penny Van Esterik, and John Van Esterik. 2001. *Cultural Anthropology.* Canadian Edition. Toronto: Pearson Education Canada.

Nanda, Serena. 1999. *Neither Man nor Woman.* Toronto: Wadsworth Publishing.

Pascoe, C.J. 2007. *Dude, You're a Fag: Masculinity and sexuality in high school.* Los Angeles: University of California Press.

Pascoe, C.J. 2011. *Dude, You're a Fag: Masculinity and Sexuality in High School.* 2nd ed. Los Angeles: University of California Press.

Pellegrini, Anthony D. 2009. *The Role of Play in Human Development.* New York: Oxford University Press. http://dx.doi.org/10.1093/acprof:oso/9780195367324.001.0001.

Phillips, Katie. 2011. "Conservative Media vs. J. CREW: The Battle of the Pink Toenails. Forbes." http://www.forbes.com/sites/shenegotiates/2011/04/13/conservative-media-vs -j-crew-the-battle-of-the-pink-toenails/.

Reddy, Gayatri. 2005. *With Respect to Sex: Negotiating Hijra identity in South India.* Chicago, London: The University of Chicago Press. http://dx.doi.org/10.7208/chicago/9780226707549.001.0001.

Thorne, Barrie. 1994. *Gender Play: girls and boys in school.* New Brunswick, NJ: Rutgers University Press.

CHAPTER 8

Alves-Silva, Juliana, M. da Silva Santos, P. Guimaraes, A. Ferreira, H. Bandelt, S. Pena, and V. Prado. 2000. "The Ancestry of Brazilian mtDNA Lineages." *American Journal of Human Genetics* 67 (2): 444–61. http://dx.doi.org/10.1086/303004.

Anderson, Kay J. 1991. *Vancouver's Chinatown: Racial discourse in Canada, 1875–1980.* Montreal, Kingston: McGill-Queen's University Press.

Benedict, Ruth. 1943. *Race: Science and politics.* New York: Viking Press.

Boas, Franz. 1916. "Eugenics." *Scientific Monthly* 3 (5): 471–78.

Boas, Franz. 1963. *The Mind of Primitive Man.* New York: The Free Press.

Boas, Franz. 1969. *Race and Democratic Society.* New York: Biblo and Tannen.

Carlson, Elof Axel. 2001. *The Unfit: A History of a Bad Idea.* Cold Spring Harbor, NY: Cold Spring Harbor Laboratory Press.

Couzin-Frankel, Jennifer. 2010. "Researchers to Return Blood Samples to the Yanomamö." *Science* 328 (5983): 1218. http://dx.doi.org/10.1126/science.328.5983.1218.

Dallaire, Roméo. 2003. *Shake Hands with the Devil: The failure of humanity in Rwanda.* Toronto: Random House Canada.

Dalton, Rex. 2002. "Tribe Blasts 'Exploitation' of Blood Samples." *Nature* 420 (6912): 111. http://dx.doi.org/10.1038/420111a.

Dalton, Rex. 2004. "When Two Tribes Go to War." *Nature* 430 (6999): 500–2. http://dx.doi.org/10.1038/430500a.

Darwin, Charles. 1998. *The Descent of Man.* Amherst, NY: Prometheus Books.

Davenport, Charles Benedict. 1911. *Heredity in Relation to Eugenics.* New York: Henry Holt. http://dx.doi.org/10.5962/bhl.title.29389.

Foster, Eugene, M.A. Jobling, P.G. Taylor, P. Donnelly, P. de Knijff, Rene Mieremet, T. Zerjal, and C. Tyler-Smith. 1998. "Jefferson Fathered Slave's Last Child." *Nature* 396 (6706): 27–28. http://dx.doi.org/10.1038/23835.

Freed, Stanley A., Ruth S. Freed, and Laila Williamson. 1988. "Capitalist Philanthropy and Russian Revolutionaries: The Jesup North Pacific Expedition (1897–1902)." *American Anthropologist* 90 (1): 7–24. http://dx.doi.org/10.1525/aa.1988.90.1.02a00010.

Galton, Sir Francis. 1909. *Essays in Eugenics.* London: Eugenics Education Society.

Gordon-Reed, Annette. 2008. *The Hemingses of Monticello: An American family.* New York: W.W. Norton.

Gould, Stephen Jay. 1996. *The Mismeasure of Man.* New York: W.W. Norton.

Hitler, Adolf. 1998. *Mein Kampf* [My Struggle]. Trans. Ralph Manheim. Boston: Houghton Mifflin.

Jefferson, Thomas. 1964. *Notes on the State of Virginia.* New York: Harper Torchbooks.

Jobling, Mark A., with Matthew Hurles and Chris Tyler-Smith. 2004. *Human Evolutionary Genetics: Origins, peoples & disease.* New York: Garland Science.

Kenny, Michael G. 1988. "Mutesa's Crime: Hubris and the control of African kings." *Comparative Studies in Society and History* 30 (4): 595–612. http://dx.doi.org/10.1017/S0010417500015450.

Kenny, Michael G. 2002. "Toward a Racial Abyss: Eugenics, Wickliffe Draper, and the origin of the Pioneer Fund." *Journal of the History of the Behavioral Sciences* 38 (3): 259–83. http://dx.doi.org/10.1002/jhbs.10063.

Kenny, Michael G. 2006. "A Question of Blood, Race, and Politics." *Journal of the History of Medicine* 61:456–91.

Kenny, Michael G. 2009. "Genomics, Genetic Identity, and the Refiguration of 'Race.'" In *Race and Science: Scientific Challenges to Racism in Modern America*, ed. Paul Farber and Hamilton Cravens, 212–27. Corvallis: Oregon State University Press.

Kevles, Daniel J. 1995. *In the Name of Eugenics: Genetics and the uses of human heredity.* Cambridge, MA: Harvard University Press.

Lee, Sandra Soo-Jin, Deborah Bolnick, Troy Duster, Pilar Ossorio, and Kimberly TallBear. 2009. "The Illusive Gold Standard in Genetic Ancestry Testing." *Science* 325 (5936): 38–39. http://dx.doi.org/10.1126/science.1173038.

Lemarchand, René. 1996. *Burundi: Ethnic conflict and genocide.* Cambridge: Cambridge University Press.

Lieberman, Arthur, Andrew Lyons, and Harriet Lyons. 1995. "An Interview with Ashley Montagu." *Current Anthropology* 36 (5): 835–44. http://dx.doi.org/10.1086/204440.

Maquet, Jacques. 1961. *The Premise of Inequality in Ruanda*. London: Oxford University Press.

Marks, Johnathan. 2008. "Race across the Physical-Cultural Divide in American Anthropology." In *A New History of Anthropology*, ed. Henrika Kuklick, 242–58. Oxford: Blackwell Publishing.

McLaren, Angus. 1990. *Our Own Master Race: The Eugenic Crusade in Canada*. Toronto: McClelland & Stewart.

Montagu, M.F. Ashley. 1942. *Man's Most Dangerous Myth: The fallacy of race*. New York: Columbia University Press.

Montagu, M.F. Ashley. 1972. *Statement on Race: An annotated elaboration and exposition of the four statements on race issued by the United Nations Educational, Scientific, and Cultural Organization*. New York: Oxford University Press.

Mourant, A.E. 1983. *Blood Relations: Blood groups and anthropology*. London: Oxford University Press.

Paul, Diane. 1995. *Controlling Human Heredity, 1865 to the Present*. Atlantic Highlands, NJ: Humanities Press.

Prunier, Gérard. 1995. *The Rwanda Crisis: History of a genocide*. New York: Columbia University Press.

Ripley, William Z. 1898. *The Races of Europe: A sociological study*. London: Kegan Paul, Trench, Trubner.

Roscoe, John. 1911. *The Baganda*. London: Macmillan.

Santos, Ricardo Ventura, and Marcos Chor Maio. 2004. "Race, Genomics, Identities and Politics in Contemporary Brazil." *Critique of Anthropology* 24 (4): 347–78.

Smith, John. 1966. *The Generall Historie of Virginia, New-England, and the Summer Isles*. London: Michael Sparkes. [facsimile edition]

Speke, John Hanning. 1863. *Journal of the Discovery of the Source of the Nile*. Edinburgh: William Blackwood and Sons.

Stepan, Nancy. 1982. *The Idea of Race in Science: Great Britain, 1800–1960*. London: McMillan.

Stocking, George. 1968. "The Critique of Racial Formalism." In *Race, Culture, and Evolution: Essays in the history of anthropology*, 160–94. Chicago: University of Chicago Press.

Stocking, George. 1982. *Victorian Anthropology*. New York: Free Press.

Wailoo, Keith, and Stephen Pemberton. 2006. *The Troubled Dream of Genetic Medicine*. Baltimore: Johns Hopkins University Press.

Wallace, Anthony F.C. 1999. *Jefferson and the Indians: The tragic fate of the first Americans*. Cambridge, MA: Harvard University Press.

Ward, R.H., with Barbara Frazier, Kerry Dew-Jager, and Svante Pääbo. 1991. "Extensive Mitochondrial Diversity within a Single Amerindian Tribe." *Proceedings of the National Academy of Sciences* 88: 8720–24. http://dx.doi.org/10.1073/pnas.88.19.8720.

CHAPTER 9

Abu-Lughod, Lila. 2012. "Living the 'Revolution' in an Egyptian Village: Moral action in a national space." *American Ethnologist* 39 (1): 21–25. http://dx.doi.org/10.1111/j.1548-1425.2011.01341.x.

Aptekar, Lewis. 1988. *Street Children of Cali*. Durham, NC: Duke University Press.

Boellstorff, Tom. 2008. *Coming of Age in Second Life: An anthropologist explores the virtually human*. Princeton, NJ: Princeton University Press.

Cairoli, M. Laetitia. 2012. *Girls of the Factory: A year with the garment workers of Morocco*. Gainsville: University Press of Florida.

Garsten, Christina. 1994. *Apple World*. Stockholm Studies in Social Anthropology 33. Stockholm: Almqvist & Wiksell International.

Hannerz, Ulf. 2003. "Being There ... and There ... and There! Reflections on multi-site ethnography." *Ethnography* 4 (2): 201–16. http://dx.doi.org/10.1177/14661381030042003.

Howell, Signe. 2003. "Kinning: The creation of life trajectories in transnational adoptive families." *Journal of the Royal Anthropological Institute* 9 (3): 465–84. http://dx.doi.org/10.1111/1467-9655.00159.

Inda, Jonathan Xavier, and Renato Rosaldo, eds. 2008. Introduction: A World in Motion. *The Anthropology of Globalization: A reader*. Malden, MA: Blackwell Publishing.

Kearney, Michael. 1995. "The Local and the Global: The anthropology of globalization and transnationalism." *Annual Review of Anthropology* 24 (1): 547–65. http://dx.doi.org/10.1146/annurev.an.24.100195.002555.

Keller, Eva. 2003. "The Banana Plant and the Moon: Conservation and the Malagasy ethos of life in Masoala, Madagascar." *American Ethnologist* 35 (4): 650–54.

Klein, C. 2003. *Cold-War Orientalism*. Berkeley: University of California Press.

Leinaweaver, Jessica. 2007. "On Moving Children: The social implications of Andean child circulation." *American Ethnologist* 34 (1): 163–80. http://dx.doi.org/10.1525/ae.2007.34.1.163.

Marre, D., and L. Briggs, eds. 2009. "Introduction: The Circulation of Children." In *International Adoption: Global inequalities and the circulation of children*, 1–28. New York, London: New York University Press.

Miller, Barbara D., Penny Van Esterik, and John Van Esterik. 2001. *Cultural Anthropology*. Canadian Edition. Toronto: Pearson Education Canada.

Nagy, Sharon. 1998. "'This Time I Think I'll Try a Filipina:' Global and local influences on relations between foreign household workers and their employers in Doha, Qatar." *City & Society* 10 (1): 83–103. http://dx.doi.org/10.1525/city.1998.10.1.83.

Nagy, Sharon. 2006. "Making Room for Migrants, Making Sense of Difference: Spatial and ideological expressions of social diversity in urban Qatar." *Urban Studies* 43 (1): 119–37. http://dx.doi.org/10.1080/00420980500409300.

Pelto, Pertti J. 1973. *The Snowmobile Revolution: Technology and social change in the arctic*. Menlo Park, CA: Cummings.

Selman, P. 2009. "The Movement of Children for International Adoption: Developments and trends in receiving states and states of origins, 1998–2004." In *International Adoption: Global inequalities and the circulation of children*, ed. D. Marre and L. Briggs, 32–51. New York, London: New York University Press.

Sintos Coloma, Roland, Bonnie McElhinny, Ethel Tungohan, John Paul C. Catungal, and Lisa M. Davidson, eds. 2012. *Filipinos in Canada: Disturbing invisibility*. Toronto: University of Toronto Press.

United Nations, Department of Economic and Social Affairs. *The World's Women: 2010 Trends and Statistics*. United Nations, New York, 2010. Retrieved from: http://unstats.un.org/unsd/demographic/products/Worldswomen/WW2010pub.htm.

Volkman, Toby Alice, ed. 2005. "Introduction: New Geographies of Kinship." In *Cultures of Transnational Adoption*, 1–24. Durham, NC and London: Duke University Press.

Walsh, Andrew. 2012. *Made in Madagascar: Sapphires, ecotourism, and the global bazaar.* Toronto: University of Toronto Press.

Weismantel, Mary. November 1995. "Making Kin: Kinship theory and Zumbagua adoptions." *American Ethnologist* 22 (4): 685–704. http://dx.doi.org/10.1525/ae.1995.22 .4.02a00010.

Yngvesson, B. 2009. "Refiguring kinship in the space of adoption." In *International Adoption: Global Inequalities and the Circulation of Children*, ed. D. Marre and L. Briggs, 103–18. New York, London: New York University Press.

Glossary

Genscript. http://www.genscript.com/product_003/molecular_biology_glossary/id/11715/ category/glossary/typological_thinking.html.

Goldman, Ruth. 1996. "Who is that *Queer* Queer? Exploring norms around sexuality, race and class in queer theory." In *Queer Studies: A lesbian, gay, bisexual and transgender anthology*, ed. Brett Beemyn and Mickey Eliason, 169–83. New York and London: New York University Press.

Hulan, Renée, and Renate Eigenbrod, eds. 2008. *Aboriginal Oral Traditions: Theory, practice, ethics.* Halifax: Fernwood Publishing.

Kearney, Michael. 1995. "The Local and the Global: The anthropology of globalization and transnationalism." *Annual Review of Anthropology* 24 (1): 547–65. http://dx.doi.org/ 10.1146/annurev.an.24.100195.002555.

Oxford Dictionaries. http://www.oxforddictionaries.com/definition/english/deterritorialization.

Satterfield, Terre. 2002. *Anatomy of a Conflict: Identity, knowledge, and emotion in old-growth forests.* Vancouver, Toronto: UBC Press.

Smith, C. 1996. "What Is This Thing Called Queer?" In *The Material Queer: A LesBiGay Cultural Studies Reader*, ed. D. Morton, 277–85. Boulder, CO: Westview Press.

Theodore, P.S., and S.A. Basow. 2000. "Heterosexual Masculinity and Homophobia: A reaction to the self?" *Journal of Homosexuality* 40 (2): 31–48. http://dx.doi.org/10.1300/ J082v40n02_03.

Wallace, Anthony F.C. 1956. "Revitalization Movements." *American Anthropologist* 58 (2): 264–81.

Winthrop, Robert H. 1991. *Dictionary of Concepts in Cultural Anthropology.* New York: Greenwood Press.

World Health Organization. http://www.who.int/gender/whatisgender/en/.

Sources

Plates

0.1 The Monstrous Races. "Specula physico-mathematico-historica ..." by Johann Zahn, 1696. Library Call No. Q155.Z33 1696. *Strange Versions of Humanity*. Image courtesy of the National Oceanic and Atmospheric Administration/Department of Commerce.

0.3 James Teit and Wife. Image #11686, American Museum of Natural History Library.

1.1 Anthropologist Charlotte Whitby-Coles in India. Film still from Black Mountain (2008); Charlotte Whitby-Coles undertaking her PhD research in India, at pilgrimage site of Kalo Dungar, Rann of Kutch, Gujarat. Photographer: Amin Hajee. Reproduced by permission of the Royal Anthropological Institute. https://www.therai.org.uk/film/film-sales.

2.1 Bronislaw Malinowski. "Malinowski with Trobriand Islanders during fieldwork, 1918," Image MALINOWSKI/3/18/2, reproduced by permission of the Library of the London School of Economics & Political Science.

2.2 Franz Boas. bpk, Berlin/Art Resource.

2.3 Margaret Mead, with Manus Mother and Child. © Bettmann/CORBIS.

3.1 Charles Darwin. Charles Darwin, 1840 (w/c on paper), by George Richmond. Down House, Downe, Kent, UK/© English Heritage Photo Library/Bridgeman Images.

3.2 Robert Fitzroy. Vice Admiral Robert Fitzroy (1805–65), Admiral Fitzroy led the expedition to South America 1834–36 with Charles Darwin, Lane, Samuel (1780–1859)/Royal Naval College, Greenwich, London, UK/Bridgeman Images.

3.3 A Fuegian. A native of Tierra del Fuego, from *Narrative of the Surveying Voyages of His Majesty's Ships* Adventure *and* Beagle (1839). © British Library Board/Robana/Art Resource, NY.

3.4 Aboriginals. CAPTAIN COOK'S LANDING AT BOTANY, A.D. 1770. National Library of Australia, 2141 #S4470. Reproduced by permission.

3.5 Lewis Henry Morgan. National Anthropological Archives, Smithsonian Institution, INV 02863100, Photo Lot 33. Reproduced by permission.

3.6 Joseph Brant: Mohawk Leader. Joseph Brant, Chief of the Mohawks, 1742–1807, Romney, George (1734–1802)/National Gallery of Canada, Ottawa, Ontario, Canada/Bridgeman Images.

4.1 Cave of the Patriarchs. Cave of the Patriarchs, from the south, Hebron, Israel. Image courtesy of Djampa, CC BY-SA 3.0.

4.2 A.R. Radcliffe-Brown. Image courtesy of the Institute of Social & Cultural Anthropology, Oxford.

4.3 Trail of Tears. Trail of Tears Sign, Bartlett TN. Image courtesy of Thomas R. Machnitzki, CC BY-SA 3.0.

5.1   Marcel Mauss. Professor Marcel Mauss with Georges Duchemin, 1936–1937. Photo by Henri Lehmann. Print on baryta paper, 12.3 x 17.8 cm. Musee du Quai Branly/Scala/Art Resource, NY.

5.2   A Dinka Man: South Sudan. A characteristic Dinka attitude, Terrakekka to Aweil, Sudan, 1925 (1927). Artist: Thomas A Glover. HIP/Art Resource, NY.

5.3   Ruth Benedict. Ruth Benedict, half-length portrait, seated, facing front/World-Telegram photo, 1937. Library of Congress.

5.4   President Obama and Emperor Akihito. US President Barack Obama (L) bows as he shakes hands with Japanese Emperor Akihito (C) and as Empress Michiko (R) looks on upon Obama's arrival at the Imperial Palace in Tokyo on November 14, 2009. MANDEL NGAN/AFP/Getty Images.

5.5   Sir Edward Evans-Pritchard. PRM 1998.341.576, E.E. Evans-Pritchard with Azande boys, by unknown photographer. Reproduced by permission of Pitt Rivers Museum, University of Oxford.

5.6   Émile Durkheim. Portrait of Emile Durkheim (1858–1917) (b/w photo), French Photographer/Bibliothèque Nationale, Paris, France/Bridgeman Images.

6.1   Nootka Village. Habitations in Nootka Sound, from drawings executed by John Webber during the Third Voyage of Captain Cook 1777–1779. © British Library Board/Robana/Art Resource, NY.

6.2   Nootka House. Nootka Group in Interior of House, Nootka Sound, British Columbia, from *Atlas to Accompany A Voyage of Discovery of the North Pacific Ocean and Round the World*, 1784. Washington State Historical Society/Art Resource, NY.

6.3   Yuquot Totem Pole. Fallen totem pole, Yuquot, Vancouver Island, British Columbia, Canada. Chris Cheadle/All Canada Photos/SuperStock.

6.4   Makah Whaler. University of Washington Libraries, Special Collections, NA740. Reproduced by permission.

6.5   Gitksan Village. Image E-08391 courtesy of Royal BC Museum, BC Archives.

6.6   Greenpeace Protester. Logging Road Blockade Oregon USA. Greenpeace activist Jennifer Kirby locks herself to a large yellow container blockading a logging road at the site of the Soukow Timber Sale in the Medford Bureau of Land Management District in southwest Oregon. © Greenpeace/Dang Ngo.

7.1   Children in Gender-Specific Hallowe'en Costumes. FREDERIC J. BROWN/AFP/Getty Images.

7.2   Hijra. Reproduced by permission of Mike Garten. CC BY-SA 3.0.

8.4   King of Rwanda. Mutara III Rudahigwa, Mwami (King) of Rwanda (1931–1959). Portrait photo, 1957. akg-images/Paul Almasy.

9.1   Burmese Refugees Waiting to be Registered by a Thai Policeman. Thierry Falise/LightRocket via Getty Images.

9.2   Korean Children with Their American Parents. © Bettmann/CORBIS.

Map

0.1   Columbus's First Voyage 1492–93. CC BY-SA 3.0.

Index

Page numbers for plates, maps, and figures are in italics.

Patterns of Culture (Benedict), 96,
100–2, 103–4, 127
PEPFAR (Emergency Plan for AIDS
Relief), 41
perception, theory shaping, xx, 148
Peru, 203–4
physical anthropology, 5, 171–73
Pizarro, Francisco, xix
Pocahontas, 179
polygynous marriage, 76
Polynesia, 163
possession, spirit, 115n5
Post, Emily, 100, 115n3
potlatch, 125, 127, 132–33
Powhatan, 81, 179
primatology, 5
"primitive" people
artifacts of, 128
European perception of, xiii, 59, 60–61
as focus of study, xiii–xiv, 37, 70,
102, 219
Franz Boas on, 176
kinship and, 70
race and culture and, 176
religious practice and, 110
Ruth Benedict on, 102
in social evolutionism, 26
progress, concept of, 196
property, private, 61–62, 63, 125. *See
also* ownership, land
protests, *see* activism; Arab Spring;
environmental activism
psychoanalysis, 115n5
purposeful sampling, 35–36

Qatar, 201–2
qualitative approach, 36
queer theory, 152

race
classification by, 171–73
culture and, 176–77

meaning of, 173
overview of, 168, 190
physical anthropology and, 5, 171–73
statements on, 191n6, 191n11
theories of, 168–69
See also biological determinism;
eugenics; genetics; heredity; racism
race mixing, 175–76
Races of Mankind (Benedict and
Weltfish), 176–77
Rachel (Isaac's wife), 79
racial determinism, *see* biological
determinism
Racial Integrity Act, 181
racism
Boasians against, 26, 33–34, 48, 101,
164, 174, 186
ethnocentrism as, 13
race and, 168
in Rwandan genocide, 186
Radcliffe-Brown, A.R., 26, 27, 28,
77–78, 90n9
Rana Plaza, Bangladesh, 198
reciprocity, 102–3
Reddy, Gayatri, 159, 160, 161
reflexive thinking, 6
religion, nature of, 109–11. *See also*
Evangelical Christians
Repatriation Act (US), 128, 142n5
research, power of, 38
research questions, 14, 17, 32, 39
residential schools, 85
revitalization movement, 122, 128–29,
130–31, 137
Richards, Audrey Isabel, 26, 28–31, 78,
100
rites of passage, 17, 74
Rolfe, John, 179
Rosaldo, Renato, 195
Rousseau, Jean-Jacques, 60, 134
Russia, 206
Rwandan genocide, 168, 183–86